Praise for *Golden Past, Red Future*

"The book is written unashamedly through the eyes of a fan, but a fan whose analysis and grasp of the team's progress almost mirrors that of Rafa Benitez himself. Rather than look through rose-tinted glasses, Tomkins examines the reawakening of Liverpool Football Club with a keen eye, balancing raw emotion with a rare sense of perspective, even when it comes to reflecting on that incredible night in Istanbul."

Oliver Kay, The Times

"A must-read for Liverpool supporters, particularly those with an open mind for considering issues confronting the club other than which multi-million pound player might be arriving in the next transfer window, *Golden Past Red Future* will appeal to fans of clubs other than Liverpool interested in examining the long, strange saga of a club with tremendous history trying to adjust to the demands of both a modern, financially-centered league competition and a support base firmly in touch with the time when the club swept all before them.

Golden Past Red Future is worth every penny for both committed Liverpool supporters and modern football fans alike."

Bill Urban, Squarefootball

" A wonderful insight into Liverpool's Champions League-winning season . The chapter on the final is exceptional"

Stephen Davies, Editor, Red and White Kop

FourFourTwo

Red Revival:
Rafa Benítez's Liverpool Revolution

Paul Tomkins

Website: *www.paultomkins.com*

Email: *tomkins_lfcbook@btinternet.com*

Harcourt
Publishing

For my family — thank you for the wonderful support.

Thanks once again to Jonathan Swain, for assisting with this, my second book.
Also, a big hand to Chris Hadley, for helping with the proofing, even during
difficult personal times.

Next, a massive thanks to Oliver Anderson, whose statistical contribution was so
impressive I was more than happy to return the favour and help with his own book
on the Reds (see final page for details).

Thanks to Garreth Cummins and Sandra Ireland, for performing various invaluable
admin tasks. Thanks to Matt Clare, for sorting the Cardiff trip.

Special thanks and hugs to Nikki Murphy.

A big thanks to everyone at **liverpoolfc.tv**, especially Paul Rogers and Paul Eaton.

Next, everyone connected to the websites which have published and championed
my work, especially everyone at **redandwhitekop.com**, as well as James Carroll
at **shanklygates.com**, Matt Ladson at **thisisanfield.com**, Eric Cordina at
bootroom.org, the gang at **ynwa.tv,** and Robbie Amins at **talklfc.com**.

ISBN 0-9549580-3-9

Published by Harcourt Publishing
© Paul Tomkins 2006

First edition published 2006

Printed in Great Britain by AnchorPrint Group Limited

Contents

Preface

The Lion Kings

Morgan's Landing, a hotel bar directly opposite the Millennium Stadium and beside the River Taff. As the night of May 13th 2006 wears on, thirty or so Liverpool fans carouse with ten West Ham fans, exchanging friendly chants and good-natured banter.

I'm forever blowing bubbles, sing the Hammers.

You can stick your fucking bubbles up your arse, mock the Scousers.

You've only got one player, retort the Hammers.

Steve Gerrard, Gerrard . . . comes the reply.

And so on, for an hour or more.

The most surreal of event of the day then occurs, eclipsing the rather bizarre game from which the fans are still recovering: fans of both West Ham and Liverpool try to coerce a slim, curly-haired Welshman into singing their respective club anthems. He has a go, then instead insists on belting out *The Lion Sleeps Tonight*, with an amazing baritone that booms from a body seemingly too slim for such sonority. Just as he gets to the chorus, both sets of fans jump around dementedly singing *o-wim-o-weh o-wim-o-weh*.

For the second season running, Rafael Benítez's team has pulled an elephant-sized rabbit from a hat, and given the fans something special to celebrate. The West Ham fans can't help but join in.

This is the story of a season that culminated with the FA Cup in the club's possession, and the most points in a Liverpool league campaign for almost 20 years. It is the story of a *Red Revival*.

Paul Tomkins
May 2006

Part One

Chapter One

Introduction

How do you top *that?* Istanbul, AC Milan, Jerzy Dudek and all the unscriptable drama. Such an amazing game that simply no other could ever be fit to follow. Unfortunately, time could not be frozen at that precise moment, and we all had to return to reality sooner or later. You could move to a flat in Istanbul overlooking Taksim Square; change your name to John Xabi Luis Smith or Jimmy Jerzy Jamie Djimi Djibril Jones; have the *Road To Istanbul* DVD on constant repeat; but life was going to move on, whether you were ready or not.

The higher the high, the harder the subsequent comedown. When it came time to resume competitive football in July (yes, *July*), many Reds were still struggling to come to terms with the previous season's mixture of baffling underachievement and mind-boggling overachievement.

Winning the Champions League did something really bizarre; it just made Kopites unhappy. Or rather, it made them ecstatically happy for a couple of months and then, once the football resumed, it became a memory — a feeling that everyone wanted to recreate week after week. Men were waking from a one night stand with Angelina Jolie, and forced to head home to Hilda Ogden. The problem with a new season is that its arrival consigns the previous one to the history books; by mid-July, the Reds' last game was no longer the most miraculous occasion against the mighty and glamourous AC Milan, but a low-key affair against Total Network Solutions of the Welsh league.

There's a very realistic chance that Istanbul will represent the high-water mark in the foreseeable future for Liverpool. Winning the league, while no longer an unthinkable proposition now Rafa Benítez is in charge, remains a tall order, and a sixth European Cup is always going to be a long shot considering the strength of the top dozen or so clubs on the continent. In the last ten years, it has eluded Chelsea, Arsenal and perennial French champions, Lens, while other teams who have excelled in their domestic league for the best part of a decade —Manchester United, AC Milan, Ajax, Juventus, Barcelona and Bayern Munich — managed just one win each when in their recent pomp. As things currently stand, there are only four teams who can realistically win the Premiership in the next few years, but a lot more who can win the Champions League, where a team can always emerge from the pack, as did Porto in 2004 and Liverpool in 2005.

Istanbul could very likely sit on its own in new-Millennium Liverpool FC, an isolated accomplishment in amongst a series of decent achievements. So what will its legacy be? Something for the club to cling to in a positive sense, like a guide rope at the pinnacle of a mountain, holding you near the top and telling you that the final steps to the summit can again be taken; or something to cling to in a negative sense, as with a long-lost dream and false hopes? It shows what *can* be achieved, but does it make other great accomplishments any more likely? Will it help the club on its way to becoming regular Premiership challengers? Or will it hamper efforts, as expectations rise again?

Some clubs never return to the summit of football. Liverpool are one of those clubs that you sense will always, at the very least, hover around the top half of the top division table; after all, its lowest league position in the last 40 years, even after some dire seasons, is 8th. Like Juventus, Real Madrid, Barcelona and Manchester United, Liverpool should always feel like a 'big' club, even if not winning silverware. Its history and fanbase should guarantee as much. But it was still a quantum leap to get from recent results to European Champions. It was like the Wright Brothers fiddling around with their wooden flying machines one day, and building Concorde the next.

In 1977, when Liverpool first scaled the heights of European Cup glory, fans had grown accustomed to the routine of success, with five league titles over the previous 13 years, after Bill Shankly took the Reds back to the top of the domestic tree in 1964 following a long wait. Of course, a team had to be champions to qualify in 1977; and as champions of a major league, fans had a right to expect at least a strong European challenge. But by 2005, if not exactly starved of success, the Kop had been consuming unfulfilling fast food every few years, with only the Happy Meal of 2001 proving anywhere near as substantial as the regular feasting between 1965 and 1990.

Time doesn't necessarily help to make any more sense of Istanbul. The trophy itself could not have been any more hard-earned and thoroughly deserved, but getting into the competition in the first place was so underwhelming, so last-ditch and desperate (ten defeats on the way to 60 points), it did not serve as a natural preparation for what followed. Nor did the Premiership form of 2004/05, or indeed, the group stage of the Champions League, even if the latter did contain a couple of sparkling performances.

No-one expected the level of success that Liverpool experienced within ten months of Benítez's arrival; not after teething problems and toothless displays. Halfway through his first season, there was talk of a crisis — talk that would resurface in October 2005, just months after winning the Champions League, showing that even winning the biggest prize around does not make you immune. While most fans were optimistic about what he could do for the club in the long term, it initially appeared that Benítez had his work cut out in the short-term. The ill-feeling that cloaked Gérard Houllier's final two years in the job meant that any manager was welcome, so disillusioned had the support become, but the reversal of the team's domestic fortunes was taking longer than expected — indeed, the Reds finished with a distinctly mediocre 58 points in 2005 — and Benítez was bracketed with Houllier by some: too academic, too detached for the fire-and-brimstone English game. The difference between the two was the Spaniard's remarkable recent record and the fact that, unlike Houllier, he was very much on the rise: an up-and-coming modern coach.

What Next?

So amazing was the Champions League success, so out of the blue (or Red), that the most interesting question became: *what next?*

How 'real' had the success been? Was it part of a building process, or had this particular cathedral been constructed without foundations? Could success be sustained, and replicated on home soil, or was the Premiership form — with its disconcerting 14 defeats, and only 17 wins — the true indicator of this team's merit? Or, possibly more accurately, was the truth directly between the two extremes?

There were so many admirable attributes to Benítez's Liverpool in the course of his first season, and it included some genuinely world-class footballers. But it was also, quite clearly, a work in progress.

It was not, as some jealous rival fans inevitably suggested, the 'worst ever team to win the trophy'. The quality of the opposition vanquished (Juventus, Chelsea, AC Milan, not to mention two recent finalists and the previous season's semi-finalists); the remarkable and *essential* three-goal second halves against Olympiakos and Milan; and the core of a side that included players of the calibre of Steven Gerrard, Xabi Alonso, Jamie Carragher, Didi Hamann, Sami Hyypia, Luis Garcia and the criminally-underrated Steve Finnan — all these points go toward making that clear. But of course this was still the victory of 'outsiders', and the team, if far from the worst-ever, was also clearly not the best. Subsequent events proved that the win was not based on luck, although like all teams in cup competitions, luck played its part, in both a positive and a negative sense.

If the Reds were not a great Premiership side in 2004/05, the continuation of the European groove in the first half of the 2005/06 season — topping a group that contained Chelsea, while Manchester United belly-flopped at the first hurdle — proved that the glory of Istanbul was no fluke, even if the title of European Champions was conceded rather limply against United's conquerors, Benfica, at the stage of the season when the Reds, looking fatigued, couldn't seem to buy a goal.

Despite the setback against the Portuguese, this was still a highly-polished outfit, with a brilliant tactician at the helm. In the whole of 2005 Liverpool were quite superb in European competition, even finding another three-goal post-half-time salvo when a goal behind to CSKA Moscow in the Super Cup, eventually winning 3-1. The Reds were unbeaten in the Champions League 'proper' the entire calendar year, encompassing 13 games, seven of which had been against the highest possible calibre of opposition. A further six games were undertaken in qualifying, the only blot the home reversal to CSKA Sofia with the tie already effectively won (with three away goals already in the bag), when fielding a fairly weakened line-up was a luxury Benítez could afford. Including the Super Cup, Liverpool played 20 European games in 2005, losing only one, and winning fifteen. That is the kind of form the Reds would need to find in the Premiership to be taken seriously.

To put the calendar year's European form into context, had all the European games come with three points for a win and one point for a draw, Liverpool would have averaged 2.5 points per game — exactly the same ratio Chelsea achieved when setting their record Premiership-winning tally of 95.

Too Soon?

One question begging to be answered was: *had the success been premature?* Like a child born before term, would Benítez's team suffer from exposure and find itself unable to breathe in the full glare of rampant expectation? The answer, in the autumn of 2005, was a resounding 'yes' from some sections of the press. Liverpool seemed no better prepared to deal with the Premiership — a cursory glance at the early-autumn league table would suggest as much. The assumptions of Jekyll and Hyde tendencies were carried over from the previous season. It seemed that Chelsea could not get a goal, let alone a win against Liverpool in Europe, encompassing four Champions League games; and yet in a visit to Anfield on the 2nd of October the Londoners ran out shock 4-1 winners, even if the scoreline was a little flattering. Things would get worse in the coming weeks, with a 2-0 reverse at Fulham (this time a remarkable comeback at Craven Cottage was not forthcoming) and defeat to Crystal Palace in the Carling Cup.

Despite only one win in the first six games, Liverpool had actually been improving on the corresponding fixtures from the previous season, and dominating games without finishing off the opposition. The 0-0 draw at Boro on the opening day of the season was one of the best away performances yet under Benítez, and that was backed up with a similar display and identical result at Spurs (who would subsequently prove the season's surprise package), but the flying start everyone had been hoping for, especially after the added fitness of a competitive pre-season, never materialised. Less bang, more whimper.

So would Benítez go the same way as Gérard Houllier, and find that winning trophies had made a rod for his own back? Houllier had claimed that his Treble came 'too soon', but that was at the end of his third season. Looking back, you have to say that it came at precisely the *right* time. The following season the Reds, despite winning nothing, finished with 80 Premiership points and a quarter-final position in the Champions League. An undeniably steady progression; so 2001 hardly raised expectations too high. Most Reds were happy with the team's progress the following season, even if endeavour started to replace inspiration a little too frequently. So the problem was not the success and the raised expectations, but a failure to maintain momentum, and to continue adding elements to elevate the team. Benítez would need to make sure his signings during the summer of 2005 didn't derail progress, instead ensuring that they added missing ingredients.

In the summer of 2002, Houllier got it all wrong; mistakes saw him paint himself into a corner (bad transfers don't easily go away), and left too little leeway to redeem himself. Maybe he had taken the side as far as his abilities would allow, lacking the tactical flexibility to push on; or maybe he just screwed up that summer's rebuilding programme and, despite better subsequent efforts, was unable to rectify the damage. (Steve Finnan and Harry Kewell, Houllier's signings the following summer, both went on to become key players for Rafa Benítez, at a total cost of just £8m).

Revival

So, to the key issue: what, exactly, constitutes a revival? And what can Liverpool fans realistically expect in the coming years?

It's fairly clear that under Benítez's shrewd stewardship and under normal circumstances, Liverpool would already be challenging for the Premiership title. But these are not normal circumstances. This is the era of the billionaire oil tycoon owning a football club, and running it at a massive loss. In such circumstances there is not a lot a competing team can do, beyond trying its level-best to get close; and, if still unable to beat them, *joining* them. But wishing for an ultra-generous benefactor is a dangerous game; look at Hearts, and the soap opera that unfolded this season. Finding the right investor, and getting him to take a fairly-valued stake of a club — the stumbling block with Steve Morgan's offers in 2004 — without disrupting the apple cart, or removing the heart and soul of the club in the process, is difficult. There are plenty of fans — at all clubs — who would be grateful to see a new investor turn up with huge wads of cash, so that their wildest transfer wishes may be granted. The difficulties tend to arise later down the line, when the full implications of any deal become apparent. In an ideal world, a club would find a local investor, with a long-held passion for the club, with so much spare money that it becomes no object; the money could then be invested cleverly, and consistently, with no strings attached. But would it be 'sport'?

While Chelsea have every right to spend their money as they see fit, there can also be no denying that it is now a hugely uneven playing field. So Liverpool's revival might amount to nothing more than 2nd-placed rosettes. Even the great Bob Paisley never had to face a team who could outspend

Liverpool four times over.

What Liverpool need, in order to be fully revived, is to be firmly established in the Champions League qualification positions, and to make substantial progress in as many cups as possible. In other words, to become an undisputed *player*, rather than loitering at the fringes. So far, that is precisely what Benítez has brought to the club. Dominating English football is no longer a realistic option, but the Reds have to be in a position to take advantage of any slips by the perennial big spenders, and to take whatever chances come their way. Unlike in too many seasons since last winning the league title in 1990, Liverpool have to be capable of at least challenging for the Premiership crown.

And once firmly established within the top four on an annual basis, not be another false dawn. For two years under Gérard Houllier, at the turn of the Millennium, Liverpool were clearly an emerging force — if, ultimately, a force that fell short of capturing the most important trophies. Just when it appeared the club was set for years of top-level performance, the cracks began to appear, and then quickly spread.

This time, the revival needs to be for more than a couple of seasons. No-one can guarantee that — especially if there's an enforced managerial change, for an unforeseen reason, that affects the stability of the club. But Rafael Benítez is attempting to build a side that can compete both in the here-and-now, and yet keep a firm eye on the future and the legacy he will bequeath the club.

Chapter Two

The Clean Up Operation: A Summer of Hard Work

The dustcart moves along Walton Breck Road, men in luminous yellow vests scouring the pavements for the detritus strewn the night before. It is the party to end all parties: anywhere up to one million people lining the streets and climbing the lampposts of Liverpool to see their returning heroes, flown in from Istanbul, as the trophy — back for keeps — is paraded on its way to the Anfield trophy room.

The clean-up operation is in full swing, and it doesn't end on the streets: almost immediately after the final whistle at the Atatürk Stadium, Igor Bišćan, Jerzy Dudek, Milan Baroš, Vladimír Šmicer, and the much-derided

Antonio Núñez, who all featured significantly at some stage *en route* to the Champions League success, are consigned to the Anfield waste bin. With them go some lesser lights, such as Alou Diarra, who never actually played a competitive game for the club (on loan to three different French clubs, he had graduated to the French national team), and Mauricio Pellegrino, whose stellar reputation took a battering during his brief sojourn on Merseyside.

Of course, it's unfair to refer to some of those players, even metaphorically, as rubbish, especially so soon after contributing to the history of the club (on that one night at the very least in some cases, if not their entire careers), but the fact of the matter is that as soon as the final was over, Benítez was clearing his squad of the superfluous. He was aware of the deficiencies well before Istanbul, and none of the exits came as any great surprise — unlike the previous summer, when Michael Owen left of his own accord, and Danny Murphy was told he could find another club.

None of those offloaded in the summer of 2005 were bad players; on the contrary, each (with the exception of Núñez full internationals) had ability, just not necessarily *consistency*, or an aptitude for the Premiership. Football is such that good players can quickly look like bad players for a myriad reasons. The international goalscoring records of both Baroš and Šmicer are quite remarkable, but neither will be desperately missed. Pellegrino had experienced many highs over the years, but had passed the tipping point in his career, and a move to the frantic style of English football, when lacking match fitness, exposed a talent on the wane. Even so, he allowed Sami Hyypia to rest ahead of big European games.

Some of the players simply didn't offer what Benítez craved. Maybe they were like jazz musicians playing in a classical orchestra; in Milan Baroš's case, at times he seemed to be performing a freeform scat distinctly out of synch with the rhythm of the rest of the team. In fairness to Baroš, he had some sparkling games, but he seemed too much of an individual for Benítez's team ethic. To continue the metaphor, Igor Bišćan never seemed to settle upon one instrument (although when Lee Carsley pulled his shorts down, Igor's 'oboe' was all too apparent), while Šmicer could even tear a muscle during the pre-concert tuning-up.

The man who could perhaps feel most hard done by was Jerzy Dudek. The hero in Istanbul, he remained at the club, but did not feature again until February 2006; an injury in the summer curtained any potential sale, and the arrival of Pepe Reina signalled an end to the Pole's claims on the no.1 spot. There can be no room for sentiment in football, and in this instance Benítez demonstrated the necessary ruthlessness. Dudek is too good to be any club's number two, but not quite good enough, or at least consistent enough, to be Liverpool's no.1. But without any tempting bids in the winter transfer window, Dudek saw out the season as Reina's deputy, having spent a couple of months alternating with Scott Carson on the bench.

Dudek's return to the first team came at Stamford Bridge, when he came on to replace the red-carded Reina, on a miserable February afternoon, with the game effectively over at 2-0 to the Londoners. He didn't concede in his ten minutes on the pitch, nor did he in the final two games of his brief spell back in the side, against Wigan (where he made some smart saves) and Arsenal. In between, he conceded a penalty — somewhat harshly — away at Charlton, and could not repeat his spot-kick heroics of Istanbul against Darren Bent. Once available again, Benítez had no hesitation in Reina replacing Dudek; again, a little harsh on the Pole, but the correct decision, given the Spaniard's consistency in the first six months of the season, and that all clubs need a clear hierarchy between goalkeepers — flitting between two keepers is a sure way to make nervous wrecks of both. While good form deserves reward, Dudek hadn't done quite enough to make it a difficult decision for the manager (in fact, in the Arsenal game, he barely had to touch the ball). There was to be two more appearances, in the away wins at West Ham and Portsmouth, in what will almost certainly prove his last appearances in a Liverpool shirt. At least Dudek got a chance to keep goal for the Reds in front of the Kop one more time following his heroics in the Champions League final.

Rebuilding
So how do you go about dismantling and rebuilding a team that, just weeks earlier, won the Champions League?

Rafa Benítez's squad rebuilding began instantly upon his arrival in July 2004, but due to the limited time available to assess the squad that first summer, and the difficulty in finalising transfers during the winter break (when players are still under contract and their clubs have the rest of the season to contend with), it was the summer of 2005 before Benítez could implement his major rebuilding strategies.

Thankfully for Liverpool, even if Benítez didn't have a full idea about the players he inherited from Gérard Houllier, he knew two *La Liga* players who he simply had to have. It's hard to believe that he will ever sign a player more important than Xabi Alonso, while Luis Garcia's goals on the way to the Champions League final were worth every penny of his relatively modest transfer fee. Fernando Morientes was the most-decorated player ever to join the Reds, and for a very reasonable fee, but his failure to live up to expectations has been one of the major surprises and disappointments of Benítez's tenure to date, yet again going to prove that there is no such thing as a sure-fire hit in the transfer market.

In 2005, the rebuilding stretched across all age groups of the playing staff. But glamour signings were thin on the ground and, ahead of a ball even being kicked, the manager and the club's leaders were accused of a number of failings in the transfer market.

Benítez's record at Valencia suggested he could win the top honours in his first season, then come back and win them again, and do so in much greater style. But even over a year after he had left, the spectre of Houllier loomed large. Certainly, enough critics compared the signings of Peter Crouch, Bolo Zenden and Momo Sissoko with Houllier's ill-fated £20m haul of El Hadji Diouf, Bruno Cheyrou and Salif Diao. These were not seen as the kind of player the Champions of Europe should be looking to procure (although you'd think the man who had just won the club that trophy would have been given a little more benefit of the doubt at the time).

Each of Benítez's signings of 2005 could be written off with a dismissive 'he lacks this' or 'he can't do that'; each could be labelled flawed in one way or another, and none had the kind of individual talent — such as that possessed by Ronaldinho or Pablo Aimar — that makes you unconcerned by any shortcomings. But Benítez believes in the team, and it was a team he was building; he didn't have the budget for the world's superstars, and even if he had, there are only certain superstars who would interest him (and most of those were beyond the lure of almost any transfer bid, however outrageous the amount offered; as Chelsea, with Jose Mourinho also fussy about the kind of superstar he pursues, discovered with Thierry Henry).

There aren't any 6' 7" strikers with the pace and skill of Thierry Henry, so if you want a striker who is tall and who also has an assured touch in order to hold up the ball, he's probably going to lack speed. If you want pace as well, then it's a question of finding the right partner, or looking for quick runners from other areas of the park.

A perfectly balanced side needs passers, runners, sprinters, tacklers, dribblers, crossers, headers, scorers. Steven Gerrard aside, no one player can do *all* those things to a high level. Crouch was not brought in to do what others already in the squad could, but to add a missing element: the ability to have the ball stick in the centre forward position, and to offer an aerial presence both inside and outside the box. Away from Anfield especially, this was an essential ingredient to add.

The laziest charge — that Benítez could not adapt to English football — was levelled at him even after Peter Crouch, seen as a traditional English centre-forward (despite more cultured ball skills), had arrived. Rather than allow him a period of adjustment, both in terms of refining his own tactics and understanding the strengths and weaknesses of the other 19 teams in the league, not to mention developing a better grasp of the language, Benítez was condemned as a fish out of water. It's an easy accusation to make, and understandable up to a point — he still had to prove himself in England, after all — but the manager is nothing if not a studious learner. This was not like Sir Clive Woodward's much-publicised switch from Rugby Union to football; this was the same sport Benítez had excelled in. His approach might need refining, but not reinventing.

Having made fairly dramatic changes following success in Istanbul — the side was still broken up, as promised, despite the legendary achievement — he was then not afforded time for his adjustments to bed in and his team to take shape. His signings were quickly questioned. Bolo Zenden, so effervescent at Middlesborough in central midfield, started slowly and unspectacularly on the Liverpool left; Peter Crouch's failure to score after a £7m transfer from Southampton (where he proved he *could* score) became a tiresome and at times febrile national obsession; and Pepe Reina's poor game against Birmingham, so soon after a £6m move from Villareal, raised some doubts, following a run of games where, despite some clean sheets, he'd had very little to do. Only Momo Sissoko, snatched from Valencia from under the noses of Everton for £5.8m, started especially brightly.

In fact, one of the biggest criticisms in the wake of the Champions League success was that the club did not cash in on its rediscovered elite status. It's difficult to know what people were expecting — Ronaldinho to pitch up with giant toothbrush in hand, or Shevchenko to defect from Milan (possibly only so he could finally try to get a ball past Jerzy Dudek in training) — but the names who did arrive were not necessarily household, while Peter Crouch was mostly famous for being a laughing stock at grounds around the country. As already mentioned, Benítez has never been a believer in superstar culture, and yet the natural response from fans is to covet the most glamorous players.

If anything it was the missed targets, notably Michael Owen, Luis Figo and Simão Sabrosa, as well as a number of centre-backs, that left many fans concerned with the summer's work. Rick Parry came in for some heavy criticism, although in each case there were at least some mitigating factors in the failures: none of the signings were straightforward, as is often the case with top-end players in demand, and in the case of Simão, where a player's club doesn't want to let them leave without a fight.

Owen's position in wanting a move back to Liverpool (more of which later) was made intractable by Newcastle going far above what the Reds were prepared to pay. Luis Figo — a genuine superstar if ever there was one, formerly the most expensive player ever, but also still professional and dedicated — was genuinely interested in a move to Liverpool on a free transfer, admittedly with high wages. Tax-breaks in Italy, not to mention the more agreeable weather and the Milanese lifestyle (Liverpool may have a lot in its favour these days, but the Mersey is not Lake Como), made it an unfair fight for his services, albeit a fight that dragged on too long. With hindsight, the club might have pulled the plug on the deal at an earlier point, although that is difficult when a lot of time and energy has been spent chasing the player in the first place, while retaining the legitimate belief that he may still sign.

In the case of Simão — the player turned to once the Figo deal was finally dead in the water — a fee was agreed and the player about to board a plane for talks on the final day of the transfer window, when Benfica panicked as word leaked, and Portuguese fans revolted. The asking price was upped by 30% in response, and such an unforeseen hike was rightly seen as an end to the deal, with no time left for further haggling.

With predictable inevitability, Simão would score the tie-killing goal at Anfield for Benfica in the Champions League, a sublime curled effort into the top corner, with the player, equally predictably, cutting in from the left flank on his right foot. The extra money Liverpool were not prepared to pay for him — and more — was lost in the moment Benfica triumphed at the Reds' (literal) expense. Of course, had Simão been signed by Liverpool, Benfica would have been considerably weakened, and so it might have been Manchester United, Villareal or Lille whom the Reds ended up facing (or indeed, the Reds' results could possibly have been worse with Simão in the side, if he was slow to settle, and Liverpool may not have topped their group).

Of course, Benítez had a budget to work within, and while many fans were bemoaning the lack of a reliable goalscorer in the second half of the season (some bemoaning the failure to sign Owen, others still angry with the player), it is worth remembering the contributions made by key new players like Reina, Sissoko and Crouch. To have signed Owen and Simão without Reina, Sissoko and Crouch would still have left a series of unsolved problems. It highlighted the issues Benítez faced in comparison to Jose Mourinho, who could buy any player providing the player's club was willing to sell.

Meanwhile, 21-year-old Chilean speedster, Mark Gonzalez, injured his knee while still at Albacete. Benítez maintained his interest, and expected the player to be fit by the autumn; Gonzalez was also not eligible for a work permit, so the deal had to be put on hold. Chile were agonisingly close to the top 70 in the world rankings, but until they broke that barrier (based on an average position, over two seasons), Gonzalez would not meet the requirements stipulated by the Department of Education and Employment. "There are certain requirements they demand," explained the player in May 2006. "Firstly, the country you play for must be in the FIFA top 70. Chile were lower than that at the time we applied. Then you must have played 75% of your country's games, which I have done. So the top 70 issue was the problem. How can it be my fault that my country are not in the top 70? It is not like I play them by myself."

Despite being a success in *La Liga*, and his country's best player, the rules worked against a player whose international commitments regularly pitted his team against Brazil and Argentina, and inevitably suffered as a result. Far worse players in fractionally higher-ranked teams would qualify without any fuss after beating the minnows of world football. A deal for South African-born Gonzalez was eventually tied up in October 2005, for a fee of £4m, although the work permit problems remained — although these should be circumnavigated by the expected award of a Spanish passport in the summer of 2006.

"We are looking at two ways of getting Spanish nationality, and with that an EC Spanish passport," Gonzalez said. "Firstly through residency, and the time I spent with Albacete and now Sociedad. You need to have been here [in Spain] two years. Secondly through Spanish descendants on my father's side of the family. Now we have an application for a Spanish passport being progressed. Once I get that I don't think there will be any problem. It has all made me more determined to be a success in England with Liverpool."

In the interim, Gonzalez was loaned to Real Sociedad, who were sitting 15th in *La Liga*. After an understandably slow start, while he recovered his fitness, Gonzalez became a big success at the San Sebastián club, scoring the equaliser in a man-of-the-match performance at Real Madrid a week after scoring a 40-yard free-kick.

To solve defensive issues, bids were made by Liverpool for Argentina international Gabriel Milito in July. Real Zaragoza demanded £11.7m for their star man, with Liverpool's offers of £6m and then £7.5m not tempting the Spanish club. The 24-year-old centre-half, who had been close to joining Real Madrid in 2003 but who had failed a contentious medical due to a knee injury, signed a new deal with Zaragoza at the end of July 2005, with the release clause increasing to €30m.

Interest was shown in Brondby's promising youngster, Daniel Agger, who would later join the club in the January transfer window. Liverpool were also linked to Spartak Moscow's Nemanja Vidic, the Serbia and Montenegro defender who joined Manchester United five months later for close to double the fee stipulated in his release clause.

Outgoing

Vladimir Šmicer's fate had been sealed before his remarkable contribution to the Champions League final: he had long known that he would be finding another club when his contract expired, and like Dudek, a convincing last-minute argument resulted in no 11th hour reprieve. Nothing about Istanbul changed Benítez's view, and Šmicer opted for a return to the French league (where he'd won the title with Lens in the '90s) and Bordeaux.

While Šmicer's contribution to Liverpool will always be viewed with disappointment, and frustration at his incessant injuries, he won a lot of trophies with the club, and contributed to many of the cup wins even if, in the league, he never demonstrated convincing consistency. Of the five trophies the club won between 2001 and 2005 — League Cup (twice), FA Cup, Uefa Cup and European Cup — Šmicer featured in every single final. In the 5-4 win against Alaves in the Uefa Cup final of 2001, Šmicer had again entered the game as a sub, and made a telling contribution in drawing the free kicks that led to Alaves players being sent off and the 118th minute Golden Goal. On his return to France, Bordeaux spent much of 2005/06 as the closest challengers to Houllier's Lyon, eventually securing 2nd place in the final table.

Šmicer's Czech team-mate, Milan Baroš, was perhaps a more surprising exit, given his age and bright future in the game, although again, the writing was on the wall in Istanbul. In the private post-match celebrations, when Baroš was reported to have dropped the trophy on a piano, he was also noted to sing about being bound for Valencia. The deal to Spain fell through, and instead Baroš ended up at Aston Villa in a £6.5m transfer. It was an anti-climatic move for a player who won the Golden Boot at Euro 2004 and, twelve months later, had played a telling role in Liverpool becoming Champions of Europe (his involvement in the Luis Garcia goal against Chelsea and the smart touch to Gerrard that led to the equalising penalty in the Champions League final stand out). Such delights were not going to be on offer at Villa Park (and I say this as someone whose grandfather played for Aston Villa between the wars). Baroš had an unremarkable season, scoring a decent amount of goals (12) in a side that were still not mathematically safe from relegation when they visited Anfield in early May; Valencia, meanwhile, would be much revived in *La Liga* (although not to the levels achieved by Benítez), largely thanks to the goals of David Villa, the Real Zaragoza striker they instead ended up signing. Coincidentally, Villa had also been linked with a move to Liverpool (although, of course, it would be easier to name the Spanish players not linked with a move to Anfield).

El-Hadji Diouf was finally removed from the Anfield payroll, joining Bolton after his season-long loan for a rumoured £4m: still below half of what was paid for him, but considerably more than the club might have received in the summer of 2004, when his stock was especially low. In typical fashion, Diouf — such an unlikeable character on the pitch — scored against the Reds at the Reebok, but was less impressive in 2005/06 than in his loan spell, while his career statistics still make uninspiring reading, with one goal approaching every six games. Born just two weeks before Peter Crouch, in January 1981, in a freakish coincidence both had played the exact same number of club games by the start of March 2006: 219. Diouf had 39 goals, while Crouch had 65, at an average of fractionally over one every three games — which happened to be almost the same rate that Diouf picked up his 62 yellow cards. But it was Diouf's attitude and demeanour that most needed excising.

While no player should have to carry the burden of being a good role model — with all the unrealistic demands that that places on young human beings — players still need to avoid being conspicuously *bad* role models. Players should not have to be saints, nor the most committed, clean-living people alive. But they have a duty to avoid insalubrious nightclubs (particularly on the wrong days of the week); steer clear of sexual liaisons that stray from the vague remit of what society deems 'normal' (i.e. being caught dogging and spit-roasting is not going to help a player stay focused); to attend training on time; and on the pitch to be as honest and honourable as possible, despite human flaws and the occasional tendency to err in the heat of the moment. Basically, it shouldn't be asking too much that they conduct themselves with some of level of human decency. This does not include gobbing globular greenies at the opposition players and crowd members, and sneering and snarling your way through 90 minutes.

If Diouf proved an incredibly poor bit of business on Gérard Houllier's part, Alou 'You Ain't Seen Me, Roight' Diarra, picked up on a free transfer from Bayern Munich, was a lot more shrewd. The club owned his contract for three years, but every summer he was despatched back to France, and another club. Eventually he felt at home at Lens, and matured to the point where he represented France. With central midfield far and away the strongest area of the Liverpool squad, he made it clear that he didn't want to return, especially with the World Cup a year away, and the Reds, having not paid his wages since he joined, offloaded him for £2m profit.

Another to depart was Igor Bišćan, who looked to have earned a reprieve with his much improved performances under Benítez, but who ultimately found himself released, heading to Greek side Panathinaikos on a free transfer after 118 hit-and-miss appearances for the Reds. In Greece he again found himself playing at centre-back, a position he was forced into at times under Houllier at Liverpool.

Benítez's less successful imports from *La Liga* were promptly sent back to Spain — there was no sentiment or favouritism. Despite their short stay on Merseyside, none represented a big financial loss to the club. Antonio Núñez, valued at £2m when included in the Michael Owen deal the previous summer, was offloaded to Celta Vigo for an undisclosed fee, believed to be close to his original value. Núñez wasn't a bad player, but his immediate serious knee injury — on his first day of training — meant no seamless segue into his Liverpool career was ever going to happen; once in the team he was always struggling, although, bar a few mis-hits sent into the Kop, he was a decent crosser of the ball, and good in the air. As he got fitter he looked stronger and quicker, but all the same it made sense to replace him with someone with a little more quality; as it transpired, all attempts to sign a right winger floundered, and Núñez may have been able to supply the natural width the team lacked on that flank.

Mauricio Pellegrino, the ageing Argentine, was released after just six months, and he made his way to Alaves. Again, like Núñez he had some good games, but experienced some stinkers too. Josemi lasted until January 2006, when he was involved in a straight swap with Villareal for Dutch full-back, Jan Kromkamp. With Kromkamp valued at £4m, it meant the club effectively doubled its money on Josemi who, despite a promising start to his Liverpool career, tailed off badly and became a big liability. In such terms, £4m represents a great bit of business, while on the early evidence, Kromkamp looks a far better player (although he could still go the way of Josemi).

Other players with first-team experience were released, including Richie

Partridge, who, despite once being widely touted as a promising über-quick winger, ended up at struggling Sheffield Wednesday in the Championship, and Jon Otsemobor, who joined Rotherham, only to be released a matter of months later, ending up at Crewe; how his career nose-dived so rapidly, only he will know. As with someone like Tony Warner — the former Reds reserve now playing for Fulham in the Premiership (and in one game, as a sub, denying Liverpool's best efforts) — there's time for all these young players to eventually fulfil their potential. But a team like Liverpool can't wait for players to reach 27 before becoming good enough, and most players won't want to wait that long. Indeed, Richie Partridge was the grand old age of 24 when he departed, after just a couple of first team appearances, some four years apart.

The summer exodus ended with a couple more of Houllier's young French imports: full-back Gregory Vignal, who had done well on loan at Rangers in 2004/05, and later faced the Reds for Portsmouth; and goalkeeper Patrice Luzi, whose only involvement came as a substitute at Stamford Bridge in an unexpected 1-0 win in early 2004, courtesy of Bruno Cheyrou's goal.

Going it on loan

It's always difficult to second-guess how a loan deal involving a young player will work out. If he impresses then he will help his chances of a return to Anfield, and the possibility of forging a future at the club. However, in impressing he may get a taste for first team football, and may not want to take what he might see as a backwards step by returning to a superior side's reserve team. But without loan experience, many young players simply won't get the chance to broaden their playing experience, and improve as a result.

During Benítez's second season, an entire *team* of players was loaned out, for varying lengths of time. Chris Kirkland (West Brom), Scott Carson (Sheffield Wednesday), Zak Whitbread (Millwall), David Raven (Tranmere), Carl Medjani (Metz), John Welsh (Hull), Salif Diao (Portsmouth), Bruno Cheyrou (Bordeaux), Darren Potter (Southampton), Anthony Le Tallec (Sunderland), Robbie Foy (Wrexham), Neil Mellor (Wigan) and Florent Sinama-Pongolle (Blackburn). Nine of these players had represented the Reds in the Premiership, while the others had been involved in the Carling Cup.

Obviously, some players were sent on loan to get them off the wage bill. Players like Diao and Cheyrou, in their mid-to-late-20s, were not in need of playing experience, merely expunging. Chris Kirkland, with so much talent and such a bright future at one stage, was a more interesting example, needing to rebuild his career as his mid-20s approached, and seemingly surplus to requirements at Anfield with the arrival of Pepe Reina and Scott Carson (who, as a rookie, was more suited to, and happy to accept, the role of understudy). Of course, Jerzy Dudek was still on the books, too.

Kirkland was in that twilight zone so many promising young players eventually find themselves in: too good to be a reserve, not good enough for the first team. His loan spell to West Brom perfectly summed up his career to date: a spell in the first team ended by unfortunate injury, only to find himself warming the bench as second choice to a Polish international (in this case, Tomasz Kuszczak). Where Kirkland goes from here is anyone's guess. Should he finally solve his injury problems, or for that matter, overcome his wretched bad luck, he can get his career back on track. He's still young for a top-level goalkeeper, so he has plenty of time on his side, wherever he ends up.

John Welsh is another interesting example, having famously been 'promised' 15 games by Gérard Houllier in his final season, but having played closer to 15 minutes. Welsh was always highly touted, and did very well in Liverpool's reserves and for England at various representative levels. But for whatever reason, the necessary progression never materialised. He must have felt very old when Momo Sissoko, several months his junior, arrived, and slotted instantly into the side. Welsh went to Hull on loan at the start of 2005/06, to play for England U21 boss Peter Taylor, and did well ... so well that Taylor wanted to keep him, to the point where he was prepared to exchange 17-year-old Paul Anderson, Hull's most promising youngster. There's a good chance Anderson would have made a real name for himself at Hull, and commanded a bigger fee in a few years' time; but Welsh was a player Hull needed in their quest to remain in the Championship; one who was able to make an instant impact on the team. From Liverpool's point of view it was a great bit of business; within two months, Anderson found himself on the bench for the crucial Champions League second leg tie against Benfica. While his presence was also due to injuries, loaned-out players and the ineligibility of Kromkamp and Agger, it was also reward for some scintillating displays for the youth and reserve sides.

Welsh is one of those players who, later in his career, should find himself gravitating to the top division, and a fulfilling career.

When players are loaned to fellow Premiership clubs, you know they have a bright future in the game, even if they can't make it at a club as big and as demanding as Liverpool. Having missed the first half of the season with a knee injury that had sidelined him since January 2005, Neil Mellor found himself at high-flying Wigan, playing for another long-term Reds' reserve, Paul Jewell. Mellor scored on his debut, a dramatic last-minute winner away at Middlesborough, but once Henri Camara was back from the African Nations Cup, Mellor found himself out of the side.

Anthony Le Tallec continued his trend of loan deals at struggling top-division clubs, having endured a torrid time at St Etienne in *Ligue Une* in 2004/05; this time he was at Sunderland, who would spend the season firmly rooted to the foot of the table.

The most surprising loan exit was Le Tallec's cousin, Florent Sinama-Pongolle, the fans' favourite who went to Blackburn in the January transfer window, and helped the Ewood Park team secure 6th place. It was a good move for the youngster in terms of playing time — he went instantly into Rovers' starting XI and stayed there for a good few weeks. He scored and assisted a Craig Bellamy goal in his fourth start, against Spurs, and would make nine starts in all. But why did Benítez let him go, seeing as he spoke highly of the player? Well, Robbie Fowler had just arrived, so a place for Sinama-Pongolle on the Liverpool bench looked less likely. It was a risk though, leaving Cissé as the only quick striker the manager could call on, and he, like Sinama-Pongolle, was often utilised on the right wing. As with Mellor, Sinama-Pongolle had missed the early part of the season with a knee injury; both players being struck down after contributing to the Liverpool cause *en route* to the Champions League final, and losing momentum as a result. As against Olympiakos the previous season, Sinama-Pongolle came off the bench to dramatic effect in a cup tie, this time scoring twice against Luton, having been introduced with the Reds trailing 3-1. He scored one more goal for Liverpool in 2005/06 (a sublime lob away at Real Betis in the Champions League) in his sixteen games; although only four were started.

Chapter Three

Steven Gerrard: Footballer of the Year

He's going. He's staying. He's definitely going. He's definitely staying. For two summers, it was a Ross and Rachel *will they, won't they?* saga. And then, finally, an end to the to-ing and fro-ing: a new contract, a new commitment. A line drawn under the issue, the soap opera concluded. Friends again.

With the threat of Steven Gerrard joining Chelsea seemingly resolved in 2004, and a fifth European Cup on display at Anfield, Liverpool fans could have been forgiven for looking forward to a summer spent basking in glory, rather than wondering if, at the second time of asking, the club captain would be relocating 200 miles south.

With Chelsea back with another bid, Gerrard had to weigh up the chance of almost certain Premiership titles with the mere outside chance of them. Against that, he had to weigh up what it would mean to be 'just another' part of a Chelsea team largely resented by the masses and always likely to struggle for recognition, by virtue of how easy their wealth makes it for them, compared with the chance to become a true Liverpool legend by helping win trophies — even if that includes just one league title before he turns 30 — against the odds. It must have been tempting to join the Russian revolution at Stamford Bridge: to play in a team already dominating English football, and with other glamorous superstars certain to follow. It must also have been tempting to receive a sizeable boost in wages, although like most top players he already had enough money to live comfortably for several lifetimes.

Footballing satisfaction comes in a number of guises. Being the captain of your hometown club — when that club is also the most successful in English history (and still a big 'player' on the world stage) — has to count for something. That the club was moving in the right direction, with a manager of proven quality, also had to be important. It is ironic that with the Reds stagnating under Gérard Houllier between 2002 and 2004 it never occurred to Gerrard (or anyone else) that his future might lie elsewhere. Then, with the long overdue change of direction, in which the manager favoured by both Gerrard and Owen was duly appointed as Houllier's successor, Owen leaves and Gerrard comes close to doing likewise. A year later, with the greatest achievement secured by the club since at least 1990 — although arguably the greatest since as far back as 1984 — Gerrard again comes close to making his exit.

Communication errors were at the heart of the problem. (Another nod to the *Friends* scriptwriters? Or perhaps closer to the Aussie farces of *Neighbours?*) Gerrard stated in Istanbul that he was definitely staying. Why would he leave? But the talks didn't materialise, with an assumption made by the club's hierarchy that everything would be sorted in due course; there was no rush. Gerrard, however, felt the lack of urgency signified doubts on the manager's part. Benítez, who was not used to making special exceptions for players, eventually came to realise that Gerrard needed to be handled more with kid gloves. After all, the captain had been carrying the hopes of the club for a number of seasons; symbolically, if nothing else, he wasn't *just any other player*. There was a lot more pressure on him than on any of his team-mates, especially once Michael Owen — the other man to carry the burden of rescuing results — left the club. If Gerrard played well, Liverpool played well.

It's not that Gerrard necessarily has an enormous ego — although the 'Stevie Me' tag he picked up none-too-subtly claims otherwise — but that he is sensitive to how he is perceived, and needs to feel appreciated and rewarded for his efforts. Gérard Houllier was always very publicly supportive, and

Benítez hadn't gone to such lengths. For a midfield enforcer, the Liverpool captain is not like Roy Keane, who didn't seem to give a sod about anything other than winning. Gerrard is more emotional; he wears his heart on his sleeve (right next to the UEFA Champions League badge). At times you can see things get on top of him, whereas Keane (much like Graeme Souness) never looked hurt, just angry, very angry, or incandescent.

It's fair to say that the links with Chelsea tarnished Gerrard's reputation with the Liverpool fans. While still adored by many, and frequently serenaded with '. . . he's big, and he's fucking hard . . .', the fact that he had been so close to leaving — and joining a major rival (and a particularly disliked one at that) –– was not something that would be forgotten overnight. Despite his best-ever season in a red shirt, admiration of the captain was tinged with doubts over the way he handled the sagas of 2004 and 2005. That he lifted the European Cup after a second-half man-of-the-match performance in May 2005, and then ultimately spurned Chelsea's advances for a second time, wasn't quite enough. An issue of trust had been damaged. Reds still unquestionably wanted Gerrard in the team, but the love had been soured a little. Fans can be forgiving, but most cannot turn their emotions on and off like a tap.

In time, it will surely be forgotten. The way he responded in 2005/06 will go a long way towards healing the wounds. His match-winning contribution in the FA Cup final will also help. But he still needs a number of seasons to put distance between the events that clouded those two summers; he needs time to prove that, after two dalliances with Chelsea, a *third* will definitely not arise. The bigger a hero, the more vilified he will be for defecting, and a local hero, as Gerrard undoubtedly is, will suffer even more; the betrayal always feels that bit greater.

Frank Lampard or Steven Gerrard?

There can be no doubting that Benítez has managed to get the best out of his captain, with a more advanced role that suits his talents. There are few players in world football as devastating when facing play, and running forward with or without the ball. He doesn't have the tricks of a Ronaldinho, but such is the pace and strength in his running, allied to good control and intelligent movement, that he can be almost unstoppable.

Since Benítez arrived, Gerrard has scored 36 goals, only four of which have been penalties. In 2005/06, his general productivity was greatly increased on the season before, which in itself had been full of telling contributions. In his second season under Benítez, Gerrard scored 23 goals, and created a further 28. That works out at almost a goal or assist every single game. When you adjust the figures from every game to every 90 minutes of football (to account for time spent on the bench, from where even the best players can't influence proceedings), it works out at more than a goal or assist every 'game'. His peers were so impressed they voted him PFA Player of the Year in 2006.

Brazil manager Carlos Parreira, when asked which foreign players he wished were Brazilian, replied: "Steven Gerrard is a wonderful midfield player. He can really play." That's a pretty big compliment, given the midfield talent Parreira can call upon. When players retire, they may like to look back on their careers and count their medals, but clearly, winning the admiration of those in the game who really matter — your peers, and those who've proven they know their stuff — has to count for a lot.

Benfica head coach Ronald Koeman was effusive in his praise of the Liverpool captain, before the two teams met in the Champions League. "Steven Gerrard is one of the very best, whether he plays on the right or in midfield. He can decide games on his own. He makes the crosses, he makes passes and shoots." Former AC Milan manager, Alberto Zaccheroni, was similarly impressed: "I like the fair play of English players, their enthusiasm and the fact that the players always give everything . . . I like Rooney, Lampard and Terry but Gerrard is my favourite. Gerrard is so versatile. He is a player who makes the difference."

Birmingham manager Steve Bruce was also quick to sing Gerrard's praises. "In Steven Gerrard they have the one player I would pick from the whole world. The performance he gave at St Andrews when they beat us 3-0 [in 2004] was unbelievable, as good as I have ever seen from any individual." In 2006, Steven Gerrard was back at St Andrews, giving Bruce nightmares, this time on the right wing. He didn't score, but time and time again he terrorised the young full-back, Matthew Sadler, with his constant forays down the right wing, and had a direct involvement in five of the seven goals.

Kenny Dalglish, the man whose title 'Liverpool's Greatest' was under threat from Gerrard (according to Alan Hansen), was full of praise for the current captain after yet another supreme contribution, this time in the FA Cup final. "Steven has done more for Liverpool in the past few seasons than any other player," said Dalglish. "Never mind Ronaldinho for Barcelona or Thierry Henry for Arsenal, Steven has done more for his team and contributed more than anyone else. When you have got fantastic ability and you ally that with his courage and belief, that is one hell of an ingredient."

Would anyone without Stamford Bridge allegiances really pick Frank Lampard ahead of Gerrard? Of course, Jose Mourinho wanted the chance to pick both. It's testament to Lampard that he has improved to the point where he is considered amongst the world's elite, and with his form and consistency for Chelsea, it's merited. His record of 164 consecutive Premiership games is phenomenal. But he has been the crowning glory of a fully-balanced side that has been consistently dominating games; when Chelsea's form deteriorated towards the end of 2005/06, Lampard became fairly invisible. Gerrard has proved he can excel in a (relatively) struggling side, as Liverpool were for a couple of seasons between 2002-2004, whereas Lampard might be no better than very good in a side lacking quality throughout. Now that Liverpool are edging closer to the level of quality and balance at Stamford Bridge, Gerrard's effectiveness has surpassed Lampard's; and yet Chelsea are the finished article as a side, whereas the Reds are still working towards their own version of 'perfection'.

When comparing the two no.8s, it's fair to say that the Londoner is more composed and less excitable than his Scouse counterpart. One of Gerrard's main flaws is how he lets things affect him, and works up too much nervous tension — as happened before the Champions League final, with the management concerned at how much energy he was expending in the build up, which perhaps manifested itself in his difficulty in getting going in the first half. The Liverpool captain is more *explosive* than Lampard in all senses, with a burst of pace and aggressive attacking, or a moment of hotheadedness. That said, dismissals and bookings have diminished, with just nine yellow cards since 2003; which made his sending off against Everton after just 18 minutes, for two moments of rashness, all the more out of (his changed) character.

Gerrard can shake up a team in the way Lampard cannot. Lampard is a brilliant attacking midfielder; there is no denying that. But Gerrard is a brilliant *all-round* player who can excel in any position on the pitch. After a shellshocked first half in Istanbul, where his nervous tension — and Milan's brilliance — made him little more than a spectator, Gerrard went on to put in a monumental performance, both in an attacking sense, and then, in extra time, as a full-back who put the tricky Brazilian Serginho in the stand time and time again.

Gerrard is more versatile than his England colleague, and while both have great stamina, the Liverpool player is clearly the more athletic. He is a better crosser, and can go past people with more ease. Gerrard's versatility has actually worked against him for England; shifted to the left and to the right, and asked to play as the holding midfielder — which goes against his natural inclination to expend energy and be completely involved in the action — he has rarely been utilised in his best role, chiefly because Lampard cannot really fit in anywhere other than as the attacking central midfielder.

Before this season, Lampard was clearly seen as the more potent goal threat, although Gerrard's 13 goals the previous season, despite missing two months with a broken foot, was a long-overdue return in front of goal, freed as he was from the shackles of the previous administration under which he had more defensive responsibilities. Lampard, with 19 goals in 2004/05, was voted the Footballer of the Year by his fellow professionals and hailed for his miraculous strike rate for a midfielder. However, Gerrard actually scored more goals per start than his London-based counterpart. Take away Lampard's three penalties that season, and Gerrard's return — with no spot kicks — looks better still. Of course, taking good penalties is a handy skill, but it's not one that helps you judge a player's overall effectiveness. A goalkeeper can stroll up and score 15 penalties in a season, but it wouldn't mean he'd be taken seriously as a goalscorer. A penalty is a 'free' shot at goal that any player could convert; far different from finding the time and space in the box in open play — or, if a midfielder, the legs to get forward in the first place. Indeed, the ability to win penalties is arguably a more valuable asset, as that is what creates the chance in the first place. And were Lampard to find himself in a team with a better penalty taker, of the calibre of Matt Le Tissier (who scored 48 of his 49), then he might find his goal tally severely depleted.

In 2005/06, Gerrard ranked above Lampard in terms of goals per start, and goals from open play per start. Removing penalties (Lampard with six, Gerrard four) makes for an even bigger difference between the two. Gerrard tops total goals 23 to 20, goals per start 0.47 to 0.42 and open play goals per start 0.39 to 0.3. Over the past two seasons Lampard outscores Gerrard by 39 to 36, but from 1270 more minutes of football (more than 14 games' worth), and including five extra penalties.

Gerrard, nearing 26, has yet to reach his peak; Lampard, approaching 28, is at his, and has only come into his own since his mid-20s. In many ways, the comparison of the two players is a reverse of the teams' other major local stars, Jamie Carragher and John Terry. Whereas there's not a lot to choose between the two — both are pure defenders who'd put their bodies in the way of anything that moves — neutrals would probably opt for Terry on account of the little extra he can do, with a goal every ten games to Carragher's one every 133. (Ian Rush's goalscoring record could yet fall to Carragher, providing the current vice-captain manages to play on until the year 3044). Terry also presumably has more scope for improvement once he reaches his peak years.

Ultimately, any comparison of Gerrard with Lampard, or of Carragher with Terry, is incomplete without the final factor: that Carragher and Gerrard wouldn't be the same at Chelsea as they are at Liverpool; and vice versa with the London pair. Both pairs of players suit the clubs they play at. Chelsea fans wouldn't want to swap Terry and Lampard for anyone; the same is true of Liverpool fans with Carragher and Gerrard.

Chapter Four

Michael Owen: An Unhappy Return

December 26th 2005: Michael Owen, in fine fettle just a week after scoring a hat-trick against West Ham, returns to Anfield with Newcastle United. Managed by Graeme Souness, another ex-Red whose stock with fans has dwindled since giving up the red jersey, Owen is turning out in opposition colours for the first time against the club he joined in 1990, aged eleven and knee-high to a grasshopper. (And which he left in 2004, aged 25 and knee-high to a slightly taller grasshopper.)

It was to become a very depressing day for the 26-year-old former no.10. Finding his erstwhile teammates in a Scrooge-like spirit of unseasonal miserliness, he was shackled throughout by his best mate Jamie Carragher and Sami Hyypia, and was given merciless stick by the Kop every time the ball went near him; it cannot be said that his every touch was booed as it is hard to recall him having a touch, so comprehensively was his new team outplayed and then dispatched.

Owen had taken a gamble on pastures new in August 2004, joining Real Madrid, the world's most successful and glamorous club. Little over a year later, he was returning to Anfield clad in the colours of one of England's most underachieving 'big' clubs, a team without a major trophy in over 30 years, and without a league title in more than 50.

It appeared a marriage of short-term convenience for Owen. With the World Cup in 2006 just a year away, he wanted regular football to guarantee his place in Sven Goran Eriksson's team; he was still at a good age, while the World Cup would be in Germany, without the problems of unbearable heat, altitude and different time zones which make winning the event on a different continent all but impossible for a European team. While he'd succeeded at Real Madrid in terms of goals-per-minutes, impressing many with his attitude, he was not a first choice starter. The writing was on the wall when Madrid entered the transfer market. In his second season, had he chosen to stay, he would have kept out of the team by the three 'R's' Ronaldo, Raul and new-boy Robinho. Another Brazilian attacker, Baptista, had also joined. It was also true that Owen hadn't really settled in Spain, and longed for a return to his homeland, and a way of life he understood.

Owen had stated that a return to Liverpool was his preferred option, and Benítez was interested in having the player back. But it was never going to be straightforward for the Liverpool hierarchy. In the summer of 2004, when faced with losing him for nothing a year later, the club had sold him to Real Madrid, for a knock-down price of £8m plus Antonio Núñez. If the fee seemed paltry, it was still in keeping with the depreciation of a top player's value in the final months of his contract, ahead of the point when he can leave for free. If the joke is true — and a compromise is defined by none of the parties involved being totally satisfied — then that was the case here: Owen couldn't demand the highest wages or have total control over the transfer, without being a free agent, and Liverpool didn't receive a hefty fee. However, Owen was as good as his word by not 'doing a Bosman', and Liverpool, unlike with Steve McManaman, did at least have some money to reinvest from the deal.

Now it was one year on — the summer of 2005 — and instead of selling Owen, Parry was faced with trying to *buy* him, and for a fee that would be considerably more than the club had received twelve months earlier. Parry was prepared to go as high as £12m, in itself a bit of a slap in the face, but a slap worth taking given the benefits Owen could offer. Newcastle's intervention — an offer of £17m — was more like a punch square on the nose.

Would Liverpool have happily paid more than £12m for Owen had he not previously played for the club, and therefore not left 'on the cheap'? You can only wonder. Once Newcastle entered the race it left no room for manoeuvre for Parry. All he could hope was that Owen would turn down the Geordies' offer, and put Real Madrid in a position where they either kept him for themselves (which they clearly didn't want to do), or accepted a lower bid from Liverpool.

Owen's problem was that a game of brinkmanship was not on the cards at this particular stage of his career. Of all the years he could consider sitting tight on the Madrid bench, a World Cup year when in his prime was not one of them. Had the gamble gone wrong, he could have lost his place as a guaranteed starter in Eriksson's side. And so, rather reluctantly, Owen had little choice but to sign on the dotted line at St James' Park, the consolation being the adulation of a passionate home crowd who worshipped goalscorers and an attacking mentality at the club. And yet it was a long way from the Champions League glory Owen had set out to pursue with Real Madrid. It was easy to foresee that he'd score goals on Tyneside, and as such satisfy half of his yearly ambition in football, but he had more chance of winning the Nobel Prize for Science than the Premiership or Champions League.

It turned into a miserable season for Owen, Newcastle and Souness. First of all, Newcastle had already crashed out of the Uefa Intertoto Cup, so there was not even the consolation of European football at the less glamorous Uefa Cup level. Weeks after his depressing return to Anfield, and having already missed half of Newcastle's league games up to that point through various muscle injuries, Owen broke his foot in a game against Spurs, and his season was effectively curtailed, just ten games and seven goals in. (He returned in May for the penultimate game of the season.) In his absence the Geordies went into free-fall, taking just one point from the five games following the Anfield defeat. On 2nd February 2006, the day after Newcastle lost 3-0 at Manchester

City (in City's first game post-Robbie Fowler), Souness was sacked. The club that had spent as much money as Liverpool in the previous five years, and easily outspent the Reds in the summer of 2005, was languishing 15th in the table, having won nothing even after all that investment. With Glenn Roeder in temporary charge the Geordies rallied, but Blackburn, aided by Florent Sinama-Pongolle, secured the final Uefa Cup spot by finishing 6th.

So did Owen deserve to receive the (Liver-)'bird' from the Kop? And was it representative of what the fans really felt? The true esteem held for Owen by Liverpool fans can be seen more in the half-time applause at Anfield, during the Monaco game in September 2004, when it was announced that he had scored his first Real Madrid goal. At the time, he was an ex-Liverpool player making it in the wider world; the almost-local boy done good. Even those bitter at the circumstances of his departure could grudgingly rouse themselves to offer a show of appreciation. But once he joined Newcastle he became the potent weapon of a rival, coming to Anfield to try and score against his former employers and to rub salt in the wounds of his former followers.

Owen stated that both he and Carragher found it odd when players looked sheepish after scoring against a former club, and to a degree it's easy to see what they mean — although if, like Denis Law or Gary McAllister, your goal has just relegated your former club, there's no need to rub fans' noses in it if you left on good terms. Owen made it clear he'd be celebrating, although perhaps not doing cartwheels into the Kop. Unfortunately for him, he'd have to get a kick of the ball first.

Reading between the lines of the abuse that cascaded down, there was more frustration that Owen was at Newcastle than any real enmity. Some fans will always hate ex-players, no matter what they do (drag out that 'Judas' chant, lads). But at Liverpool, the vast majority still respected what Owen had to offer. "You should have joined a big club," says it all: you should be here, in red. "Where were you in Istanbul?" was part 'We didn't need you to be successful', part 'You should still be *here*, in red." Following the Champions League win, Owen had been honest (and generous) enough to admit that had he been in the team instead of Milan Baroš, they might not even have made the final. Cause and effect *does* apply to football, as much as people tend to ignore it in retrospective analysis. Owen understood that he could have scored a hat-trick against Chelsea in the semi-final but, given the different players would have been on the pitch, different patterns of play would have ensued from first minute to last, and maybe Liverpool would have lost 4-3. Who knows? You can't just lob a player into a team with hindsight and expect things to have panned out in the same way; it's just not logical.

It's a shame Owen was not shown more respect for his achievements at Liverpool, and it must have upset Jamie Carragher and Steven Gerrard to see their friend, who had contributed so much to the club, given a rough ride. While it will have proved to them that leaving Liverpool is never an idea welcomed by fans, they also must have wondered 'Why do we bother?' if the crowd can be so forgetful of past efforts and glories. Would it stop Owen signing for the club again, maybe in the summer of 2006 if rumours persist? If the manager still wants him to sign, hopefully not.

Which brings us to the notion of a get-out clause in his contract — an idea dismissed at the time by Newcastle chairman Freddie Shepherd, although it's not stretching things to suggest he could have been primarily concerned to ward off speculation. And yet, if you look at the circumstances surrounding Owen's move to Tyneside, it's not too hard to believe the player would have insisted on something legally binding that would allow him to bid them *adios* if, as was highly likely, the club failed to match his ambition. This is a player who craves the highest stage, and Champions League football. As an hypothesis, you can see Newcastle agreeing to the idea of a get-out clause because their need for the player was so great: to supplement the ageing Shearer, who was their only decent striker, and to appease fans who seem perennially restless. The gamble on their part would be that, with Owen at the club, they stood a better chance of reaching the Champions League; and if they did so, Owen could not — and maybe even *would not want to* — leave. So Newcastle, in their haste to have him sign, agree to a release figure in the region of £12m, crossing their fingers that it would never need to be activated.

That is not to say that such a clause exists, but the reasons behind there being one, from the player's point of view, are undeniably sound. The last thing Michael Owen wants is to spend the best remaining years of his career, before he turns 30 and the pace dims, in a team not even qualifying for the Uefa Cup. Much surely depends on who is appointed as Souness' successor — the potential on Tyneside remains huge, if only they could appoint the right manager and then stand by him. Then there's the issue of guilt; it's arguable that Owen is not the most sentimental of players, but even someone as ambitious as he might feel loath to walk away from a club where he spent most of the season injured.

Injuries are perceived to have blighted his career, but it's also true that, at just 26, he's played 420 games for club and country, scoring 213 goals in the process. So despite the dodgy hamstrings, and the ailments that hindered him in 2005/06, he remains a hugely effective and reliable goalscorer. Few are cooler in front of goal. Should Liverpool come knocking again in the summer of 2006, it'll be interesting to see what happens. As a lone striker, in the formation Benítez favoured at the start of this season, Owen would have floundered: he is no hold-up man, no great linker of play. In that particular role, he might score more goals than Peter Crouch, but the team as a whole would struggle. But alongside a target-man like Crouch, he would be in his element, as seen with all the goals he has plundered when the two have played together for England. With Benítez opting for a 4-4-2 formation more than anticipated in his second season in England, there could yet be a (mostly) united Kop behind Owen again, singing *Hallelujah*.

Stranger things have happened, as seen with the return of Robbie Fowler.

Chapter Five

Keeping Benítez

Liverpool's ability to retain the services of Rafael Benítez is clearly going to be crucial to how far the Reds progress in the coming seasons; this is *Rafa's Revival*, after all. He may not be the only top-notch manager in world football, but men of his calibre are thin on the ground, and it can become a feeding frenzy between the top clubs for their signatures when they become available. While press speculation and fans' fears in the spring of 2006 may have made Benítez seem closer to a move to Real Madrid than was actually true — after all, there was no reason to question his working relationship with the Liverpool hierarchy, or his intention to finish a job into which he had put so much effort starting — it is also clear that this is a story that will not easily go away.

Some stories in football become perennials, flowering with the daffodils. Some stories are *easy*; if you trot something out often enough, it starts to have a ring of truth about it (there's no smoke without fire), even though it could logically seem *less* true every time it surfaces and disappears without trace.

Sometimes stories fit: Owen returning to Liverpool, for instance. There are enough suspicions, given previous links, to make it all seem plausible even if denied vehemently. And in the case of Benítez and Real Madrid, the links will always remain especially strong. Perhaps one day the rumour will prove true, but there is nothing to suggest it will be in the near future. Benítez is a young manager, with time on his side; time to achieve all he possibly can in England, and only then look to his homeland, either at Madrid or with the national team.

Having tried to ignore the speculation, in an attempt to deny it any credibility, Benítez was eventually forced to confront the issue by dedicating his future to Liverpool. Madrid had allegedly made an approach, and Inter Milan were rumoured to be very interested, but it did not necessarily follow that the manager was thinking of defecting. It was widely reported on March 15th that he had signed a new contract, extending his current deal by a further year — taking it to 2010 — but there was no official confirmation of this, just a public statement reiterating his commitment to the Anfield cause. "I've never talked about demands [to the board]," Benítez said. "Sure, I want to improve and I want to see the club progressing, but I think we are working in the right way. I will be here next season, for sure. I am grateful to the people here — the supporters, the board, the chairman, the Chief Executive and also the players. If you are at a club where everything is right, the atmosphere is good, then there is no need to change."

Benítez went on to insist that while Real Madrid and Inter Milan were 'fantastic clubs', Liverpool was too. "I have a responsibility," he said, "and I must continue doing my job. I cannot say, okay, I will go because I might receive a good offer. If I am here and I want to stay here for a long time, it means I have confidence. We will have a better team next season than last season. The difference between a very good season, a fantastic season or a not so good season can be one or two players. Next season, with more players, it will be easier. We already have a better squad than last season, after all."

Annual link

Two years, two major links to Real Madrid, the club where Benítez spent his formative years as both player and coach. The first was when Benítez had taken Liverpool to the latter stages of the Champions League in 2005, with Madrid already dumped out; the second came in the spring of 2006, when Real Madrid found themselves with yet another caretaker manager and a new President. The *galactico* system may have been seen as a failure, and its mastermind, Florentino Pérez, may have fallen on his own sword, but this remains Real Madrid, the place where superstars still wield too much power, and where interference from above is an all too common occurrence.

At the height of the speculation it was reported that Real Madrid's new President, Fernando Martín, had approached Benítez's agent, Manuel García Quilón, about his client's availability. Real Madrid's fans certainly saw Benítez as the best man for the job: 35% voted for him on an internet poll, placing him ahead of Fabio Capello and Arsene Wenger.

However, Wenger summed up the scepticism top coaches feel about the role: told that Madrid's next coach will be given more power, Wenger joked, "Do you believe that?" But Wenger also highlighted the attraction the club holds: "Real Madrid is certainly a club I love because of my childhood." He just knows *not to touch*. Too many men have discovered that Real Madrid is like the beautiful, alluring woman in the nightclub: once she is taken home, out of the flattering light, the fake tan, false eyelashes, hair extensions, excessive make-up and *Wonderbra* become all too apparent. Oh, and she microwaves your cat and eats your hamster.

The political machinations at the Bernabéu make the goings-on at Westminster look like a particularly sedate kindergarten. In May 2006,

Sid Lowe, the *Guardian Unlimited*'s Spanish correspondent, described the latest events behind the scenes that took place in the final two months of the season, from the point Martín replaced Pérez: "He [Martín] had the entire team photo redone so he could be in it, sent letters to the socios [club members] from holiday telling them how great he was, refused to hold the elections that everyone demanded, and cut his hair and swapped his specs to look more statesman-like. But, however hard he tried — and he tried pretty hard — he remained a joke, haranguing players like a school-master in a classroom (a photo was briefly available on the club's website, so blind was he to the damage the image would cause); taking [the players'] holidays away; giving holidays back; bringing a new director of communications whose experience consisted of pithy statements about piles of bricks to a club with the game's biggest media stars; shouting his mouth off about signings that were never going to happen; threatening his very own footballing Big Brother; and generally getting absolutely everything wrong." This about the man who was taking over at a time of 'crisis', and whose brief was presumably to steady the ship. Martín lasted 59 days. Pérez had remained an extremely powerful figure at the club, and the board of directors were still extraordinarily loyal to him. With such power struggles taking place, building a successful team seems almost secondary. Instead of looking like an easier working environment for a manager, the activity behind the scenes continues to make it all the more difficult.

It's an unusual position for Liverpool to find themselves in: a manager courted by a more powerful, glamorous and successful club; after all, not many of those exist. In the past, British managers at Anfield were happy at what they felt was the top of the game, and nothing overseas was likely to lure all-too-British men like Bill Shankly and Bob Paisley away from where they felt at home (and years later, in the early '90s, no top continental club was ever likely to want to lure Graeme Souness). Football has changed a great deal in the last 15 years, with Europe opening up its employment boundaries and offering far greater freedom of movement. And in that time, Liverpool has slipped from its perch at the top of the English game, and while able to lift the European Cup one more time in 2005, it is no longer regarded as the best team in Europe, as it had been during the late '70s and early '80s. It remains important, but is no longer in an elite of *one*.

Not since Bob Paisley have Liverpool had one of Europe's undisputed premier managers. Kenny Dalglish did very well domestically, but never got a chance to prove himself as a manager on the European stage, while the team he created owed a large debt to Paisley and Joe Fagan; without wishing to undermine Dalglish's laudable achievements, it always takes more to build a successful team from scratch than to keep a successful team at the top (although, of course, that isn't exactly easy, either). Paisley topped Shankly's achievements by winning the European Cup not once, but three times; Dalglish added nothing new in terms of heights attained — at least in terms of trophies — although his 1987/88 side did set some records with its exhilarating brand of football, and he led the club to its only league and FA Cup 'double', in 1986.

Having a manager from the continent means that this individual, whoever he is, will have his own boyhood ideal, his own view on the 'dream' club to manage. In Gérard Houllier's case, a stint on Merseyside as a young man in the late 1960s had given him a love for Liverpool, a bond strengthened by having stood on the Kop. Houllier, even when at his most successful at Liverpool, was never quite able to escape the stigma of past failures (most notably when, as head of the French national team, his side collapsed and failed to qualify for the 1994 World Cup), and even his remarkable cup treble of 2001 did not obscure an inability to land the biggest prizes. No other club was desperate for Houllier, certainly not to the point where it felt like any predators were hovering overhead. Houllier proved with his subsequent league title with Lyon that he is a good manager. Lyon's unlucky exit to AC Milan in the Champions League, where he came within three minutes of reaching the semi-final (a handful of minutes closer than against Bayer Leverkusen with Liverpool at the same stage in 2002), was another indicator that he could do well on the highest stage. But the latter achievement was also another example of falling short, while the former — strolling to the French title — was more a case of keeping on an even keel a team that had won the league the previous four seasons. He deserves credit, especially as some rebuilding work was involved, but if there was one job in France where it was easy to win the championship, Lyon was it.

Houllier only ended up at Lyon because he was sacked by Liverpool. His homeland, France, has no club of greater stature than Liverpool, and frankly, none that comes even close; so he could not have been lured away from Anfield while still in charge. Spain, on the other hand, has Barcelona and, most notably, Real Madrid. Italy, another nation with its fair share of glamorous, successful super-clubs, was not slow in noticing Benítez's talents, with Inter Milan also linked with a swoop.

Inter Milan remain an interesting case. Or rather, an interesting *headcase*. Massimo Moratti, the Inter Milan owner who resigned as president in 2004, has signed 112 players and worked his way through an incredible 14 coaches in the past 11 years, winning only one Uefa Cup (in 1998) and one Coppa Italia. The club's spending has been astronomical, buying superstars whenever they hit the market. Compare that to Liverpool in that time: just three managers, far less expenditure, and a trophy haul of three League Cups, two FA Cups, two European Super Cups, one Uefa Cup and the *coup de grâce*: the club's fifth European Cup.

However, it's also important to remember that a foreign club often holds more mystique and romance for any individual; there's less likelihood of taking something for granted when it's not part of your own culture. The rare intensity of the Kop's passion, and Liverpool's tradition, makes it a club that excites those from countries used to more sedate crowds and more difficult working environments. Liverpool has a lot to offer, and remains unique in many ways.

Liverpool has a dignity that most other clubs lack. There is an integrity about this institution, a special respect outsiders reserve for it: from the way Peter Robinson went about his business, to how its top brass repeatedly offers new contracts to players who might instead be fearing for their futures, such as when struck down with a broken leg (Stephen Warnock) or when seriously ill in hospital (Markus Babbel); to the decided lack of haste when it comes to dismissing managers (if one sacking in nearly 50 years is anything to go by); to its refusal to charge excessive amounts for season tickets (at least when compared to some other clubs); to the continued access it offers the media, unlike other clubs who petulantly ban journalists or entire news organisations if they dare criticise; and so on.

This is not to say that the club is perfect, as its censure for illegally approaching Christian Ziege from Middlesborough in 2000 highlights, while its involvement in G14 ties the club to accusations of a self-serving interest (although there is not one football club in the world that would turn down membership; Everton's hierarchy was questioning the group's motives, but they would jump at the chance to be part of the G14). For any manager working outside Anfield, there will be an admiration for how the club generally conducts itself.

Target

Liverpool is used to losing its top players to the continent — Kevin Keegan, Graeme Souness, Ian Rush, Michael Owen, Phil Babb (old joke, but well worth recycling) — but has never before felt covetous eyes on its manager. Of course, never before had Liverpool appointed a manager so fresh from notable success, but that in itself should have served to illustrate Benítez's desire to be on Merseyside: if he had wanted to be anywhere else, he could have cherry-picked his destination after walking out on Valencia. Vacancies at Real Madrid and Inter Milan are hardly slow in coming around — Real Madrid get through coaches quicker than Ronaldo gets through *cordero asado* — so Benítez could have rebutted Liverpool's approach if it was important to be at one of these other clubs instead. If Benítez was unhappy with anything he was finding about life at Anfield, it was not going to be any better at a big Spanish or Italian club.

Of course, Real Madrid remain the real 'threat', the one that makes fans worry. And yet there simply isn't an air of stability about that club, at least in terms of management: some of the players, on the other hand, seem all too stable, safely cosseted within their comfort zones. It's debatable whether

Madrid could ever have a culture that truly respects the manager, and since Benítez's methods — like those of most top coaches — involve him being 100% in charge, he's unlikely to want to be undermined by anyone else at the club. It's not just Player Power in Spain, but President Power. And if it's not Player Power or President Power, it's Sporting Director Power — as Benítez discovered at Valencia, with Jesus Garcia Pitarch, who appeared to be acting upon his own agenda when it came to signing players. Benitez described another director, Manuel Lloren, as 'a scorpion' and added: "He would put a syringe in your neck to be sure he extracted the last drop out of you." In Spain, and possibly a small number of British clubs, so many people are in on the act, offering their views and sticking their oar in, that it must be virtually impossible for the man responsible for running the team to actually get on and do so.

Clearly Real Madrid is dear to Benítez's heart. But the role of manager at the Bernabéu remains a poisoned chalice; you can take the job, and find your career derailed months later. There is no time to build a side, no thought to long-term planning. Vicente Del Bosque, Benítez's former team-mate and the man he also worked beside as assistant manager, was sacked in 2003, having won *two* European Cups and just clinched another league title. Perez said: "I want to be sincere about this — our belief that he was not the right coach for the future." It's laughable. It was like Liverpool sacking Bob Paisley — with whom Del Bosque shared an unassuming manner and avuncular style — in 1981, and replacing him with Tommy Docherty.

You can only fully realise how well a club like Liverpool is run — at least in terms of support for its manager — when compared to some of the alternatives. At Anfield the manager gets *time*: the commodity he values more highly than money. There's no point being given £100m to spend if, after two bad results, a new manager is in charge of those players, some of whom he will find himself trying to offload at half the price. As well as allowing time for a plan to come to fruition, you don't see David Moores and Rick Parry in the dressing room at half-time, delivering team talks and deciding upon substitutions. There is a distinct lack of ego behind the scenes. Freedom is another commodity managers value more highly than money: the freedom to choose their own squad, pick their own team, and implement their own tactics.

At Liverpool, a manager will be granted time and freedom. He will also receive a sizeable amount of money — no Liverpool manager has ever not been backed in the transfer market — but of course, by spiralling standards elsewhere, the budget will pale in comparison with that of other teams, and Chelsea's expenditure in particular. Money is still important in football. Any manager will struggle if he cannot get the players he wants at a price his club can afford. Just how much money any manager needs is like asking *how long is a piece of string?* There are no hard and fast rules, and each target has his own circumstances, and his own monetary value.

What is true is that, Xabi Alonso aside, none of Liverpool's best players have ever cost more than £10m. Above that figure, the Reds have seen diminishing returns on their outlay: Emile Heskey, El- Hadji Diouf and Djbril Cissé have not proved good value for money. Other teams have successfully spent large sums, but nearly all clubs have had their fingers burnt when writing large cheques, and some disastrously so. Alex Ferguson had a no-brainer with Wayne Rooney, with the only danger being that of him going off the rails, but Juan Sebastian Veron cost even more and delivered far less; Arsene Wenger bought arguably English football's finest-ever player, Thierry Henry, for less than he paid for Sylvan Wiltord; while Chelsea have paid £10m+ on players like Chris Sutton, Adrian Mutu, Scott Parker and Veron (again), all of whom offered nothing to the club.

What Liverpool has done is to succeed in finding more than its fair share of bargains: players who, if sold on at their prime, would be *fetching* £10m+ from other clubs (in other words, the club has had its 'expensive' players, it just got them on the cheap). There is nothing to say that good scouting cannot deliver more like Hyypia, Riise, Reina, Finnan, Kewell and Alonso: all of whom could have been put up for sale for at least double their original transfer fee quickly after their arrival, and as such, made an almost instant mockery of their transfer fee. Shrewd buying is what counts, even if certain players, with the exception of those who are out of contract, will always be in the top price bracket, and as such, out of range. Gary McAllister and Markus Babbel were two of Gérard Houllier's best signings, but also his cheapest; Robbie Fowler, back at Anfield on a free transfer, could prove of equal value if he remains fit, while Bolo Zenden is another Bosman transfer who could yet have a big influence on the club. Of course, sometimes a free transfer disguises the inflated £6m-a-year salary, but all of these players would be on relatively 'normal' pay-packets for top-end players.

Value for money is everything. Whatever else Luis Garcia contributes to Liverpool's cause, the decision to pay £6m for him was vindicated by his goals *en route* to the Champions League success; it's daft whenever commentators trot out the cliché that a new player has repaid 'a large part of his transfer fee' after one single goal, but the little Spaniard's five strikes in the knockout stages of the competition not only generated the club a sum greater that his transfer fee, but also 'bought' the club one of the best nights in its history, ensuring that the Champions League trophy would never again leave Anfield. Of course it wasn't Luis Garcia alone who won the trophy, but his goals were the most visible contribution of the whole cup run.

On top of this, Liverpool has promoted enough notable talent from its youth ranks, particularly in the '90s, to make a difference. If Liverpool had wanted to buy Robbie Fowler, Steve McManaman, Michael Owen, Jamie Carragher and Steven Gerrard from a rival club when at their peak — had they been groomed by Blackburn, for example — then that could easily have set the club back £100m. Irrespective of how much these players generate in transfer fees (so far it stands at around just £20m, with McManaman leaving for nothing a year after being valued at £12m, and Owen for less than half his true value), their contribution to the club cannot be questioned. To date those five players have totalled 1,700 games in a red shirt. Their contributions to Champions League qualifications, and in a number of cup successes (eight since 1992, when McManaman featured heavily), have earned the club money and kudos, and saved the board millions in expenditure in not having to look elsewhere for players of comparable quality.

Money

In March 2006, when the rumours about Real Madrid courting Benítez became back-page headlines, the newspapers were reporting that the Anfield transfer kitty was an issue for the Spaniard.

Up to that point — just over 18 months into his tenure — Benítez had spent approximately £52m on senior players, plus up to £5m (depending on subsequent appearances) on a series of teenagers. A further £6m was committed to Gabriel Paletta and Mark Gonzalez, two players yet to arrive at the club. Considering the amount of players this covers — nearly 25 — as part of the extensive rebuilding work everyone acknowledged was required, it's a fairly modest sum. Chelsea and Manchester United spent such sums on just two players each. The £4m spent on 'failures' Josemi and Antonio Núñez was more than recouped, and only the £6.5m spent on Fernando Morientes looks poor value for money, when, given Morientes' pedigree, it should have proved great business. Such are the vagaries of transfer success and failure.

Since Benítez's arrival in the summer of 2004, the club has recouped £30m in transfer fees, although in the case of Emile Heskey it was the previous regime which organised the sale, and it was they who also committed to an outlay of £14.2m on Djibril Cissé. Excluding deals done by Houllier and his staff, the net spend of Benítez works out at around £30m: a fraction more than Rio Ferdinand cost Manchester United.

So would Benítez seriously have considered leaving Liverpool if he did not think there was enough money to spend? Much depends on what he was promised by Rick Parry in the negotiations preceding his appointment, but it's unlikely he was told there would be extravagant amounts on offer. Even had the club been in better financial shape, following the expected investment that summer, it's unlikely to have radically altered the manager's plans as to who he bought; players like Alonso and Luis Garcia were targets from the get-go. And yet it could have made the crucial difference regarding a number of targets that were ultimately deemed too expensive, most notably Michael Owen and Simão Sabrosa.

At other clubs — certainly on the continent — Benítez might have more cash, only to discover that it's not actually down to him to spend it. When Benítez arrived at Liverpool, the club appeared on the brink of securing an investment deal that would allow the Spaniard a fairly substantial war-chest; the club then won the Champions League, with all its financial rewards, and qualified for the following season, too. (As it did for a third successive season, in 2006.) So he would have been expecting money to spend. However, his success at Valencia was based on tactics and workrate, not the chequebook. The option of money would be welcome; but it need not be a limitless supply. Already in two years he has spent more at Liverpool — and has had greater control over that spending — than in three years at Valencia. It's also clear that at Liverpool he needed to spend more than at his previous club, where he inherited a more talented and capable unit.

"I am happy here," Benítez reiterated in March, "and if we continue progressing I think I will be here for a long time. I've spoken with [the Chief Executive] Rick Parry, the Chairman [David Moores] and the board, and they've told me they have the same idea as me. They want to progress, to win trophies and keep the club going forward. For me, that is enough."

The sense of satisfaction gained from making Liverpool consistently successful again would surely outweigh spending megabucks at Madrid. Jose Mourinho has discovered with Chelsea that even winning the major honours doesn't necessarily guarantee full respect, if it's been achieved with what others may deem an unfair advantage. Benítez can make history at Liverpool — or rather, continue to reunite Liverpool with its own illustrious history — but at Madrid, the recent history still includes three European Cups and a number of league titles, and the continuous expectation of glory each and every season. It's difficult to see a man as driven and as committed as Benítez walk away from a job having failed, and that's what he would be doing if he were to leave before his vision is complete. So far he has not failed in his development of the club, but he was brought in to finish a job, not leave one half-started.

Benítez has always had the air of an honourable man. Despite serious internal pressures while managing Valencia, he clearly did not find it easy to walk away, even breaking down in tears in an unusual moment of public emotion. That he had exceeded his ambitions with Valencia — it's doubtful that even in his wildest dreams he expected to win two *La Liga* titles in just three years, as well as the Uefa Cup — made it possible for him to walk away with his head held high. He has not yet achieved such aims at Liverpool. The Champions League success, however remarkable, was not the sum of his work, but the result of his instant impact on a mostly inherited squad. It ensures his place in Liverpool's history, but he will know in his heart that he has to achieve more in the coming seasons to one day walk away as an unqualified success.

Chapter Six

The Two Year Search for Overnight Riches

Many Liverpool fans, when faced with the long-running saga of investment in their club, have understandably craved a Roman Abramovich-type investor, having seen how dramatically the Russian's money has boosted Chelsea. In many ways, Abramovich is the apotheosis of Sugar Daddies. Most people invest money with the hope of seeing financial reward; in his case, the Russian is almost like Richard Prior in Brewster's Millions: trying to give it away (except Abramovich has a few billion set aside for those harsh Siberian winters). Maybe his ambition is to ultimately make a very tidy profit from Chelsea, but from the outside it appears he is simply happy to have found an expensive hobby that can put him at the epicentre of the footballing world, with all the kudos and glamour that provides. But it's easy, as a fan of a rival club, to wish for a stranger to appear from out of nowhere, bestow a billion pounds, and lurk mostly in the background without interfering.

The reality is that most investment simply isn't like that. Clubs sell a stake in order to raise capital, and that tends to be a limited amount that, in truth, doesn't go an awfully long way in the modern age; certainly nowhere near as far as Abramovich's money. Once the stake is sold, there's no going back. And if the entire club is sold, it can end up in the hands of people who don't have the fans' best interests at heart. Success on the field reaps financial rewards, but some big clubs can remain money-making machines for their shareholders even in the face of mediocrity.

Heart of Midlothian is a painful example. With the Edinburgh team starting the season in impressive form, coming out of the traps flying — the best start in their 132-year history leaving them six points clear of Celtic — it all looked so rosy. Vladimir Romanov, the Lithuania-based majority shareholder, had invested money in the team, and it looked like a match made in heaven. However, with George Burley doing an apparently perfect job as manager, there were still allegations of interference. Riding high, the Tynecastle side abruptly sacked Burley, and replaced him with Graham Rix — a bizarre choice, given the latter's unremarkable record as a manager, and the baggage of a prison sentence for statutory rape. Rix was sacked after just a few months, amid claims that Romanov wanted the axe to fall even quicker; hardly an example of appointing the correct manager and giving him time to go about his work. Rix had previously held a team meeting to inform the players that Romanov had picked the team for the 1-1 draw against Dundee United, and that he had been 'powerless' to act. To fans, it's a powerful example of the old adage "be careful what you wish for, as it might come true." Investors who are not prepared to give the team the necessary amount of time can undermine the most crucial pre-requisites for success: patience and stability.

It's clear that Liverpool could have sold shares, or indeed the entire club, to some of the suitors who came sniffing. It is to the credit of Rick Parry and David Moores that they did not sell in haste only to repent at their leisure, although it obviously leaves them open to the criticism of procrastination; certainly the issue dragged on longer than would have been ideal. Any resolution had to represent the best deal for the club, not only the investor.

Rick Parry defended the club's position on the issue: "It's been frustrating for us and we make no secrets about that. We'd like to have got it done sooner but when you're Liverpool then you have to be incredibly careful that you get it right. It's not about selling the family silver and walking away. At the end of the day we're all trustees really and making sure the club's future is in safe hands is of paramount importance. Along the way we have picked up the Champions League so it hasn't been a wasted couple of years."

The men behind the scenes at any club will invariably come in for criticism. They are often the easy, 'faceless' targets. "Sack the board" is a common refrain at football grounds. And yet, most people don't know *precisely* what a board does; certainly few fans, aside from shareholders and those who form Supporters Trusts to get a place on their club's board, get to glean a true insight into what takes place behind closed oak doors. Often the criticisms are guesswork.

Rick Parry, for example, gets his fair share of criticism. However, he might feel compelled to point to his record since becoming Chief Executive of Liverpool FC in July 1998 (having been Chief Executive Designate from June 1997). Liverpool's CV does not read as impressively as it did during the halcyon days, but the club is certainly in a healthier position in the new millennium than it was in the final decade of the old one. Since 2001, the club has won two League Cups, two FA Cups, a Uefa Cup, and, the crowning glory, the Champions League (adding two European Super Cups in the process). Having not played in the European Cup once during the 1990s, following a return to European competition in 1991 after a six-year exile, the club has just managed to secure its fifth qualification this decade. While it's now easier to qualify for the competition, with more places up for grabs in the Champions League format, others teams, such as Newcastle, have spent as much money and ultimately proven less successful. For much of the '90s, Liverpool fans had their noses pressed enviously to the window of the Champions League, watching Manchester United gain experience at the top level, and ultimately win the trophy in 1999. Now the Reds are once again their betters in this arena, having won the tournament in 2005 — for the fifth time — and progressed further than United in 2006.

Whether or not another CEO might have done a better job than Parry is, as with all conjecture, open to debate; but it's also clear that Liverpool could be in far worse shape than it currently finds itself (even ignoring any potential investment). The appointment of Gérard Houllier in 1998 was a good one — if ultimately a working partnership that turned sour as it moved past its sell-by date. Houllier, despite losing impetus in his final two years (and the support and goodwill of many of the fans), stabilised the club and made a series of essential changes with regard to professionalism and preparation. He modernised the club. Most importantly, he got Liverpool back into the habit of garnering silverware, and left enough good players for his successor, Rafa Benítez, to use them as the basis for his Champions League-winning team. Benítez still had a lot of work to do, some of which was down to the Frenchman's failings, but many problems from the '90s are no longer an issue. Again, hindsight suggests that a better manager than Houllier should have been secured if the club wanted to quickly reach its ultimate goals; just who that might have been, however, is hard to say with any certainty.

It is worth remembering how highly Houllier was regarded at the time of his collapse with a dissected aorta in October 2001; until then, Houllier and his assistant, Phil Thompson, had appeared the 'Dream Team'. Liverpool were headed in only one direction. In the end, Houllier and Thompson outstayed their welcome by at least a year — with hindsight they might have been replaced in 2003, when the rot was setting in — but at the time it wasn't 100% conclusive that the downward trend was anything more than a blip; just a year earlier the club had finished in 2nd place with 80 points.

2003/04 confirmed that the dip was no mere blip, but it's admirable that the club did not fire the management team at the first sign of a reversal of fortune; all top managers have sticky periods, and it has to be determined that the manager is no longer up to the job, rather than experiencing a poor run of luck. And while the club was clearly stagnating by the end of 2003/04, Houllier still managed to drag it over the finishing line in 4th place; a success of sorts. Such trust from the boardroom also helps attract men of substance when the job becomes available; why else do so many top coaches turn down Real Madrid? With Houllier sacked, Parry acted swiftly to procure Rafa Benítez: a coup, if ever there was one.

Investment

Between March 2004 — when Liverpool appointed financial advisors Hawkpoint — and the summer of 2006, the list of those linked to possible investment in the club consistently grew longer, from a local building magnate to a Thai, an American and a Spaniard. All it lacked was a Greek bearing gifts to complete the cosmopolitan line-up.

It all began in 2004, with Thaksin Shinawatra, the Thai Prime Minister, who was looking to take a 30% stake in the club, with what appeared to be his government's money (an idea that, two years on, seems totally insane). Deputy Commerce Minister Pongsak Raktapongpaisarn (who is in desperate need of a catchy nickname) claimed an agreement "on all aspects" of the deal had been reached, which was rumoured to include two seats on the Anfield board. But the deal never materialised.

Existing shareholder Steve Morgan was also in the running over a number of months, although his subsequent offers were not believed to be as attractive to the club as he would have had the media believe. His often rancorous run-ins with David Moores were in danger of dragging the club's name through the mud, but hostilities managed to stop just short of all-out war.

In November 2005, American billionaire Robert Kraft became the next name mentioned. The Kraft Group, which specialises in paper and packaging, sports and entertainment, and venture investment, bought the New England Patriots for £98m in 1994 and also owns Major League Soccer team New England Revolution. Speaking to the BBC's *Radio Five Live*, Kraft refused to rule out investment in Liverpool after a meeting with Anfield Chief Executive Rick Parry. "Liverpool is a great brand," he said. "It's something our family respects a lot." Parry had been in the US to hold talks with the Krafts about the proposed new stadium. Kraft told *Five Live*: "We're always interested in opportunities and growing, so you never know what can happen." Parry, without totally rejecting the possibility of future investment, stressed no deal was imminent. "I've known them since 2001 and had an invitation to visit the Gillette Stadium, one of the USA's few privately-funded stadia," said Parry. "It gave us a chance to discuss the way they funded the ground's construction. Being an international break, it was a convenient time to accept the invitation and it proved an interesting trip. It was hardly a secret mission. I attended an NFL match with 80,000 spectators."

London-based Spanish millionaire, Juan Villalonga, was the next person to appear, with claims he was aiming to buy a £42m stake in the club. In March 2006, Mr Villalonga pledged: "I want Liverpool to change from a domestically-focused club into a global force." Yet again, nothing was forthcoming.

The next group to be linked with investment was a consortium of Norwegian businessmen, who included in their number an environmental activist who once chained himself to the gates of Sellafield; as if the cast couldn't get any more bizarre. The consortium was put together by Oystein Stray Spetalen, a financial investor worth an estimated £150m, with their principal backer the hotel magnate Petter Stordalen. The 43-year-old Stordalen once tied himself to a footbridge over a drainage pipe at Sellafield after claiming radioactive emissions from the nuclear power plant were polluting the Norwegian coast. The Norwegian pair sought advice on English football and Liverpool's future potential from the former Swindon, Sheffield United, Middlesbrough and Barnsley striker Jan Aage Fjortoft on the scheme. It was reported that Spetalen hoped Fjortoft, at the time the manager at Lillestrom, would play some role at Liverpool. Quite where that would have left Rafa Benítez, the man behind Liverpool's resurgence, is anyone's guess, but it does highlight the extremely alarming potential for investment to do more harm than good. (As yet there is no confirmation on the bid from a consortium comprising Stig Inge Bjornebye, a Parisian fan dancer, the president of Greenpeace and Mr Burns from the Simpsons.)

The list of potential suitors did not end there. Robin Herd, who helped design *Concorde* as well as a series of motor racing cars, was another name linked to a takeover bid. The 67-year-old was acting as figurehead for a consortium believed to include American businessmen and key players from motor sport. Herd, a friend of Parry, became Oxford United's chairman in 1991, but lost a lot of money when his plans to build a new stadium did not come to fruition. Will Herd's group buy into Liverpool, or is it yet another red herring?

Stalemate

David Moores, the Liverpool Chairman, has so far declined to reduce his stake in the club below 51%, the amount that gives him an automatic majority. It's fair to say that, whether or not his judgement is clouded, Moores has the interests of the club at heart. He is not some overseas tycoon in it only for the money; he is not some fly-by-night fan, but a genuine dyed-in-the-wool Red.

Steve Morgan, a fierce critic of Moores, used the Annual General Meeting to claim that the Reds were over £70m in debt — a shocking announcement that painted a grim picture of the club's financial status, with the sense of impending doom heightened by the spiralling costs for the proposed new stadium. The figure was made up of £45.8m for net current liabilities and £26.1m for creditors — amounts falling due after more than one year — resulting in debts of £71.9m. However, included in the net current liabilities was an amount of £19.5m that is referred to as 'deferred income', which is monies received in advance of providing goods and services. This deferred income relates to season ticket revenue received in July and sponsorship revenue received at the start of the season. The goods and services the club provides for this deferred income is the staging of 19 home league matches (for the season ticket revenue), and the use, advertisement and stocking of sponsors' products. It is a paper debt on the balance sheet and as such, as is common with football clubs, is not regarded as an actual debt since it is highly unlikely that the staging of matches will not occur; it is just a requirement to post the income as a liability. Also not included in the accounts for the financial year were the sales of Milan Baroš and El-Hadji Diouf, for a combined fee of around £10m, covering over half of the trade creditors due within one year.

Net debt increased by £1.757m in the year, due partly to the non-payment by Reebok of sponsorship revenue. Reports stated that Reebok owed in the region of £7.5m. The kit manufacturers were unhappy over delays in Liverpool signing a new sponsorship deal with Carlsberg. Had the club received

Reebok's money then net debt would have been significantly reduced, with the overdraft cleared and net debt reduced to under £10m. Also, had the transfers of Diouf and Baroš been before the year end, the net debt would theoretically have been cleared. The club would still have had loans but they would also have had cash in the bank.

Rick Parry said that Morgan was 'technically correct' to use the figure of £71.9m, but that he had overlooked a corresponding asset on the balance sheet as well. "When you use credit to buy players," Parry said, "you're obviously offsetting the debt with the value of the players you're putting on the balance sheet. If we're spreading payments over a number of years then we still owe the money but it only gives part of the story." In other words, it's like buying a car on credit: you owe money, but you have an asset that has a value. As with cars, players' values may depreciate; although, as with classic cars, their value may equally double or treble. There is also the fact that while Liverpool buys players with payments spread over a number of years, it also sells them under the same conditions.

Just how much the Liverpool squad is worth is debatable. It changes from day to day; a good performance by a certain player will inevitably lead to suggestions of increased value. Is Steven Gerrard worth £30m, £35m or £40m? Is Xabi Alonso worth £10m, £15m or £20m? What price Jamie Carragher? Bar career-ending injuries (which would be covered by insurance pay-outs) or players running down their contracts (which the club tries to avoid), the players currently in the Liverpool squad all retain significant financial value as assets. Benítez's unsuccessful signings have tended to be players who cost negligible amounts, and these failures have been sold with money recouped; in the case of Josemi, he was swapped with Jan Kromkamp, a player valued at £4m, meaning that the manager effectively doubled his investment. At present, with the possible exception of Fernando Morientes, whose form and age leaves his value lower than £6.5m, all of Benítez's signings have either held or increased their value. Of course, Benítez didn't buy these players in order for their value to increase merely to precipitate a sale; he bought them to succeed, and as a result of their success, their values have risen.

A football club doesn't exist to make money, and all clubs rack up manageable debts. It's like an individual shopping with a credit card: provided he or she sticks to the agreed limit, which is calculated based on the individual's financial situation, then it's not a problem; monthly or annual repayments are made, and the process continues. The trouble comes when borrowing far exceeds current or expected income. Leeds United suffered because they factored on-going Champions League qualification into their projected earnings. While every club can guarantee it will experience a domestic league campaign, for which it can sell tickets, there is no way it can count on money from the bonus of European competition. Not only did Leeds fail to qualify for Europe, their overspending meant a desperate necessity to off-load players — and desperation leaves a club in a poor bargaining position, and so open to exploitation. Selling its best individuals without the facility to replace them with players of anything approaching the same calibre led to the club subsequently losing what it would have felt was a safe source of income: the riches for being in the Premiership.

Running a football club is about weighing up a certain amount of risk against the likelihood of reaping dividends. The link between success and money is strong, and it becomes a beneficial cycle, with the former begetting the latter, but the latter is often required to ensure the former. It's certainly not an exact science; surprises are thrown up constantly. In 2001, could the Liverpool board have expected the club's manager — who was riding the crest of a wave — to come within minutes of dying, and as a result, never quite appear the same in the job afterwards? How do you legislate for such a turn of events? Long-term planning in football is constantly undermined by changing circumstances, not least the players' form and fitness, and their own ambitions (which might lead them elsewhere).

The challenge remains unchanged: Liverpool has to secure beneficial investment without jeopardising its long-term future. That's easier said than done.

Part Two

Chapter 7

The Reinforcements

There was no shortage of transfer market activity in Rafa Benítez's second season. A total of 17 players were signed — almost an entire squad —either to go straight into the first team set-up or, in the case of highly sought-after teenagers, for an education in the reserves. In the twelve months since winning the Champions League, Benítez's outlay in transfer fees, including two swap deals, totalled approximately £34m: not a lot more than the kind of fees Manchester United had paid for a single player (on three separate occasions), and those that Chelsea paid for numerous pairs of players in recent seasons, with their litany of £13m-£24m signings. Benítez's 2005/06 outlay worked out at an average of £2m per player, which represented excellent value for money, considering it was spread over a number of the world's best young prospects and eight full international footballers: Peter Crouch, Pepe Reina, Daniel Agger, Momo Sissoko, Jan Kromkamp, Bolo Zenden, Mark Gonzalez and Robbie Fowler.

Gonzalez, who was signed in October 2005 ahead of hopefully becoming eligible for the Premiership in July 2006 — should a Spanish passport be granted, otherwise it will need another work permit appeal — will be joined by Gabriel Paletta, the highly-rated young Argentine defender who will also arrive in July. Another player who wouldn't get a chance to make much of an impact in '05/06 was Bolo Zenden, who would start only 11 matches before a knee ligament injury in November curtailed his season, just as he was starting to find some form.

Pace in wide positions remained an area in need of addressing. Steven Gerrard, while superb in the right-midfield role, will always be marginally more effective in a central area, while Harry Kewell, coming back to his best, hasn't quite rediscovered his former pace. Djibril Cissé has the pace, but not the positional sense to prove a consistent threat on the flank, although he had some bright moments. Two young players may yet solve this shortcoming, although neither Gonzalez nor Paul Anderson, both signed during 2005/06, will have a smooth passage into the Liverpool first team, for contrasting reasons: the former needs to circumnavigate a sturdy defensive wall of red tape, while the latter is still a raw young player, albeit one with bags of potential. Anderson and Gonzalez are similar types of player: small, tenacious, turbo-charged wingers capable of scoring goals, and happy to work hard for the team. While there are other wide men already at the club, and possibly more to follow, it may not be too long before Gonzalez and Anderson line up on opposite flanks. While fans may end up having their breath taken away, opposing full-backs will be laid out in oxygen tents afterwards.

Gonzalez proved the hero for *La Liga*'s Real Sociedad, where he ended up on loan, as the club battled relegation. The Chilean scored a superb winner against Racing Santander on April 15th (such a poignant date), to follow his poacher's effort against Real Madrid a week earlier, and his fulminating 45-yard direct free-kick against Getafe a couple of weeks before that. (Picture Riise's ferocious free-kick against Manchester United in 2001, and double the distance.) A week after his winner against Racing, he scored again, this time at Villarreal, the Champions League semi-finalists. Not only Sociedad's star player, Gonzalez was playing as well as anyone in *La Liga*.

Winter work

Winter is never the easiest time for a manager to make signings, given that the best players will be wanted by their clubs until the end of the season (at least), while plenty will still be in action in European competition and, as such, going nowhere.

Arriving in the winter transfer window means a player has no pre-season to gel with his team-mates. He is also likely to be lacking fitness if, like Fernando Morientes, Mauricio Pellegrino, Daniel Agger, Robbie Fowler and Jan Kromkamp, he has not been playing regular football in the months before arriving, for whatever reason (injury, being out of favour, or, in Agger's case, his league being closed down for the winter). The Premiership is particularly unforgiving in its physical demands, and winter arrivals need to hit the ground running. The bonus is that, once match fit, such players should be fresher than those who have already played 50-or-so mostly high-intensity games as the season draws to its conclusion. If a player settles quickly, it's a big bonus; if he doesn't, it doesn't mean he won't, given time. There has to be time for him to relocate his life, and to integrate himself into the team while learning what the manager requires.

As with the summer, there were signings which appeared completed, only for the deals to fall through at the 11th hour. One player who came close to signing for the Reds in January 2006 was Deportivo La Coruña's right-sided midfielder, Victor, who joined a long list of players specialising in that particular position who ultimately slipped through the net. With the player out of contract at the Riazor just six months later, it was reported that Liverpool refused to pay the full fee the Spanish club were holding out for. But soon after the deal collapsed, Victor revealed that a disagreement between himself and Deportivo ended his hopes of moving to Anfield, with the player hoping that his employers would pay him a fee for moving on; they refused to meet his request. "It was impossible to pardon the money and in these circumstances I've preferred to stay in La Coruña and finish my contract in June," explained Victor. Available on a free transfer in the summer of 2006, the Reds' interest could yet be revived, although a pre-contract could have been signed in the winter had Liverpool still been keen. That the player chose to not come to Liverpool because of money may well end up working against him.

Jan Kromkamp

If replacing Steve Finnan will prove a tall order for Jan Kromkamp, faring better than Josemi, the rather hapless defender he replaced in a direct swap, shouldn't prove too problematic. Despite looking a little ungainly in his running style, Kromkamp appears a fine all-round footballer on the early evidence in a red shirt: big, strong, fairly quick, good in the tackle and very comfortable on the ball. He reads the game well, and that's always one of the first things a manager looks for in a defender. Although played out of position on the right of midfield on several occasions, where he was often average at best, it was in his handful of appearances at right-back that the Dutchman really caught the eye. Some players are better at driving forward from deeper areas, as seen with many attacking midfielders who suddenly look lost when shifted into the forward line. It's often the same with attacking full-backs, who seem less sure of the timing of their runs when starting from a more advanced position. Kromkamp made his name in Holland with his forward bursts from the back, but not at the expense of his defensive duties.

It's difficult for an attacking full-back to not get caught out of position, given he cannot be in line with the rest of the defence if he's just gone on an overlap, so he needs to do everything possible to give himself the best chance of succeeding. So far the Dutchman appears to have that ability to know when to go forward, and when to hold his run. Bombing mindlessly forward is a certain way to put the team under pressure, and despite the need for others to cover the space, it's also a full-back's duty to get back as quickly as possible.

When he did get forward, Kromkamp's use of the ball was mostly exemplary. His cross for Peter Crouch's goal at Newcastle was judged to perfection, and was clearly a deliberate attempt to hit that exact space between back four and goalkeeper: he sized up the situation before delivering the chipped cross, rather than just hitting and hoping. There was a similar amount of composure to his second-half volley that forced Shay Given into a top-class save.

Kromkamp's settling-in period at Liverpool wasn't helped by the Dutch coach, the legendary striker Marco van Basten, criticising the move and swiftly leaving the man who had hitherto been his first-choice right-back out of his next squad. "It is annoying that Kromkamp, who is a good player, made the wrong choices for his career," van Basten told ANP. "It is sad when someone throws away his own chances and also doesn't help us. It seems to us that Jan is more busy with peripheral events."

No matter how many times you read these quotes, they refuse to make sense. Whether or not Kromkamp will ever get enough games at Liverpool to satisfy van Basten is debatable, but you cannot criticise a player for joining a big club in the hope furthering his career and trying to make the grade; leaving Holland for AC Milan never harmed van Basten — although, of course, he was one of the greatest strikers the game has ever seen, and less likely to struggle to hold down a place in a top side. As it was, it took Kromkamp just three months to exceed the eleven appearances he made for Villarreal, even if displacing Steve Finnan — Liverpool's Mr Reliable (alongside Mr Dependable, Jamie Carragher) — will prove difficult. While Kromkamp played more times for Liverpool than Villarreal, he started fewer games; of course, in the second half of the season there are fewer games available in which to play, especially for a player cup-tied in Europe. And as a newcomer, he was never going to be thrown straight into a defence that was keeping so many clean sheets.

Kromkamp had to look long-term, rather than return to Holland for a few months just to appease his manager and cement his World Cup spot with half a season of regular appearances at a 'lesser' club. In the modern day, apart from a few weeks every other summer, international football is the peripheral event, with often fewer than ten games each calendar year; club football is the week-in, week-out lifeblood of the game. After a four year wait, the World Cup is over in a month for all players, maybe even ten days if all goes pear-shaped. The World Cup boosts club football, of course, but club football supports the international game. Club football is where players make their living. So it seems a little rich for an international manager to criticise what, from the outside, looks a very exciting and challenging move for the player; joining the reigning champions of Europe, and the fastest-improving team in England. Kromkamp ended the season playing an important role in the FA Cup final victory over West Ham, as the right wing outlet in a tiring team. From his point of view, the decision to join Liverpool had been vindicated.

Daniel Agger

Daniel Agger was the quarry Benítez eventually seized at the second time of asking. In the Great Summer of Centre-Backs, Agger had been one of the small number of genuine targets amongst the many names linked to the club. The timing wasn't right, but six months later the Reds were back in with a bid of £5.8m, and the cultured Danish centre-back was finally paraded as a Red.

Agger's gait and playing style is somewhat reminiscent of Jonathan Woodgate, the ex-Leeds and Newcastle player Benítez tried to sign when he first arrived, and who, when he wasn't injured at Real Madrid, won rave reviews in the Spanish press. Agger possesses a similar air of insouciance, in never seeming rushed or panicked. He plays the game at his own pace, and his passing is extremely assured: one 50-yard ball at St James' Park (coincidentally

Woodgate's last English port of call) was like watching Xabi Alonso spread play from the defence. But as Agger will have learned against Fulham, when he played a loose ball straight to a white shirt in an error that cost a goal, stray passes in more dangerous areas are quickly seized upon in England, where opponents nip in quicker than in the more sedate league he was used to.

At 21, Agger has plenty of time to learn and adjust. He already possesses the appearance of a thoroughbred — a *real* footballer (as opposed to an athlete or a bruiser) — and seems especially composed for a central defender of his age. Centre-back, along with goalkeeper, is the position where youngsters can really suffer, as it's the one area of the pitch where mistakes are instantly punishable. An inexperienced striker can give the ball away and miss chances, but if he does just one thing right in a game — namely tucking away a chance, even if mis-kicked — everyone will praise him; it just takes one mistake for a young defender, one piece of poor control, to be remembered for all the wrong reasons. It can be even riskier for ball-playing centre-backs, since being constructive with the ball at the back is always inviting more danger than simply whacking it into Row Z. (Word of advice: never buy a ticket in Row Z.)

With Benítez fielding three centre-backs at Newcastle, as he had a year earlier (with less success), it was important that at least one of them was prepared to move into the midfield space when the opportunity presented itself. Agger did this in the build–up to the second goal, advancing 40 yards with the ball before delivering a fine pass out to the right. When Gerrard eventually struck the shot, Agger was so far advanced that he had to get out of the way of the goal-bound effort.

It may take the Dane time to come to terms with the physical nature of English football, but he's started as well as could have been hoped for. His rise to prominence has been spectacularly meteoric, and his lack of experience should not be overlooked. He had only played 24 club games before signing for Liverpool, having burst onto the scene in Denmark and almost instantly become a full-international. While in all probability not ready to replace Sami Hyypia for a season or two, he is already at a level where he can provide more than adequate cover, while also offering the opportunity to rest the two stalwarts of the Reds' defence.

Bolo Zenden

It was a fairly slow and unspectacular start for Boudewijn 'Bolo' Zenden at Liverpool. Then, just as he scored a couple of goals and started to look settled, he suffered a serious knee injury that ended his season in November. Fortunately for Rafa Benítez, Harry Kewell finally returned to form and fitness on the left, but even so, Zenden would have been an important member of his squad.

Bolo Zenden is a difficult player to categorise: he has a little bit of everything, and seems to excel at nothing in particular. A *Johannes of all trades*, if you will: quick, but not blisteringly so; good on the ball, but not supremely skilful; hard-working, but no Momo Sissoko; a fine crosser, but unlikely to whip in a number of devastating deliveries; can score goals, but has not been especially prolific since leaving Holland in 1998 (where he scored an impressive one goal every three games). In many ways he is reminiscent of Ray Houghton, with a busy style on the flank and an ability to pop up in different areas of the pitch to good effect.

In the summer of 2005, when Benítez came calling, the Dutchman had just experienced an excellent season for Middlesborough in the centre of midfield, but he was never going to get a sniff of that position at Anfield, given the depth of talent already available — although his versatility may one day come in handy, should an injury crisis arise. Having played at left-back and left-midfield during his career, he can certainly fill a number of roles. If anything, it's Zenden's experience — as he approaches his 30th birthday — that could prove his biggest asset at Anfield. He's played at some of Europe's most successful clubs, with stints at PSV Eindhoven, Barcelona and Chelsea, not to mention representing Holland 54 times. He could yet prove a canny free signing, now that expectations have been lowered a little due to the long lay-off.

Chapter Eight

Momo Sissoko – Midfield Destroyer

French-born Mali international Momo Sissoko arrived at Anfield in a £5.8m deal from Valencia, where, as an 18-year-old, he'd featured during the title-winning season of 2003/04. The following season, following Rafa Benítez's departure and the arrival of Claudio 'Crazy Eyes' Ranieri, Sissoko featured less, increasing the likelihood of a move away from the Mestalla.

Benítez, in making an approach for the player, was mining his old club for the second time, following the recruitment of Mauricio Pellegrino, a player at the other end of his career and the other end of the spectrum regarding pace and energy. Sissoko's transfer was made all the more sweet for Liverpool fans by the club beating Everton and Chelsea to the punch. "We had an advantage over Everton," Benítez admitted shortly after the deal was concluded. "I already knew the player. He had good memories of winning trophies with me at Valencia. We knew Everton were interested, but it was easy to sign him." Benítez was also buying Sissoko for the second time, having been in charge when Valencia signed him in the first place, from the impressive production line at Auxerre, in August 2003.

Sissoko was in no doubt he was right to eschew the advances of Everton in order to move to Liverpool. "Any player in the world would have done the same as me. Between the two offers, I had to go for the Reds because they are the champions of Europe and I already knew Rafa Benítez."

When the approach for Sissoko was made, Benítez did not know whether or not Steven Gerrard would be staying; in fact, it looked certain he would be heading to Chelsea. Sissoko, rather than ending up as Gerrard's successor, arrived and helped free up the Liverpool captain in a more advanced, attack-minded role.

In many ways, Sissoko — whose physique and running style, on top of the way he plays the game, draws inevitable comparisons to Patrick Vieira — seems purpose-built to be the ultimate modern midfield enforcer. "In a couple of years he will be more dynamic than Vieira and a better player," Benítez said upon signing him, unafraid to burden the player with the kind of comparison that weighed down previous French signings: Bruno Cheyrou will never live down Gérard Houllier's comparisons with Zinedine Zidane (it might have been kinder to liken him to Marcel Marceau). While Sissoko is not at the level Vieira is remembered for, it's also true that, since Vieira was also aged only 20 upon his arrival in England, Sissoko should only currently be compared (if there *have* to be comparisons) with Vieira when he arrived at Arsenal, and not when he was at his pomp in his mid-20s.

Sissoko had actually started his career in France as a striker, scoring 50 times in two seasons in the Auxerre youth team. There has been precious little to suggest this in his play at Liverpool, which has been almost completely defence-oriented. In fact, until Sissoko headed on Steven Gerrard's first-minute cross at Birmingham in the FA Cup, for Sami Hyypia to finish off, Sissoko was at the foot of the table in terms of direct involvement in Liverpool's goals; going into that game, even Pepe Reina had more assists (two).

Sissoko's reinvention as a midfielder came against Swiss side St Gallen in a pre-season friendly, soon after he joined Valencia. With all of his substitutes used, and another player injured, Benítez asked the referee's permission to return Sissoko to the pitch as a midfielder, after he spent the first half as a striker. "We put him in the middle and it was like, 'Wow! What is this?'" Benítez said. "After that we started working with him as a midfielder. We were looking at the numbers after each game in astonishment. Every game he was running 11 or 12 kilometres so it just required us to work on certain tactical situations with him because he'd always been a striker before."

Despite being predominately a destroyer, Sissoko's ball skills are very tidy, he has the capability to go past players, as witnessed in a few mazy runs, and the technical ability to pass well, which he has on many occasions. However, a rashness in his decision-making has led him to squander possession far too cheaply at times; perhaps partly due to his tender years, and partly due to the shock of English football, where the pace of the game forces errors. He also has a hint of a youthful Steven Gerrard about him, in that he tries to do things too quickly, in an attempt to keep the tempo at breakneck speed. When a player is haring about, chasing all over the park for 90 minutes, he will be in an excited state, and as such it can be hard for him to find the calmness to pick the right option. He needs to learn to switch from fixated harrier when not in possession, to cool-headed passer when the ball ends up at his feet. That should come with age and experience.

However, the young Malian covers so much ground and puts in such an incredible number of tackles — at one stage of the season he'd made twice as many successful tackles as the next best Premiership player — that he isn't close to being a liability. The main concern is the amount of yellow cards he picks up, although the more tackles a player makes, the greater the risk of mistiming one or two. In his case it is an occupational hazard, although one maturity will help lessen the impact of, again as evinced by Gerrard, who received the vast majority of his yellow cards in the first few seasons of his career.

It was perhaps a surprise that Sissoko usurped Didi Hamann in the pecking order so quickly, but Benítez was not judging between the two on individual talent or experience; instead, his concern was for the balance Sissoko provided the midfield. Sissoko could not only offer pace in deeper areas to allow Gerrard to move into more advanced positions, but was also required because Hamann and Xabi Alonso are not the most natural pairing, given that both like to play as the deepest midfielder, and that neither is the quickest. "When we have Momo, Xabi and Gerrard available," said Benítez in March, "we have the right balance of skill and energy, pace and power, and they bring the best qualities out of each other."

Hamann, a master in picking off opposition attacks before they reach the Liverpool back line, was arguably a victim of the lack of genuine pace in Liverpool's defensive areas, and of the fact that Alonso had become the playmaker from the very area Hamann liked to patrol in a defensive mindset. (Although Alonso was also exceptionally good at reading the opposition's play and intercepting. You only had to look at him against West Brom at the Hawthorns for confirmation of this: dropping so far back as to become the deepest outfield player to receive a ball from Pepe Reina, before sending a glorious 60-yard pass to Cissé, who rounded the keeper to score the Reds' second goal.)

It also seems paradoxically true that the German is far more impressive in fast-tempo games when he can put his foot on the ball in his ultra-composed manner (and draw free-kicks as he wanders off with the ball on one of his deceptively 'aimless' runs). In slower games, he can look more pedestrian, especially as he is not someone who can add pace or tempo to a match with his passing (which is mostly simple and effective) or his running with the ball. However, Hamann, who turns 33 in August 2006, remained an important squad player in 2005/06, featuring enough times to activate a contract clause that meant an automatic one-year extension. Nonetheless, he has clearly no longer a first-team regular and is now more of an understudy to the man almost twelve years his junior.

Sissoko quickly made himself an essential element in Benítez's high-pressing game, in which teams aren't allowed to settle on the ball in midfield in order to find time to bring their strikers into play. His ability to run quickly to close down the player in possession, then the player passed to, then back again without needing to pause and draw breath can almost be like having two players. In fact, his impressive early-season tackling stats indicate it was indeed like having two effective midfield destroyers, given the Premiership's 2nd- and 3rd-best tacklers at that stage were, only when combined, making as many successful tackles as Sissoko (whose rate was one every eight minutes, to his rivals' one every 15/16 minutes).

By the end of his first campaign, Sissoko had made 78 million tackles (or so it seemed), and run to the sun and back.

Eye Contact

Momo Sissoko's season was not without unwelcome drama. Not only did Liverpool effectively lose their grip on the European Cup at Benfica's Stadium of Light, but for a few weeks it looked like the Reds might also permanently lose the services of their new recruit, after he took a kick in the eye from the Portuguese club's midfielder, Beto, which left the area badly cut. The eye-lid went into reflex spasm, meaning he couldn't open it. For the next 36 hours there was no sight in the eye at all, with the retina damaged.

It presented some unwelcome symmetry with the previous season: a young African-French graduate of the Auxerre academy lying in a hospital bed fearing his career could be over, only to make a miraculously quick recovery. (If Sissoko and Cissé share an ability to cheaply surrender possession, they also share an ability to fight the odds in adversity.) "It was an awful time," Sissoko told Liverpool's official website. "There were lots of lonely hours at home when I was very worried and very scared about what was going to happen. It was such a bad injury."

The initial prognosis didn't help lift his spirits: a Portuguese specialist announced to the media that there was an 80% chance of Sissoko losing the sight in his right eye. "I wasn't happy when the Portuguese doctor told me that," Sissoko added. "All I want to do is play football. He said that football was finished for me. I didn't like that. I didn't believe that. We went to see other specialists and thankfully things have got a lot better."

Gradually the sight returned to his eye, and within a month he returned to the first team, complete with Edgar Davids-style protective eyewear. It coincided with the 7-0 demolition of Birmingham, and within 50 seconds of the start he had headed the ball on to Sami Hyypia for the opening goal. Sissoko remained in the first team until the end of the season, although the glasses lasted only a few minutes.

"The glasses were steaming up for the first 10 minutes I wore them, so I took them off," he told the *Sunday Times'* Jonathan Northcroft. "I was taking a risk and I'm still taking a risk, but if you try something and it just doesn't work, what can you do? I just can't physically play in the glasses. That's all there is to it. I want to play and I can't play wearing them, so this is what I have to do. Our doctor spoke to the Spurs doctor about Edgar Davids and his glasses and we've tried ones like his and different types, styles and makes, but I can't manage with them. I can't be doing with them. I haven't spoken too much about the consequences of what might happen if I get kicked in the eye again. The doctors have just told me to take care and try not to get a knock."

The leggy Malian had been missed, especially with the team looking heavy-legged after such a gruelling schedule. If he continues to cover the ground that allows Gerrard and Alonso to shine with the ball at their feet, his effectiveness will be appreciated for years to come, and he will rank among the canniest of Benitez's acquisitions.

Chapter Nine

Pepe Reina –– the 25-1 Shot Stopper

April 19th, 2001. The buzz goes up from all four sides of the ground as, at the Anfield Road end, the award of a first-half penalty — courtesy of a bizarre Patrick Kluivert handball — gives Liverpool the chance to take a crucial lead in the second leg of a European semi-final; the highest stakes for the club in a decade. For a moment the young Barcelona keeper stands at the back of the net, before edging up to the goal line to face Gary McAllister, the man who famously missed his highest-pressure penalty, for Scotland against England in Euro'96. It might easily be father versus son: bald man faces a prematurely balding keeper literally half his age. This time Gary 'baldy' Mac makes no mistake, and sends the ball high to the top right corner, as the 18-year-old — who, later in his career, would save seven out of nine penalties in a single Spanish season, and three out of four in an FA Cup Final shoot-out — dives the wrong way.

It's fair to say that Jose 'Pepe' Reina would go on to have a lot more joy at Anfield in Liverpool's colours than he did in his first appearance at the famous ground. However, this would be after yet another visit with Barça, a year on from the first, this time in an impressive 3-1 victory for the Catalans. It would take a third appearance — his first for the Reds — to finally register a clean sheet, in the 3-0 win over TNS, but that 2002 Champions League victory had already introduced him to what would become a familiar habit: winning at Anfield.

Summer steal

Several months after his arrival from Villarreal in the summer of 2005 for £6m, and with a number of clean sheets under his belt (assuming the belt is the accepted storage method for clean sheets), the jury was still out on Pepe Reina. This was mostly through no fault of his own; he just hadn't had a lot to do. Then there was the game against Birmingham at St Andrews, in which he had a very poor match in a 2-2 draw. One nervous, flapping performance was enough to make fans concerned; after all, it had been a depressingly familiar theme throughout the previous 15 years. However, within a few months, most fans were won over by his impressive all-round game and his ice-cool temperament, which let him down only once, when he confronted Arjen Robben and (perhaps harshly) received a red card for brushing his cheek. The Spaniard's arrival effectively ended the Liverpool career of Istanbul hero Jerzy Dudek — whose only subsequent games came during Reina's ban following the Robben incident, plus a couple of token appearances in the spring — as well as consigning Chris Kirkland to a loan spell at a struggling West Brom.

The *Daily Mirror*'s Oliver Holt, when discussing Kirkland's bad luck with injuries as 2005/06 approached its conclusion, stated that the English keeper had earlier put in the goalkeeping performance of the season for West Brom against Arsenal. But such praise, while richly merited, also reflected the type of club Kirkland was now representing; i.e. one where he was always going to be called into action. Reina, whose arrival at Anfield ended any remaining hopes that boyhood Red Kirkland had of making the no.1 jersey his, never got the chance to put in 'the goalkeeping performance of the season', because in most games he had only a couple of shots to save. He was certainly never asked to perform the kind of heroics demanded of Arsenal's Jens Lehmann at Anfield in February. (It is interesting to note that Lehmann finally won over his critics this season, with his team's league losses into double figures, and yet, paradoxically, he was never trusted during the season when they went the full league campaign unbeaten. Did he need to be playing behind a struggling defence to receive positive press?)

Of course, it is precisely how Reina dealt with what he did have to do that marked him out as the perfect keeper for Rafa Benítez's side. It is said that the sign of a good goalkeeper is the ability to make a save after having had nothing else to do in a game — to summon action out of forced inaction — and Reina certainly proved the maxim true. In the 1-0 home win against Spurs, he made two excellent saves, denying Robbie Keane and Mido; against Birmingham at Anfield, he pulled off an exceptional save from Emile Heskey's last-minute header to protect the 1-0 lead, which would have ensured all three points but for Xabi Alonso's unpredictable and unstoppable chested own-goal a minute later; and against Middlesborough at Anfield in December 2005 he was troubled just once, when Mark Viduka broke free and Reina denied him with a superb save with an outstretched boot. Even the late, late Rio Ferdinand header which stole three points for Manchester United had its positives; few 'keepers would have got near the ball at all.

Kirkland's inability to stay fit undermines his undoubted talent; while he still has up to 15 years ahead of him in the game (if he can rid himself of his ailments), it's also interesting to note that this 'young' English goalkeeper is, at 25, two years older than Reina. Whereas the Spaniard has an incredible 250 club games under his (increasingly burgeoning) belt — due to starting his first team career early with Barcelona and finding regular football with Villarreal — Kirkland had totalled just 86 club games by the end of 2005/06.

Despite buying a goalkeeper who was still essentially a 'junior' — in terms of a position where maturity comes later than for outfield players — Benítez knew he was getting an experienced and accomplished individual. To put Reina's experience into context, Tottenham's Paul Robinson, who turns 27 in October 2006 and who was playing for Leeds as a young man, has 50 fewer club appearances, as does Chelsea's Petr Cech, who is several months older than Reina; Aston Villa's Thomas Sorensen, at 30, has played only 60 more games, while Jerzy Dudek, a full ten years Reina's senior, has only 100 more club games to his name.

It tends to be African players whose age is questioned, due to the rudimentary birth records of much of that particular continent, combined with the overactive imaginations of conspiracy theorists. Claims were made that Kanu was far older than was stated (perhaps due to cardiac trouble combined with the running style of an old man), and rumours circulated that El-Hadji Diouf was a decade older than the age on his passport when he signed for Liverpool, while Cameroon international Roger Milla, who starred in the 1990 World Cup, was believed to be aged anywhere from 38 to 103. Looking at Pepe Reina — at the way he plays and his physical appearance — the desire is to see irrefutable evidence that he really was born on 31 August 1982, and not ten years earlier.

As well as knowing Reina's qualities from his time in Spanish football, Benítez also had a valuable 'inside track' on the player. Jose Ochotorena, the goalkeeping coach brought to Liverpool from Valencia by Benítez, knew Reina from the Spanish national team set-up, where he also coached on a part-time basis. The keeper's character, habits, dedication and professionalism could also be accurately assessed.

There is very much a 'type' of goalkeeper Benítez likes, and Ochotorena's knowledge is a key part of finding such keepers, and then, once at the club, honing their talent. A lot of the work Ochotorena does with his charges involves them saving shots, then getting up quickly to face the rebound; more than ever, the importance of reacting following a save is crucial, given how hard it is to hold onto shots that move unpredictably in flight. This was seen in Jerzy Dudek's stunning double save from Andriy Shevchenko in the Champions League final. Without the incessant training drills run by Ochotorena, Dudek may have been a fraction slower to get up after the first attempt. The reason Shevchenko didn't try to conclusively bury the second chance was because, with Dudek prostrate, he thought he was merely aiming at an empty net from a couple of yards; in such situations, a more gentle, controlled effort is all that seems required, concentrating on getting a good clean contact and not risking a mis-kick (the more a player tries to blast the ball, the less control he has). Had the Ukrainian known Dudek was capable of getting off the ground so quickly, he would surely have opted for a different kind of finish, either going higher or harder. Even so, Shevchenko, and the watching world, thought he had done enough to score. It still beggars belief that he didn't.

As the ball seems lighter with each season's latest model — rumours abound that the 2009 version will be an inflated Nike-branded condom — goalkeepers are increasingly having to punch and parry rather than catch. Sometimes the ball will change direction at the last nanosecond, as if there has been a touch by an invisible striker. The English game, where catching was always the be-all and end-all, has moved more towards continental-type goalkeeping, which of course makes having continental keepers and coaches less of a risk. Having said that, it's also refreshing to see Benítez prepared to pay fees for two young English goalkeepers: Scott Carson and David Martin.

A big feature of Reina's game is his punching. The Spaniard regularly gets a quite remarkable distance when required to fist a ball. (Indeed, for the power of the man, see the game at Stamford Bridge: his gentle slap of Arjen Robben sent the little Dutchman flying an unprecedented distance.) Punching a cross will lead to the occasional mistake, as a clean contact isn't always possible — just as players will sometimes mis-time a volley — but there are times when, with the area crowded, a catch cannot be taken above a collection of bodies, and trying to do so means that the keeper risks dropping the ball and presenting an open goal. Even a bad punch will travel further from harm's way than a dropped cross. There were a couple of games in which Reina appeared to have no need to punch — such as at the Hawthorns on a slightly blustery April Fool's Day — although he tended to get away with it when he erred.

Benítez explained the reasoning behind the keeper's style: "Pepe punches the ball because I told him to. I said 'Be careful, it is different here in England.' In Spain he was the best goalkeeper in the air, but it is more difficult here, more physical. Players do attack the goalkeeper more so it is better to punch the ball. You watch the TV highlights and you see how many goals are conceded when goalkeepers try to catch the ball and fail, instead of punching it away. He is so quick off his line and reads the game very well and has made some good saves for us this season. He gets good distance with his punches and it is very important for us."

Reina is positive, but not reckless like someone such as David James, whose brilliant physical gifts and undeniable natural talent were undermined — certainly at Reina's age, if a little less so later in his career — by a tendency to make drastically incorrect decisions that only served to increase the pressure on himself and, consequently, the team. James seemed to lose concentration, whereas Reina is able to stay focused.

Alertness is such a big asset in a goalkeeper: cutting off the danger by reacting before a threatening situation develops, and having the presence of mind when in possession to be aware of team-mates' positions in order to start attacks. When receiving the ball, Reina is alive to what's happening, looking to release a quick throw whilst having the strength to hurl it great distances and the skill to do so accurately; it's the same story with his kicking. Not once in the previous season had Jerzy Dudek or Scott Carson 'assisted' a goal, while Kirkland did so only once. In 2005/06, Reina contributed four assists; it may not seem like a big deal, but it is a small piece of evidence that attests to the improvement in this area. In the Anfield derby, with Liverpool down to ten men, Jamie Carragher visibly instructed the keeper to aim for Peter Crouch from his first goalkick of the second half; the ball travelled 70 yards onto Crouch's head, and Luis Garcia, having read the flick — the little Spaniard being a lively anticipator — found himself in on goal and able to lob exquisitely over the onrushing Richard Wright. Crouch clearly gives a Liverpool goalkeeper an option to call upon when he has the ball in his possession, but it takes accuracy to make sure Crouch retains his advantage and isn't forced to try to win aimless punts. Reina's quick-thinking and accurate use of the ball — both in throwing and kicking, and in the ability to sweep behind the back four — make him closer to an eleventh outfield player.

A fraction taller than the lithe Jerzy Dudek, Reina has a sturdier build than his Polish counterpart. In fact, the Spaniard is a fairly unremarkable looking for a goalkeeper: medium height, medium build. He doesn't stand out, or grab the attention. (Having been present for both Barcelona's visits to Gérard

Houllier's Liverpool, I have to confess to not at all remembering Reina; not that you tend to remember unfamiliar opposing European goalkeepers unless on the day they are exceptional, eccentric, erratic, or they look like some über-freak with a snake tattoo on their face and a Worzel Gummidge haircut.)

Despite a fairly solid physique, Reina clearly felt intimidated by some of the strikers he faced in the English game, describing them as being built more like boxers. Although the odd targetman appears in *La Liga* from time to time, such as John Carew (who Benítez had at Valencia) and the former Blackburn player, Yordi, there aren't anywhere near as many tall, robust and physical opponents as there are in England, with the likes of Emile Heskey, Chris Sutton, Duncan Ferguson, James Beattie, Shefki Kuqi, Kevin Davies, Henrik Pedersen, Darren Bent, Collins John, Georgios Samaras, Aiyegbeni Yakubu, Mark Viduka, Jason Roberts, Alan Shearer, Nwankwo Kanu, Marlon Harewood and Kevin Kyle. Even Arsenal eventually got in on the act, by signing Monaco's Emmanuel Adebayor.

Not the tallest, standing several inches shorter than a number of his outfield colleagues — although one of whom, Crouch, is taller than any of the division's keepers — Reina is an athletic, agile goalkeeper whose alertness and general football intelligence are his main strengths. He clearly had a good education in the art-form from a young age, with his father, Miguel, being a former Atlético Madrid goalkeeper. The position could be said to be in his blood. Before making it into the Barcelona B-team, young Pepe had been part of the national side that won the 1999 Uefa European Under-16 Championship, and within two years he had graduated to the Barcelona first team: clear evidence that Reina possessed precocious talent, to be keeping goal for one of the world's major clubs at such a tender age. Teenage goalkeepers who can handle such pressure are thin on the ground, and most big clubs don't even risk playing them, although at the same time Real Madrid were defying convention, with Iker Casillas — the man currently keeping Reina from the Spanish no.1 jersey — especially impressive between the sticks (but also more prone to moments of madness).

Reina went on to make 30 league and 11 European appearances for the Catalan club, in a period of alternation with Roberto Bonano and Richard Dutruel. In 2002, Louis Van Gaal arrived at Barcelona and loaned the 19-year-old Reina to Villarreal, a move that would ultimately be the making of the young keeper, with it eventually becoming a permanent transfer. With less pressure and lower expectations at a smaller club, and less competition for his place, Reina could blossom as undisputed first choice, without the dreaded uncertainty that always comes when a manager can't seem to make up his mind who his main custodian will be. He played 32 out of 38 league games in his first season and didn't miss a single league game in his next two campaigns. In 2004/05, Villarreal finished an impressive 3rd in *La Liga*, and in so doing, qualified for the Champions League for the first time. And yet by the time the Spanish team arrived on Merseyside in July — to knock out Everton in the preliminary qualifying round — Reina was already keeping clean sheets in the competition for Liverpool.

Accolades

There was no shortage of accolades for Reina as the season reached its conclusion. The most important judge — the manager himself — was clearly happy at the way things panned out. Benítez said: "When we signed Pepe, I said he was the best goalkeeper in Spain, now I believe he is among the top two or three in England." This also goes to show the quality of goalkeeping talent that gravitates towards the Premiership. Whereas Spain and Italy tend to have the best Spanish and Italian goalkeepers — at least until Reina departed *La Liga* — England, on top of its home-grown elite like James and Robinson, has world-class imports such as Petr Cech and Edwin van der Sar, as well as newly-installed German no.1, Jens Lehman. Add Reina, and you have the best goalkeepers from a number of major footballing nations, while goalkeepers like Thomas Sorensen and Mark Schwarzer are extremely steady and reliable. "For me," Benítez concluded, "Pepe is the complete goalkeeper and he has done a very good job for the team."

Kenny Dalglish, a man whose views on the club are second to none — as its best-ever player and also a hugely successful manager — was in no doubt of the Spanish keeper's quality. "He's superb. The hardest thing for a goalkeeper to adjust to at Liverpool are the long periods of inactivity. Those gaps in action test a goalkeeper's concentration and that's when you see those little slips that sometimes cost points. But Reina's powers of concentration are top drawer and that's why you can count his mistakes on the fingers of one hand."

Alan Hansen was equally impressed. "He's done exceptionally well. He's worked out when to come for crosses and when to stay on his line. Basically, he's worked out what the right thing to do is. No-one should ever underestimate how important having a good goalkeeper is to a team, and Rafa Benítez has signed a really good one. He said at the time that Reina was a great goalkeeper and that has been proved right. Anyone will tell you what a world-class goalkeeper is there for, and the big teams have all got them. Liverpool have been missing that, but that's no longer the case."

Maybe the most telling testimony came from Ray Clemence, the most decorated goalkeeper in the club's history, with three European Cups, five league titles and two Uefa Cups during his 14 years at the Anfield. "From what I've seen so far, it's his shot-stopping and decision making which has impressed me most. There are still one or two areas he needs to work on, particularly when dangerous balls are put into the box and there are a lot of bodies around, but he seems to have an ability to see danger and he reads balls over the top of the defence quickly."

But Clemence also added a proviso: "He's done very well over his first 50 games, but at Liverpool that's still only a short amount of time. What's important now is he continues this."

Clemence, like Bruce Grobbelaar, was watching Reina eclipse a number of his long-standing personal bests with the club. Reina kept 30 clean sheets in his first 50 games: four more than Clemence achieved over the same period following his debut in 1969. He also conceded two fewer goals than 'Clem' in that time. But the Spaniard has a long way to go to match the defensive parsimony of the 1978/79 side, which conceded just 16 league goals all season, and a mere four at Anfield.

However, one major record tumbled: the longest period without the Reds conceding a goal, as the team compiled eleven consecutive clean sheets that lasted an incredible 1,014 minutes of football. Brazlian side São Paulo would eventually end the run at the World Club Championship, just as it was starting to look possible that Liverpool could break the English and all-time world records. Reading's Steve Death — who strikers could be excused for giving a wide berth — managed 11 consecutive clean sheets in 1979, going 1,103 minutes without conceding in all. The British record stands at 1,196 minutes, by former England goalkeeper Chris Woods, playing for Rangers in 1986-87. And the world record stands at 1,275 minutes, and was set by a fellow Spaniard: Abel Resino of Atlético Madrid in 1990-91.

So Reina fell one game short of the English record, and three games short of the world best. While much of it was down to the improved defending, it can't be coincidental that the defence improved so dramatically as a whole after he arrived. How much of it was down purely to the keeper is impossible to say, as is the case with any of the defenders — it really was a team effort — but as a regular part of the unit he deserves his share of the acclaim. While Reina was still seen by many as inferior to his Chelsea counterpart, Petr Cech, Reina finished the season with more clean sheets, and the amount of on-target shots the two keepers saved was virtually identical, both around the 87% mark.

It was also the first time in 22 years that a Liverpool team collected 30 clean sheets in a single season. Three times in the club's history had the defence put together 34 clean sheets, never more. In 2005/06, the Reds ended with 33 clean sheets, falling just one short of a place in the history books; 30 were gathered with Reina between the sticks. Still, the Spaniard won the Premier League's Golden Gloves award, after 20 Premiership clean sheets, two more than Edwin van der Sar and three more than Petr Cech.

The overall goalkeeping situation

Had things been different, Chris Kirkland could have rendered the signing of Pepe Reina unnecessary. Kirkland's injury record, at a time when he should have been ready to take over the no.1 role, ultimately gave Benítez no option but to look elsewhere: whatever his ability, the former Coventry City keeper could not be relied upon, and was no closer to fulfilling his substantial potential than when signed. Meanwhile, Scott Carson, at just 20, and with only a handful of games to his name, was not yet ready for the responsibility of being Liverpool's no.1. Jerzy Dudek's days were numbered long before his outstanding contribution to the Champions League final in Istanbul. A very good goalkeeper, and at times appearing to be a great one, he never convinced Benítez he was *quite* good enough.

Kirkland must be left with the most regrets. He had been responsible for a high percentage of the goals conceded during his stint between the sticks in Benítez's first season. Much of this was down to playing with an inhibiting injury — at times you could see how difficult he was finding diving, getting down like a geriatric trying to pick up a dropped penny. Whilst being brave in playing in the first place, none of his mistakes gave the manager reason to believe in him.

Of course, mistakes range in their severity, from the obvious 'Djimi Traore's Burnley Come Dancing Spectacular' catastrophe — where, it can safely be said, the Frenchman, rather than the keeper, was at fault as he pirouetted the ball into his own net with almost Maradona-like footwork — through to the more subjective areas, such as errors of positioning, marking or a failure to anticipate, including when a goalkeeper is slow off his line. And indeed, more than one player can make an error in the build-up to a goal: if one defender falls over, another is out of position, and the goalkeeper compounds the slips by making a pig's ear of the shot.

In 2004/05, Scott Carson was at fault for one goal in his five games (a real howler, against Juventus); Jerzy Dudek had the exact same ratio — one every five games — with eight crucial mistakes in 40 games. Kirkland, however, made nine goal-costing errors in just 14 games. A season later, and in six games Dudek was at fault for two goals.

In his first season at Liverpool, Reina clearly bettered all of the other keepers Benítez had called upon in terms of errors costing goals: in 51 games, only four were down to the Spaniard (although one of which was a high-profile error in the FA Cup Final). As with any goalkeeper, you could nit-pickingly argue that there were more goals that he could possibly have done better with, but a shot always looks easier to save when you're watching it back with the knowledge of what the striker is going to do; a keeper has no such luxury, having to react in the moment.

Number one

Pepe Reina is solving a problem position for the club dating back almost twenty years, to when Bruce Grobbelaar was in his prime. Since the start of the 1990s, the club has moved unsuccessfully through Grobbelaar, David

James, Mike Hooper, Brad Friedel, Sander Westerveld, Jerzy Dudek and Chris Kirkland as first choice custodians, with none showing more than temporary brilliance, and none proving a satisfactory long-term solution.

Before getting carried away with Reina's very promising start, it's worth noting that in his own debut season, Jerzy Dudek was quite outstanding — before the cracks appeared. But Reina appears to have what it takes to be around for the long haul. Looking at his game, there are no areas that need radical intervention. He's a good shot stopper; he commands his area; he seems mentally strong; when he chooses to catch, his handling is excellent; he anticipates danger and is quick to deal with on-rushing strikers; his distribution is top-rate; he has an excellent record with saving penalties; and his communication with his defence rarely seems lacking. While there's room for improvement, there are no glaring weaknesses to his game. He will almost certainly get even better in the coming years — a 23-year-old keeper is akin to a 19-year-old outfield player — and, sooner rather than later, the number on his back will change from 25 to 1.

Chapter Ten

Peter Crouch: A Tall Order

It's fair to say that more than a few eyebrows were raised when Rafa Benítez opted to sign Southampton's Peter Crouch. For both good and bad reasons, Crouch became a major talking point during his inaugural season at Anfield.

If fans were expecting 'glamour' signings upon the Reds becoming European Champions, they were in for a shock; Crouch has always been seen at quite the other end of the spectrum. In fact, many have seen him as a joke figure: freakishly tall, and with all the muscle bulk of a malnourished stick insect. It's easy to overlook how good a footballer Crouch is; his height makes him a target for ridicule, but also, quite clearly, an equally effective *target-man*. Wish for a *big* signing, and sometimes it will come true.

It's impossible to talk about Crouch and not make reference to his height. It's his defining characteristic. However, it's one thing poking some light-hearted fun at him, another entirely to ridicule him to the lengths some people have. He's a very good footballer; he just happens also to be a *very tall* footballer.

Benítez was happy to pay £7m for Crouch, in the knowledge that the 24-

year-old was coming into form, and his best years were ahead of him. The previous season had seen Crouch finally find his feet in the Premiership (and no, not because they were so far away from the rest of his body). He scored 16 goals for Southampton, a poor team ultimately unable to escape relegation; 13 of those goals came in a flurry in the second half of the season, when Harry Redknapp had arrived as the Saints' third manager since August, and the striker was finally getting a regular game.

Redknapp's son, ex-Liverpool captain Jamie, was in the same side. Himself an accomplished technical player, he was in no doubt about Crouch's ability: "Peter has got the feet of a Wayne Rooney or a Ronaldo. He has a lot of skills. But I don't think he realised how well he could play. Now he does. People laughed when I said that he would play for England but I always knew he would offer something. Not necessarily starting but if you have got 20 minutes to go in a World Cup qualifier or even the tournament itself, you can bring him on and just give yourself another option. He is better than just making a nuisance of himself. That's unfair, because he is a genuinely good footballer."

Crouch made his top-flight bow at a young age, joining Graham Taylor's Aston Villa in a £4.5m move in March 2002, shortly after his 21st birthday, having impressed under Harry Redknapp at Portsmouth. It was to prove the wrong move at the wrong time. Crouch suffered from the burden of pressure, receiving dog's abuse from opposing fans, and was undermined by the Villains' too-apparent eagerness to hit him early with the long ball. Even Taylor, not noted for his purist tactics, was frustrated by how his team failed to get the best out of the player by neglecting to play in to his feet as well. Whereas Redknapp could get his teams to make the best use of what Crouch had to offer, other managers proved less successful, and Taylor's successor, David O'Leary, seemed to have little time for the striker, finally offloading him to Southampton after a loan spell at Norwich. His career appeared to be in reverse, although he was no stranger to disappointment, having been released by Spurs, whom had joined as a trainee in July 2000, without making a senior appearance.

Even Crouch's harshest critics would accept that his has not been the easiest ascent to the top, and that, in order to keep bouncing back from the knocks and rising above the persistent jibes, he has had to possess a special mental fortitude.

Golden touch

Crouch does not have a good touch 'for a big man'; he has a good touch *full stop*. In truth, he is a footballing thoroughbred in an emaciated basketball player's body. Imagine Bergkamp stretched on a medieval rack for several years: the balance slightly more clumsy as a result, a higher centre of gravity, and instead of smooth lines, you see jagged, angular joints jutting awkwardly out as he runs. Many of the same qualities are present, with the same end result, just a failure to make the game look so effortless and, well, *beautiful*.

An example of Crouch's skill was evident in his first Anfield Mersey derby. Receiving a ball played down the touchline towards the corner flag, with two defenders for company, he controlled on his chest, then thigh, then foot, in a seamless act of assured juggling; swiftly followed by a 'Cruyff turn' that reverse-nutmegged the full-back and, in almost one movement, delivered an accurate low cross. Then there was the thigh control followed by the deft lay-off to Robbie Fowler against Bolton, when setting up his strike partner for a match-winning goal.

Despite such skill, Crouch will never be poetry in motion. He will never be the easiest on the eye. But if his touch and his passing were bound up in a player who was 5ft 10", everyone would be much more complimentary about it. But of course, if he was 5ft 10", he'd be much less of a threat in the air. So while he may never get the credit he deserves, the team he plays for will always enjoy the benefits.

While Bergkamp has never scored prolifically for Arsenal, especially in recent years, he played his part in a successful team creating chances. Obviously Crouch doesn't quite have the Dutchman's vision, but he does share with him a great ability to know what's going on around him, and to bring others into the game (perhaps because, like a giraffe, he can see above his habitat). With such long legs, Crouch can deal with wayward high passes; imagine John Cleese's goosestep in *Fawlty Towers*, but with a ball controlled on the end of a foot lifted higher than most people's heads. He can jump high to chest the ball, to control it in situations where others may have to head it, or he can get above defenders to win headers. Anything knocked into Crouch, however bad a pass, stands a chance of being turned into retained possession, because of the mix of height and control. The key is to not start hitting passes to him out of desperation.

While Crouch can be out-muscled, and needs to work on his aggression, if he gets his body into the right position, as he's learning to do, his marker can only get to the ball by fouling. And that's the main benefit of Peter Crouch: he enables team-mates to get up with play, either by holding the ball up or by winning free-kicks. Whereas Milan Baroš, the man he effectively replaced, would constantly look to spin in behind defenders, which often meant he had to take on an entire defence single-handedly (leading to the occasional spectacular goal or, more often, a corner at best), Crouch keeps the ball in a dangerous area until the cavalry arrives — most likely in the form of Steven Gerrard, but also in any number of attacking midfielders. In essence, Crouch has become the lynchpin of the attack: the man who holds the forward play together.

Lynchpins are often easy to overlook, in football as in machinery. They do not perform a glamorous task; they perform an *essential* task. Their role is

71

not to dazzle, but to unite. People don't fall in love with houses because of firm foundations or sturdy walls; they love the flourishes, the details. Midfield lynchpins have often been under-appreciated (initially at least), from Ronnie Whelan to Didi Hamann. Their job is to allow others to shine.

It's always important to look at what benefits a player offers, and weigh them up, rather than fixate about his faults. In the case of Crouch this is especially true, as the positives he offers are so unique. Sure, he can't run particularly fast — but so what? He is ideal for someone fast to play off, as Michael Owen discovered for England. Crouch is not your bog-standard, average footballer. Clearly. Like Didier Drogba at Chelsea, who regularly got a game ahead of the far more cultured and admired Hernan Crespo, Crouch is in the team for a reason. Purists may balk at the prospect of Drogba being preferred to Crespo, but his effectiveness in the Premiership is undeniable. Where Crouch is concerned, it's also been a journey of discovery, for him and for his teammates.

Crouch's early appearances for Liverpool arguably involved too much running into wide and deep areas. In one game he even covered more ground than Momo Sissoko, and something is not quite right when a target-man is covering more ground than a hard-running midfielder. It seemed that the desire to impress as a footballer was taking him into areas where, whilst he could show his deft touch, he wasn't going to hurt teams. There's a limit to how far he should drop off the front line. When dropping deep in the opening Champions League game, away at Real Betis, he showed how he could pick up the ball 40 yards from goal and, with vision and precision, play an unlikely pass, in this instance to Bolo Zenden; the ball ended up being crossed, and Luis Garcia scored a poacher's goal. Any deeper, however, and Crouch runs the risk of taking himself out of the equation — unless, as he demonstrated with some perceptive passes to Michael Owen when partnering him for England, he has a quick striker to pass forward to.

As the season progressed, Crouch wandered less and less from the central area of the final third, although in a passing team you cannot afford to be static and predictable, and as such he didn't simply become an immobile totem pole. It was notable that his two goals in the 7-0 drubbing of Birmingham involved sprints from deep after being involved in quick breaks from the halfway line. There wasn't a sense of 'I've done my part,' but a desire to conclude the move, not merely start it.

It is not *necessarily* the job of every forward to score goals: it is his job to help ensure the team wins games, and thereafter, wins trophies. Obviously it cannot be overlooked that goals play a big part, especially as a striker will be one of the players closest to the opposition goal over the course of a game. Without the right team-mates, a forward who doesn't score enough is a liability. But a forward who can help a series of attacking midfielders — or a prolific partner — to score an abundance of goals is a valuable commodity.

It depends on the system, and it depends on the team-mates; you cannot judge an individual like Crouch out of the context of the team, because he is primarily a team player. Until football becomes a one-on-one sport, with a forward playing on his own against a goalkeeper (like the alternative to penalties experimented with in countries like America), then there is room in a team for a range of talents.

Comparisons with Emile Heskey were quickly made: the great under-achieving striker offloaded in 2004, who never seemed to score enough goals. Such comparisons are lazy and ill-conceived. First of all, Heskey was playing in a team that utilised the quick ball over the top; often it was only he or Michael Owen who stood a chance of scoring, with the midfield often too far adrift of the play to have any chance of joining it. Then there is the fact that, after four seasons, it was time for Houllier to try something new, hence the signing of Djibril Cissé and Heskey's sale to Birmingham; little did Houllier know he'd not be around long enough to see it transpire.

If Liverpool had won the league under Houllier, it wouldn't have mattered if Heskey didn't score a single goal as it would have meant the *team* scored enough: his inclusion would have been vindicated by results. (Having a forward who doesn't score many goals could well make winning the league difficult, but Bergkamp barely scored during Arsenal's 'Invincibles' season of 2003/04.) The problem was that, with Heskey a regular starter, Liverpool were getting further away from winning the league, not closer; again, this is not to say it was all the former Leicester man's fault, just that he had to take his share of culpability in the overall failure.

Four years is more than enough time to decide something isn't working; four months, which was roughly the time it took for many to write off Crouch (indeed, some took less than four minutes), is not. It's fair to say that his confidence suffered during that time, as he approached 24 hours in a Liverpool shirt without a goal, and the pressure to break his duck — as hysteria raged in the newspapers — started to affect his overall game. But 12 goals in his next 24 games (many of which lasted only 70 minutes) showed that, when confident and supplied with the right kind of service, he *could* get goals at a ratio that would appease even those who choose to look less closely at his other abilities. That those goals included crucial opening strikes against Everton and Manchester United didn't hurt, either.

His duck was broken on December 3rd by the flukiest of goals, but by then he deserved any slice of luck prepared to head his way. Running towards the Wigan goal, his shot cannoned off a defender before the goalkeeper, Mike Pollitt, parried the ball into his own net. Even then the Press Association was quick to take it from him, marking it down as an own goal; it took the Premiership's Dubious Goal's Panel to re-credit Crouch with the strike, given it had been on target before the deflection. If every time a keeper got his hands to a shot that crossed the line was pegged as an O.G., then all the strikers in the land would see half their strikes chalked off. It seemed petty on behalf of the Press Association, and fuelled suspicions of an agenda by some journalists, who had staked their reputations on his failure and were not about to help him prove them wrong. Fortunately Crouch himself wasn't aware during the game that it had been taken from him, and with his confidence boosted and the millstone lifted, he quickly lobbed home the kind of subtle finish that would have felt impossible for him even to attempt just minutes earlier. He ended December with seven goals.

But he had to fight to claim other strikes, too. A header against Newcastle was tipped against the post by Shay Given and, as it span back towards the goalline, passed by the prostrate Geordie custodian, possibly brushing his shoulder but with video evidence inconclusive; it too was awarded as an own goal to the goalkeeper by the Press Association, even though, at Euro 2004, Wayne Rooney had been given a goal where his shot cannoned off the post and was headed away from goal at speed — and therefore with no possibility of it going in of its own accord — when it crashed into the keeper. (Crouch's goal was finally credited to him four months later, by the Dubious Goals Panel.)

Effective

Peter Crouch was the Reds' second-most effective attacking player in 2005/06 when adding goals and assists to form an overall contribution in the final third. For the second season running, Steven Gerrard was the main man, scoring 23 goals and weighing in with 28 assists: a quite phenomenal return. Crouch, after a slow start, ended the season with 13 goals and 18 assists: a valuable all-round contribution, especially considering his attacking 'partnership' with Gerrard was of an exceptionally symbiotic nature. Those statistics — 36 goals and 54 assists — from a pair of strikers would be celebrated as evidence of a successful pairing; instead they come from the two attacking players who featured most for Liverpool in the season, and who linked time and time again in the Reds' best moves, but neither of whom is considered an out-and-out goalscorer, and one is a midfielder.

Gerrard's contribution and output was akin to the sportsman who pipped him for the BBC's Sports Personality of the Year in 2005: Andrew Flintoff. In cricket, the team is happy if the runs come from lower down the order; the opening batsmen, like strikers in football, are expected to score the majority of the runs, but if the team wins the test, then the ends justify the means. In many ways, Crouch plays the role of the steady batsman whose ability to fend off the bowlers, while scoring at a steady rate himself, enables him to keep the more flamboyant man company at the crease, as they build up a winning margin.

Statistics that prove Crouch's effectiveness will never be enough to win over his doubters. Niall Quinn, another tall striker who struggled to score goals early in his career, is someone worth listening to when it comes to Crouch. The big Irishman obviously sees a kindred spirit. Quinn, in both his *Guardian* column and his television commentaries, steadfastly defended Crouch, but also offered words of advice. He felt Crouch should be looking to station himself against the opposing full-back to enable a diagonal ball from left to right, or vice versa. Facing play, on the other side of the pitch from where the ball was delivered, he would then be able to see runners while also keeping his eye on the ball as it arrives, opening the game up for himself.

Many pundits felt Crouch should be taking up areas at the back post, to isolate smaller full-backs. Against Newcastle at St James' Park, it paid dividends, as Jan Kromkamp's cross was headed home as Crouch ghosted past Peter Ramage, who stood a full half-foot shorter. This was also seen when Crouch headed back to Gerrard in the FA Cup Final. Graham Taylor, however, felt Crouch should be attacking the near post. "Get him in front of people. The back post is no good. Peter's so tall he has never had to jump. He doesn't get the power from his back to head the ball with any force."

Crouch's headed lay-offs are not aimless flicks, but often closer to headed passes. He's not a brilliant header of the ball, technically speaking, but also not as bad as some people make out: his height raises expectations about his ability to connect cleanly with the ball every time. To compensate, he tries to head the ball *intelligently*. As Taylor implies, he doesn't have the neck muscles of an Alan Shearer or a Les Ferdinand, nor the power in the leap to generate sufficient force. His timing can be awry at times, but he tends to go for accuracy — aiming for the corners of the net, knowing he can't bullet a header past a keeper. When he misses it's rarely by much; when high or wide, it's usually by no more than a foot, while two of the headers he's scored have gone in off the post.

International man of mystery

Peter Crouch will always have to run the gauntlet of hate, or ridicule at the very least. The England situation following his debut only exacerbated the problem. His Liverpool form was the only thing of concern to most Kopites, but in becoming part of the England squad, Crouch was being opened up to more psychological abuse, from both fans and press.

Unless you watch Crouch week in, week out, you will not appreciate just how good he is, and how effective he can be; he will never be a superstar like Wayne Rooney. He will never be quick, or a 30-goal-a-season man. But then not every player is the same, and nor would you want them to be. As soon as fans of other clubs saw Crouch in an England shirt, it was their invitation to either bitch about how their club's striker was better, or indeed, to boo the player, as did fans during his first two international appearances on English soil. 'Whipping boy' is not a new concept.

"He is not Rooney," said Benítez in May 2006, with Crouch once again the target of harsh criticism — this time as the likely candidate to fill in for the injured Rooney at the World Cup. "He's a different player. He hasn't got the pace of Rooney, but he is a little bit better than Rooney in the air, wouldn't you say? Rooney is a fantastic footballer, he can change a game, he can win games, but Crouch can do the same. He can give an assist, win in the air, keep the ball, play good passes. He's not the kind of target-man you can say, 'Okay, stay there, we'll only pass you long balls'."

Benítez went further, explaining how his new striker was not merely a target-man. "The first time he was with us, when we were preparing to play Olympiacos in pre-season, a Spanish coach was watching our training and he said, 'Hey, he is really good, this player. Look at him, short passes, both feet'. And against Olympiacos he did what we call in Spanish a 'bicycle'; you call it a stepover; and went on a dribble. Maybe in other countries as a manager you might prefer another player, but the way you play in England, to have a target-man but with his game intelligence and qualities, it's difficult to find better."

In club football, whether or not you like a player, he represents your club and is 'one of yours'. For England, those club players who own your loyalties are suddenly in competition with the very opposition players you spend your time loathing. It has to be a very special player indeed to cross that dividing line, so that someone who is royally disliked in club football can at least be respected in an England shirt.

It didn't stop with opposing fans. Too many members of the national press seemed to have an agenda against Crouch; others in their profession confessed to being embarrassed at the treatment he received. Nothing anyone could say, or indeed Crouch could do, would alter that fact. The better Crouch played for Liverpool and England, the less they were going to go back on their beliefs and actually admit it.

If you look at Crouch's international record during 2005/06 (starting with the Columbia game in the summer of 2005, when he made his debut), then it amounts to just one goal in five games, in a season in which England played a further three times. But the two games he started for his country both ended in wins; the three in which he came on saw England end up winning a game they were either losing (on two occasions) or drawing (once). Two of the three games in which he didn't feature at all — against Northern Ireland and Denmark — ended with humiliating defeats.

England's scoring rate is far more impressive with Crouch in the team than when he has been absent. In the 502 minutes when Crouch didn't feature for his country, England scored just four goals — at a rate of one every 126 minutes. In the 218 minutes when Crouch featured, England scored a staggering *nine* times — at a rate of one every 24 minutes. Put more simply, when Crouch is absent it's almost a game-and-a-half between goals for the national side; when he's playing, it's worth almost four goals for every 90 minutes.

Statistically speaking, that's a fairly small sample. But it's also still worthy of consideration, as it covers the course of international football over one calendar year. Over time the figures — even if they continue to prove positive — will surely become less dramatic, as no player can maintain such an impact; England will not average four goals a game with Crouch in the side over a 50 game period, as no top team averages four goals a game, and clearly part of his effectiveness has been as an impact player from the bench. But in the meantime, Crouch has the right to say, "Judge me on how many goals England have scored and how games they have won with me in the side". For Liverpool, neither he nor the team have proved outrageously prolific over the season, but since his arrival, the Reds' results and consistency have significantly improved, and after a couple of barren spells, Liverpool ended up with 104 goals in 2005/06. The part he has played in this, as a key man in the spine of the side, cannot be overlooked. He is also a brilliant asset at defending set pieces, and while it's hard to argue that any striker should be in the team purely on his defensive contribution, if Crouch (while playing his part in the attacking third) also saves the team 5-10 goals a season with his headed clearances, then that can be as good as him scoring 5-10 more. If you add the goals he scores to the goals he creates and to the goals he saves, you have an overall package that helps his team win games. And surely that's all that counts?

The future
There's a lot more to come from Peter Crouch; he is not the finished article. His is a role that grows with experience, and an increased knowledge of how best to utilise his unique physical gifts. Each season he should become increasingly 'unplayable', as he learns which positions are impossible to defend against. His first season at Liverpool was a steep learning curve, with his first taste of a world-class club and an equally gifted manager. It was his first taste of working at an English club under a continental manager, and coincided with his England career commencing. With it came his introduction to the Champions League and World Club Championship.

Niall Quinn was not particularly effective as a young player, but came of age once leaving Arsenal for Manchester City, and in his later years at Sunderland was the perfect foil for Kevin Phillips, the prolific goalscorer.

While Crouch will never win over *all* Liverpool fans — there will always be those too blind to see, and those to whose taste Crouch will never appeal — but his attitude and endeavour was winning over the Kop well before he broke his dreaded duck, 19 games into his career with the Reds. The Liverpool faithful love a trier — an Erik Meijer, for example — but will quickly tire if the ability does not match the effort. Meijer was a nice novelty, a cult hero for a while, but God help him if he had stayed at the club for a number of seasons without improving on his output or showing more skill.

Peter Crouch will be judged over a longer period than one season, but the potential to be an even more dangerous and effective player is clearly present.

Chapter Eleven

Fowler - Robbie's Return

Clearly one of the greatest stories of 2005/06 was the re-signing of Robbie Fowler, the former number nine arriving on a shock free transfer from Manchester City at the end of the January transfer window. Short of Kenny Dalglish reclaiming the number seven shirt, there couldn't have been a more unexpected or welcome comeback at Anfield — at least in terms of symbolism.

'God' was back. Such was the hysteria surrounding the news, it was hard to gauge if fans saw it as a great signing for the future, or an excuse to wallow in the past. While plenty accepted that he would not breeze in and replicate the form from when he was 21, others seemed to think he did indeed possess mythical powers; while a more surreal reaction was 'I don't care if he never scores another goal for us, he's *home*'.

What did seem certain was that if Fowler was going to rediscover anything approaching the form of his youth, he would not get a better place to do so than his spiritual home, playing in a team that was clearly on the rise, and who were still the reigning Champions of Europe (indeed, Fowler had been in Istanbul as a fan). A profligacy in front of goal had been noted as the side's Achilles' Heel in the first half of the season — although it hadn't stopped a domestic run of 13 wins in 15 games — and Fowler was of course a hugely clinical finisher in his youth. At 30 he was far from finished, but injuries and an apparent loss of desire had made Fowler look a shadow of his former self in recent years.

The deal started off as a rumour in the weeks beforehand, but it seemed a rehash of a 'wishful thinking' story that had appeared many times before, without substance. In fact, arch-rivals Everton had made a move for the player in the transfer window. Such was the abuse Fowler received over the years from Evertonians, he was never going to entertain the notion of playing for his childhood favourites. His heart is decidedly Red these days.

Rick Parry denied Liverpool were interested on Thursday 28th January, while Benítez said that he could neither confirm nor deny that a return was on the cards — which seemed to indicate at least some form of interest. At this stage none of the newspapers picked up on it as a legitimate story. At 4pm on Friday 27th January the news broke, and was confirmed by the club shortly after. "I've never known a transfer happen quite so quickly," Parry told BBC Radio Five. "It was all done within 24 hours. I had to persuade Robbie to look at the contract. I think I could have put a contract in front of him with no money on it and he'd have signed it!"

"Signing Robbie has obviously given everyone at the club a major lift but

I want to make it clear that this isn't a PR exercise," Parry added. "Robbie's return is down to Rafa. It was his decision to bring in Robbie and he's done it because he believes that he can improve us as a team. Rafa hasn't let his heart rule his head because he's not that type of manager. This transfer has happened because Rafa believes Robbie can offer us something that we haven't currently got at the club."

Benítez explained his reasoning thus: "Robbie is a great finisher, which is why we signed him. If we continue our attacking play, especially at home, controlling games and creating chances, he will score a lot of goals for us. My scouts told me that bringing him in would be a good option and as soon as I started talking to him I knew he wanted to come back."

The deal had its genesis after the semi-final victory over Chelsea at Anfield in May 2005. Benítez explained: "I first thought of the idea after the Chelsea game, he was in a pub — only with a soft drink — with us and we were talking about football. Steve McManaman was also there and you could hear all the fans saying 'you should sign Robbie again' and things like that."

McManaman offered his version: "Rafael Benitez has said he formed the idea of re-signing him when he had a drink with Robbie and myself after Liverpool's defeat of Chelsea in the Champions League semi-final last May. We were celebrating with fans in the Pan American pub in the Albert Dock. I knew Rafa when I played for Real Madrid and he was manager of Valencia, and he loves talking football. Five minutes after reaching the Champions League final and he's thinking about where there is room for improvement. I can't recall any words that hinted at his interest in re-signing Robbie. Maybe it was Robbie down on his knees that gave him the idea!"

Fowler himself was in no doubt as to what he had to do. "If I'm honest I've got six months to get a contract and I'm doing everything I can to get it. If it takes me being what's seen as a good boy for six months, that's what I've got to do. I suppose I've got to live a bit like a monk for a while," said Fowler. Of course, it does need pointing out that a footballer shouldn't only be looking after himself for six months; that it should be a permanent concern during a playing career and that, perhaps in the past, the player hadn't helped himself by falling short of such standards of abstinence.

The second coming
The time on the Anfield clock was 9.23pm, the date 1st February 2006. The number 16 was displayed on the electronic substitution board, and Peter Crouch made way for the new number 11: Robbie Fowler. Anfield went wild.

It was strange watching Fowler in the red of Liverpool again; in many ways it was hard to comprehend that he'd ever been away. It was just so *familiar*. But it was Emile Heskey — the man who, in Fowler's previous game for Liverpool in November 2001 had kept his place in the second half when Fowler was hauled off at half-time — who had the final word, heading a ball across the box that Xabi Alonso inadvertently chested into his own net with only a minute left. Fowler almost had the *final* final word, deep into injury time, when his spectacular overhead kick at the Kop end was correctly ruled out for offside. If there was a scriptwriter penning the fairytale comeback, it wasn't the linesman.

The next real glimpse of the Fowler of old came against Arsenal, the club he routinely terrorised during the 1990s, and with whom he was linked for a number of years as rumours of his discontent under Gérard Houllier surfaced. Reacting quicker than Philippe Senderos to a ball played into the area, Fowler skipped past the Swiss with such clever movement he left the defender rocking on his heels, and then almost instantaneously fired a right-footed shot back across Jens Lehman, intent on nestling in the far corner of the net. The German keeper somehow managed to paw the shot away, just as the Kop was rising in celebration. Fowler himself had spun away with arms raised, believing he'd done enough to score his first goal in his second spell with the Reds. It was a game that showcased his wonderful passing, as had the previous fixture — his first start under Benítez, away at Wigan Athletic. In both games Fowler supplied inch-perfect crosses.

Two further disallowed Kop-end goals were chalked off before Fowler would finally get off the mark in legitimate fashion. While the Birmingham goal had rightly been ruled out, the next two decisions were harsh. The first was yet another last-minute effort, this time against Charlton, where Fowler received a pass in the area and quickly smashed home a low shot that the keeper stood no chance of saving. The flag was raised against Djibril Cissé in the centre, and while he may have been a fraction offside, the pass had been fed wide to Fowler; under the current interpretation of the law, Cissé was 'inactive' (weeks later the Reds would concede in an almost identical manner at Newcastle, with Shearer standing offside beside the scorer, Shola Ameobi, but that goal stood). It cost the Reds two points, and also the confidence of their new striker, who was desperate to score what would have been his 172nd goal in Liverpool colours, to draw level with Kenny Dalglish. Then came another late, late disallowed goal, this time against Benfica, when Xabi Alonso's corner was penalised for drifting out of play before it ricocheted off Fowler and into the net. Television replays did not back up the linesman's assertion, but it was too late for the Reds to rescue the tie. However, it would have got Fowler off the mark, and sparked some confidence into the team. But the new no.11 would only have to wait 16 minutes into his next Anfield appearance to score his first goal for the club in his second spell, and with typical symmetry, it would come against Fulham, the team against whom he had scored his very first Liverpool goal, thirteen years earlier.

One-thousand, six-hundred and eight days after last registering a goal for the club, Robbie Fowler was back on the scoresheet. It came from a Harry Kewell corner, flicked on at the near post by Luis Garcia into an area where

Fowler, who had been standing in front of the keeper at the moment the kick had been taken, had cleverly backed away into space. A firm header, and Tony Warner — the man who set a Premiership record for most appearances as an unused substitute during Fowler's heyday — could do nothing to stop his former team-mate (or *bench*-mate, to be more accurate) from celebrating. Warner, who must have experienced Fowler's finishing in training countless times, would not need reminding of what the striker was capable of doing with time and space. And so Robbie was off and running again, but only after a nervous glance towards the linesman.

His new team-mates were suitably impressed by the returning hero, none more so than Xabi Alonso. "Robbie is a great player," enthused the Spaniard. "There has been a lot of talk about whether he will be with us next season but he is doing his job very well. As a finisher, he is an absolute killer inside the penalty area. What sets him apart is the way he takes advantage of half chances when the ball is loose. He is lethal when that happens."

The goal against Fulham set Fowler on a run of four goals in four starts; each aiding his quest to earn a new contract. His second goal came at West Bromich Albion, when he showed impressive fitness levels, determination and pace in keeping up with Djibril Cissé, whose hard and low centre was turned home by the unmarked no.11. (Admittedly Fowler looked like he was going to have a coronary 30 seconds later.) Next came the winner in the home game against Bolton, when good combination play with Peter Crouch saw 'God' strike home a left-footed grubber that, as of old, nestled tight to the side netting; in no way a clean strike, as it bobbled home, it showed that accuracy is everything with Fowler. Then came the winner at Blackburn, in what would replace Patrick Kluivert's Anfield effort for Newcastle in 2004 as the Most Offside Goal in the history of the game. But with two unfairly disallowed goals in earlier games, the striker was due a bit of good fortune. As with his previous effort against Bolton, Fowler played a key part in the move: this time chesting John Arne Riise's throw into the path of Cissé, who was standing yards offside. The Frenchman waved a foot at the ball as it approached, then pulled his foot away, effectively throwing a dummy. Quite how this was not interfering with play is anyone's guess, but Fowler was not complaining when the ball broke to Fernando Morientes, whose smart cut-back was drilled home by the gleeful no.11, who had held the perfect position in order for the Spaniard to pick him out without risk of interception. Yet again it was a relatively simple strike, but as with the others it owed everything to an advanced positional sense and the ability to lose a marker for that essential split second. If a finisher is clever enough, he can make it a lot easier for himself.

After drawing a couple of blanks, a 5th goal soon followed, away at Portsmouth. Again Morientes was the supplier, with a cute flick that Fowler controlled and, as expected, tucked away into the corner of the net.

Each was an important goal — either deciding a match on its own, or setting the Reds on the way to victory; all five goals were scored with the score at 0-0. And his first — at Fulham — totally reversed the fortunes of the strikers at the club. They would net 20 goals between them in the next eight weeks. Fowler could take pride from the fact that he could have done nothing more — he gave it his all, scored some crucial goals, and vindicated Benítez's gamble. He could only sit tight and hope that the longed-for contract was forthcoming — and indeed it was. That he would be staying for at least one extra season was confirmed by the club on May 5th. "Robbie has done really well and he deserves this," said Benítez. "He has scored vital goals for us and has worked really hard. I am delighted to have him with us for next season, he is an important member of our squad."

Later in May, Benítez expanded on his decision: "We have thought long and hard about the future with him. We have balanced the positives against the negatives and we know he can do even better next season. He is a natural finisher, he has good game intelligence, he is very good for the team, he is a good worker, and he has great passion for this club. It is important for him to do his job and work hard over the summer on his fitness. We will work with him by providing a special programme. But if he does that, then he can go on for a long time."

Fowler vs Houllier

Robbie Fowler's 'resurrection' came just over four years after Gérard Houllier sold him to Leeds for £11m. Whatever the rights and wrongs of offloading Fowler — and from a purely business point of view, it was very profitable (although the reinvesting of the transfer fee was less shrewd) — Houllier had long been in a difficult position, inasmuch as Fowler's presence seemed to overshadow the club. The very fact that the boy once known as the 'Toxteth Terror' was now known as 'God' made all dealings with him, and about him, fraught with peril. Many fans could see no wrong in anything Fowler did; he was worshipped unconditionally.

Houllier's heart operation in October 2001, so soon after securing five trophies in that one calendar year, meant he would never be in a stronger position to take on his bête noire. The manager had public sympathy on his side, and trust in his leadership from the fans. It seemed an emblematic sale, a marker set down by the French boss.

Looking back, Houllier never seemed able to cope with the more opinionated and experienced players, and Fowler, wittingly or otherwise, could apparently undermine his manager. Any manager has to be *Numero Uno*, and it is his right to excise someone he feels threatens his authority; other managers may have embraced a 'difficult' character if he could still deliver the goods on the pitch (as did Alex Ferguson with Eric Cantona and Roy Keane), but Houllier's style seemed based on getting the most out of more submissive types, who happily toed the line. And, of course, with discontent rife between manager and player, and a succession of injuries, Fowler was no longer looking like the top-class striker of the mid-'90s. At times it was clear that Fowler wasn't helping himself, certainly when going nose-to-nose with Phil Thompson on the training ground, but he'd been able to get away with things under previous managers, only for Houllier, an 'outsider', to now be laying down a far stricter law. Fowler was a local, part of the furniture. Liverpool was *his* club, after all. At Newcastle in 1999, Alan Shearer went head-to-head with Ruud Gullit, and the player won, with the Dutchman losing his job; although the circumstances were different, no player is allowed to be bigger than the club at Liverpool.

Chris Bascombe, who has been covering the club's fortunes for the *Liverpool Echo* since the late '90s, claimed Houllier wanted him to be less than complimentary about Fowler in the paper. Talking to *The Liverpool Way* website in 2004, he said, "Let's just say I wasn't discouraged [by Houllier] from being more critical of him [Fowler]. On many occasions, the first question to me on a Monday morning at Melwood was 'what have you written about Robbie's performance?' Looking back, I feel certain people wanted the idea of Robbie being sold to slowly enter the public consciousness. I should say I agreed with the decision to sell Robbie at the time, although in retrospect I'd rather he'd stayed than have him replaced by Mr Diouf. I know the manager wanted him out for a long time but wanted to do it when public opinion was on his side.

"I recognised this before Robbie left and he was fully aware of what was going on. With more experience, I realised I should have been backing him through the difficult period, not criticising so much. When I felt a similar tactic was being used on other players a few years later, it made me want to defend them even more. I'll never be used in that way again."

Even had Fowler's talent (or rather, fitness and confidence) not been diminished by injuries, he would have struggled to find his best form with rotation — which, as it was a new phenomenon at the club, he presumably took as a personal, demoralising snub — and the prevalent feeling of unease with his superiors. As a result, the hunger seemed to vanish and the smile of his youth had been replaced with a scowl. (How many times did he tear off that breathe-easy nose strip in a fit of pique after being withdrawn? No player enjoys being taken off, but you could see Fowler felt it was just the latest instalment in a personal agenda.) From then on, he was sold against his will to Leeds and then, as they sank into financial ruin, sold on once more to Manchester City. His destiny seemed out of his own hands, a pawn in football's game; unable to any longer tap into the old devastating marksmanship at will, and therefore no longer able to call any of the shots.

Clearly, Houllier's tactical approach to games did not suit Fowler. Houllier's task was to build a successful team, not to get the best out of one individual.

Owen was the in-form striker, winning the European Footballer of the Year at the time Fowler was offloaded; Emile Heskey, with his bulk and brute strength, was the more natural foil for Owen, even if the two never struck up a partnership in the truest sense, in the way Fowler and Stan Collymore linked almost telepathically. Until Houllier's tactics passed their sell-by date, and grew increasingly predictable, Owen was clearly the best option.

While Owen and Heskey had become Houllier's first-choice pairing in the Treble season of 2000/01, Fowler's contribution should not be overlooked. Fowler is a 'big game' player. Despite being third choice, he scored in two different semi-finals, two different finals, and bagged two crucial goals in the 'final final' at Charlton. While Heskey's contribution to the success was also notable, the goals dried up in the Premiership run-in, and he scored in none of the finals, and only one of the semi-finals.

It's plausible that Benítez would have been far less happy inheriting the Fowler of 2001, had he taken charge of the club back then. It perhaps took Fowler the shock of leaving his beloved club, and realising what it meant to him *in absentia*, to complete a stage in growing up. He certainly seemed a different person upon his return, the old fires rekindled, allied to a new sense of perspective on both his career and the football club he would be playing for. It's possible that at the time of his sale, he felt Liverpool owed him, after all those goals; now he was under no illusions. If Rafa needed Fowler's finishing, it was equally true that Fowler owed Benítez for taking a chance on a player who, just weeks earlier, had been disparaged by Nigel Worthington, manager of Championship side Norwich — the Norfolk side's boss feeling Fowler had too many houses, and not enough desire.

It's important to remember that Houllier wasn't given the smoothest of rides by his number nine. The Frenchman was in charge during Fowler's distasteful baiting of Graeme Le Saux (as annoying as Le Saux can be, homophobic taunts were not the way to de-spike the full-back's pricked-up hairdo), not to mention the ill-advised white line snorting against Everton (again under extreme provocation, and admittedly a humorous riposte at the vicious cocaine rumours, but not the actions of someone thinking clearly). There were training ground bust-ups with Phil Thompson, and attacks from Everton fans in Liverpool nightspots (not necessarily Fowler's fault, but the headlines were not the kind a manager wants to read). Houllier certainly had his hands full.

Often players who've been at a club since they were young boys need to break out on their own, just as a young adult can never fully grow until he or she flies the family nest. In life you can get cast in a certain role, and never be allowed to outgrow it. Fowler needed to escape, if only to return home a different person. It's worth remembering that Houllier also cast aside impish local 'scally', David Thompson — another player who caused a personality clash. While injuries would also hamper Thompson's career, there were signs when at Blackburn that the player could become a full England international, so inspirational was he for the Lancashire club, following a very promising spell for Coventry. The move away from Anfield sparked a new desire and confidence in the little terrier.

It is clear that Fowler was a victim of the changing culture at Liverpool — albeit an essential transformation — as well as the sea-change in English football that took place in the second half of the 1990s. He grew up in a far less 'professional' era, and seemed left behind as football became more athletic, more health-conscious, and less about having fun. Football had become big business, and as such, ticket prices soared and media interest expanded almost exponentially. While most fans still want to see players enjoying themselves, all will feel insulted if those players aren't taking it seriously enough (and playing 'pass the pound coin', as occurred during Roy Evans' reign, is patently not taking it seriously enough). At his best, Fowler seemed to perform like he was still in the playground, three-and-in, jumpers for goalposts, rush goalie, etc.

In some ways the entertainment level of football has increased, as technically superior players continue to arrive from overseas, meaning only the finest local talents flourish (the death of the journeyman), and as the pace grows more frenetic by the week; in other ways, players are given less room to express themselves as more and more teams seek to nullify, through fear of failure, while sometimes the game is far too quick for its own good. Winning the league is an ambition shared by perhaps only four teams at most; the other 16 teams seem to set their aim at avoiding relegation, and making the Uefa Cup if lucky.

And yet the game always has room for players who can find time and space, no matter how quick their legs or how capacious their lungs. The first yards have always been in a player's head. And it all depends on how you utilise that player, after all. If you don't — or can't — play to his strengths, he will never flourish.

"I can see he is mature now, and clever," said Benitez, days after Fowler arrived. "He's got game intelligence. It's not like playing basketball where you need to be fit. In football, if you're clever, you can play. He's so clever he can get a goal walking, where other players wouldn't running."

Was he past his best, or had the teams he'd played in since the Evans-era Liverpool not suited his strengths? A lot of what Robbie Fowler showed in the past is simply not lost. A player cannot 'unlearn' how to strike a ball so exquisitely, and if you are a natural finisher at 18 you are a natural finisher at 30. His record at Leeds in his first season was 12 league goals in 22 appearances — a fine return, aided by playing in a good side, shortly before the great Elland Road fire sale. But as part of an inconsistent Manchester City set up, he struggled with injuries and never really got a consistent run in the side. But his record, with a goal every three starts, was still highly respectable.

A footballer's thinking should improve with age, and Fowler was always a very clever player with great movement, capable of finding space on any part of the pitch. But what can evanesce is a sense of self-belief and confidence, and those things are what enable a player to *access* his true ability. Sometimes certain environments and specific managers can get the best out of a player, and the combination of Fowler, Benítez and Liverpool instantly looked interesting on paper.

Fowler and Owen

Inextricably linked to the Robbie Fowler story is that of Michael Owen. It was ironic that in the season when Owen returned to England — and so nearly to Liverpool — it should be Fowler, whom he had overshadowed in recent years, who instead made the return to Anfield.

Linked to the transfer merry-go-round is another ex-Red, Graeme Souness — the man who, to complete the symmetry, gave Robbie Fowler his Liverpool debut in 1993, and who was in charge at Anfield during Michael Owen's early years in the youth academy. Had Souness' Newcastle not driven up Owen's price, there's a good chance the former no. 10 would have been back at Liverpool, leaving no vacancy for the former no. 9 to fill.

In many ways Owen was inadvertently instrumental in the decline of Fowler in the late '90s. Whereas the former stood little chance of lodging as firm a place in the fans' affections, it is also true that Owen's emergence put a lot of pressure on Fowler. In life there is nothing like the arrival of a younger, sharper, fitter, faster or hungrier person in our position to make us feel threatened at best, old and creaking at worst. Owen sped past Fowler in the race to be Alan Shearer's partner for England, and soon usurped 'God' in the Liverpool side. The two Liverpool strikers, who at first were considered a mouth-watering prospect in partnership, became rivals for the role of 'finisher' alongside the target-man, Emile Heskey. Although their games differed, Fowler and Owen were never going to be a match made in heaven given neither was the natural foil for the other. One was quick and right-footed, the other canny and left-footed, but neither wanted to be creator and each required a different kind of player to bring out the best in them.

Owen never possessed the impish charm of Fowler. He was not *as* local, and unlike Fowler, Owen was adopted as a national icon at the age of just 18 — making him seem more concerned with the national team in some fans' eyes, when in truth he was like all footballers in being fiercely determined to play international football and go to World Cups. Fowler never became a regular for England, and as such, remained very much a local hero; Liverpool fans could keep him all to themselves. Fowler was one of the fans' own, a kid from nearby streets, whereas Owen always seemed far more a product of today's 'branded' Premiership, a clean-cut, airbrushed, media-savvy advertiser's dream package.

The two may end up as teammates once again, if rumours of buy-out clauses in Owen's contract are true. So apparently desperate were Newcastle to sign another 'trophy' player, to appease their fans (it works fairly well when actual trophies are thin on the ground), it's hard to believe that Owen, who surely doesn't see Newcastle as a long-term option, wouldn't have put provisions in place to make an escape. But that remains to be seen.

Chapter Twelve

Disappointments

During the winter of 2005/06 doctors were baffled by an outbreak of severe alopecia among Reds everywhere, with water sources checked for pollutants and the air tested for unusual chemicals, until someone finally linked it to Luis Garcia, a one-man anxiety machine. Hair had been pulled out in clumps by fans as baffled by his inconsistency as opponents were by his skills when one of his tricks came off. But he wasn't the only frustration.

It was a strange season in many ways, with a good number of individual players 'disappointing' in a variety of ways, and yet the team, as a whole, clearly progressing. Perhaps it was because, after the success in Istanbul, people expected more; after all, everyone was pleasantly surprised when Djimi Traoré played so well during 2004/05 — fans had come to expect very little from him. Once expectations were higher, he reverted to disappointing people, despite pulling the occasional impressive display out of the hat, as he did at home to Fulham.

Luis Garcia — who had also been inconsistent in his first season — and Xabi Alonso saw their levels dip a little at certain times during their second season, especially over the winter months. Alonso was now a marked man, as teams cottoned onto the fact that he was the Reds' move-starter, while Garcia continued to beguile and bemuse in equal measure. But again, expectations of these two were a lot higher in 2005/06. Unlike in the previous season, when Garcia (with hamstring trouble) and Alonso (broken ankle) had enforced mid-season breaks — something they would have been used to their entire careers, albeit in the more standard format organised by the Spanish FA — there was no period of time over the winter months to rest and recuperate.

Second seasons are notoriously difficult: the dreaded 'sophomore slump'. In some respects, a player should be more settled and adjusted, both at the club and, if from overseas, in the country. But the surprise factor will have diminished significantly. On top of this, the excitement of impressing new fans, and the thrill of a fresh adventure, will have worn off somewhat. With both Alonso and Garcia, there was quite a lot to live up to: Alonso's brilliance in controlling games and hitting exquisite passes, and his little compatriot's hugely important goals in Europe (plus a crucial strike in a Merseyside derby) on his way to a very impressive 13 goals in total.

The main difference between Liverpool reaching the Champions League final in 2005 and going out without a goal against Benfica in 2006 was the ability of Garcia to pop up with crucial first-half goals that changed games. On the way to the final in Istanbul, the former Barcelona player scored the opening goal in the 15th minute in the first knockout game, at home to Bayer Leverkusen. In the away leg he scored the first two goals, in the 26th and 32nd minutes. Against Juventus at Anfield, his brilliant volley in the 25th minute really confirmed the Reds' superiority, and ended up as the tie-winning goal. And finally, against Chelsea, his 4th-minute strike took the Reds to the final. So it wasn't just that he scored — while the strikers drew blanks (other than Baroš scoring an inconsequential goal in Germany) — but that he scored the goals that either put the Reds in the driving seat, or in the next round. Such regular match-winning effectiveness at such a high level of football cannot be maintained, especially for a player coming from deeper positions, and when, a year later, the strikers were still drawing blanks in Europe, Garcia could not come to the rescue again.

Was Garcia a flop in his second season? Well, statistics suggest he was actually more productive, scoring slightly fewer goals but creating more than in his first season: scoring 11, and having a direct involvement in a further 15 (ignoring the clever goal-creating dummies, such as the one that led to Morientes' goal in the FA Cup victory over Birmingham). Again Garcia got into double figures for goals, and as with his first season, none of them were free-kicks or penalties — the means by which a lot of goal-scoring midfielders gain impressive tallies. (Frank Lampard's record would be far less impressive without all his penalties.) Compared to other tricky attacking players who frustrated in recent seasons, such as Vladimir Šmicer and El Hadji Diouf, Garcia remains positively prolific. So for all his faults, such as an inexplicable insistence on passing to the opposition, Garcia remains a potent weapon in the Reds' armoury.

His fellow Spaniard, Xabi Alonso, had more of a mixed season than first time around, looking very fit and covering lots of ground in some games, and then looking tired in others. However, he remained a hugely influential player when on top of his game, and a damned good one even when playing below par. Despite some disappointing displays in the middle of the season, he ended the campaign in imperious form — at least until an ankle injury in the final league game inhibited his FA Cup Final performance.

Alonso's game proved more rounded than in his inaugural season. The no.14 developed into a very effective defensive midfielder, mirroring the way Didi Hamann made a career from reading play and picking off danger as the deepest midfielder, but unlike the German, offering more creativity on the ball once it was won. Alonso did a lot of good work in his own box, something not seen so much during his inaugural season, and an aspect of his play for which he still receives insufficient credit. Many times he was on hand to make crucial last-ditch blocks and interceptions. Indeed, he ended the season as the league's second-highest tackle maker, with 126 of his 175 tackles won — a higher success rate than his closest rivals.

In terms of his creative stats, his direct involvement in goals was more-or-less exactly the same as in 2004/05. He scored more — five, to add to the three in his first season — but created a fraction fewer. So it's fair to say that Alonso was at least equally as effective as in his inaugural season, and arguably performed even better — but that such an incredible amount was expected of the Iberian playmaker. A lot of the best teams in the world would love their midfielders to be as 'disappointing' as Alonso.

With Garcia and Alonso, any disappointment was more to do with perceptions than any real dip in the high standards they had set in their first seasons.

Stephen Warnock

With Gérard Houllier sacked, and Rafael Benítez arriving in the summer of 2004, it was inevitable that some players were playing above themselves to impress the new manager. Players like Stephen Warnock were on a high having been given their chance by Benítez, after having looked to be heading to the exit, and as a result, were giving their all, but at a level they could not sustain. Warnock failed to build upon a promising first season, and his performances at left back contained too many mistakes. He looked nervous, perhaps now aware of what was expected of him as a Liverpool player, rather than pleasantly surprised to *still be* a Liverpool player. Warnock, who still managed over 20 starts for the Reds and a number of substitute appearances, never came close to making the position his own. A ferocious and utterly undaunted tackler — despite thrice breaking a leg in his teens — he had a habit of diving in, and trying to make it a physical contest; as a result, he found himself outwitted by trickier, quicker wingers. Warnock made the England squad, but at a time when Ashley Cole and Wayne Bridge were both injured, and Sven Goran Eriksson's options were severely limited.

Just when it appeared Warnock was regressing, he came on as a late sub against Fulham in March and struck a bobbling last-minute shot at the Kop end that evaded Tony Warner — one of the Academy recruits long-since shown the door — to make the score 5-1; and the Liverpool no.28 found himself celebrating like he'd scored the winning penalty in the Champions League final. A few days later he started as a wing-back at Newcastle, with licence to get forward at will — the Geordies' ineptitude on the day allowing Warnock to play more like a left winger — and he was suddenly impressing again, especially in an enterprising first half. But at present he's caught between two stalls: lapses at left back make him a slight liability, while he's not quite good enough as an attacking player to stand a realistic chance of usurping Harry Kewell, Mark Gonzalez, Bolo Zenden and John Arne Riise, all of whom will be ahead in the pecking order for left midfield. Whatever happens, Warnock has the ability to remain a handy squad player. It's just a question of whether he's happy with that, and whether or not the manager thinks he can find someone to provide stiffer competition for Riise.

Fernando Morientes

When he arrived in January 2005, Fernando Morientes looked to be worth his weight in silver: a whole career spent gathering silverware and scoring a steady stream of goals. But it never quite happened for 'El Moro'. There were times when he seemed to click into gear, such as when he scored a superb opening goal against Anderlecht, and an assured brace against Boro, but these never resulted in a sustained run of form or goals. Having previously been hampered by niggling injuries that occurred just as he was looking the part, the one time he was finally able to put together a consistent run in the side — at the start of 2006 — coincided with the kind of extended goal drought all strikers experience from time to time. In the Spaniard's case, it meant that, finally physically fit, he was now struggling *mentally*. The timing was hugely unfortunate. Fans grew frustrated, but Benítez stood by his charge, keeping him on the pitch as long as possible in the hope that he'd break the hoodoo and go on to flourish.

The booing of the manager's decision to replace first Peter Crouch, against Manchester City, and then Robbie Fowler against Fulham, must have been taken by Morientes as a clear sign of the fans' disapproval, the one striker left on the pitch on both occasions despite looking less productive than his withdrawn colleagues. When he finally ended a 15-game barren spell (after Fowler had been removed against Fulham) — smashing home a rebound at the Kop end — the Spaniard looked rather dejected, and turned to his team-mates rather than go celebrate with the crowd. Back on the score-sheet, he was one of the players to help themselves to goals against Birmingham, turning the ball home confidently after excellent work from Luis Garcia and Steven Gerrard.

Often Morientes played his part in the best football the Reds played, linking well with the other attackers, and in his second season he scored nine goals; almost respectable for a striker who isn't an out-and-out goalscorer (who also doesn't take penalties), and one who was often expected to drop deep to link play. He also weighed in with 11 assists. Fifteen goals would have been the upper limit of what could be expected from the no.19; in his career he'd managed mostly between 15 and 20 goals a season, but when playing every game.

The way a manager uses strikers has changed over the years. Individual strikers will struggle to get 25-goals when, effectively, there are four or five players sharing the duties over the course of a season. In the old days, it was mostly just the first-choice pairing. Also, Benítez often changes his front players around the 70-minute mark. While Morientes' overall strike rate was approximately one goal every five games, when the figure is adjusted to take into account incomplete appearances, his ratio is closer to one goal every three 90 minute periods — far more respectable, and closer to what would be expected.

Despite this, there remained widespread belief that Morientes wasn't ideally suited to English football. At times he didn't look tough enough, and lacked sufficient dynamism — there were numerous frustrating occasions when he seemed to be running in quicksand as he chased a ball in the box. His reactions at times seemed a little sluggish, especially when anticipating Peter Crouch's flick-ons. His heading — which had been his stock-in-trade in Spain — was strangely inconsistent. In his first season, he powerfully glanced a header against Fulham, showing the timing and power he could find. But that timing seemed to desert him, with only one more headed goal, away at CSKA Sofia, to his name. He just kept missing the target, or hitting the keeper. His confidence in front of goal just wasn't there. In one *La Liga* game he scored five times for Real Madrid; incredibly, *four* were with his head. He still awaits his fourth headed goal for the Reds, 18 months after his arrival.

Will that arrive? It remains to be seen. Often touted as one heading for the exit, he also remains a favourite of the manager, getting more time as a striker as the season progressed than the more prolific Djibril Cissé. Morientes is a thinking footballer, and a good influence on the other players with his experience and professionalism. What's clear is that Morientes is a winner, and will not easily walk away from Anfield without having proved just why the manager bought him in the first place. However, with his last-minute omission from the Spanish World Cup squad, having been in the original slightly larger party, he seemed to see the writing on the wall.

"People are saying that Liverpool are going to sign forwards and Benítez does not count on me any more," said Morientes just three days after being a substitute in the FA Cup Final, in which he'd looked fairly sharp having been introduced early in the second half. "But if I don't play, I can't stay. I've been at Liverpool a year-and-a-half, and with injuries and other things I've never felt right. I will have to speak to the manager to see if he wants me. But I cannot stay if I don't play, if I do not feel useful. That's the reason I left Madrid. If

I'd played more, if I'd scored 15 or 20 more goals, I'd have been able to expect something better but I haven't played well."

Djibril Cissé

I think it's fair to say that, as with Fernando Morientes, Djibril Cissé is a better player than he has shown in a Liverpool shirt. I think it's apparent to anyone who has closely followed his career, both at Auxerre and for the French national side, that he can offer a lot more than he did during his first (and possibly only?) two years at Anfield.

His technique for most of those goals in France was top class, his reactions first-rate. He produced all manner of finishes, from the powerful to the subtle and cheeky. His strike-rate, in a top league, was phenomenal. Cissé is a natural finisher in many respects, as his record in France and for France shows, but one who has never quite found his feet at Liverpool.

Obviously much of the first season at Anfield was a write-off, with the terrible broken leg, but when he returned at the back end of 2004/05 — miraculously quickly, a feat for which he deserves great credit — he looked like he'd finally cracked it, and had both settled at the club and settled the issues in his own mind that he would be a success in England.

He was superb in his first start after the injury, scoring a brace against Aston Villa at Anfield, and was close to getting a start the Champions League final; Benítez eventually deciding that Cissé would be happy just to be involved at some point, whereas Milan Baroš would not be in such a good psychological state if asked to drop down and take a place on the bench. As it was, Baroš' running opened up space in the Milan defence during the remarkable comeback, while Cissé came on at the end of normal time, and although he had little chance to shine in extra time, with Liverpool completely on the back foot, his cool penalty in the shootout will surely remain a personal highlight when he looks back on his career. He had played his part, and his unhinged celebrations were a delight for the crowd to behold. As much as anyone, he epitomised what the night was about: achievement against the steepest odds.

It should have been a platform on which to build. Baroš — and not Cissé — was the striker offloaded. Whether or not Cissé was kept because, following his injury (and his limited run-outs), his value had not significantly recovered, is open to debate. Baroš, while at times very effective, seemed to frustrate Benítez. Cissé remained more of an unknown quantity, and as such, could perhaps pleasantly surprise his manager. As it transpired, he seemed to please Benítez no more than Baroš had, given that he spent much of the season in and out of the side, and back and forth between the right wing and his favoured central striking berth.

Cissé started the season in great shape, firing four goals in the Champions League qualifiers, albeit against fairly weak opposition. Despite being rotated, he added two goals in the Champions League proper, including a thumping volley against Anderlecht, and, having come on as a sub, added two more in the Super Cup final against CSKA Moscow, to win the cup. His league tally wasn't quite as impressive, although in the early months of the season he did score a penalty at Birmingham, a free-kick against Blackburn (following which he ran to shake Benítez's hand) and a fluke from a mis-hit cross against Portsmouth. In the summer and autumn of 2005 he also added three goals for the French national side, taking his tally for *Les Bleus* to nine, in only eight starts (and a further fifteen substitute appearances).

Despite the promising start, and a return to full fitness, what he delivered didn't amount to what was promised. The winter saw only one goal, albeit a brilliant finish that killed off Everton's hopes of a comeback at Goodison Park. Even then he seemed to stumble past the defender, lacking conviction (he didn't provide a trick, or even drop his shoulder), and in the surprise of doing so unleashed a brilliant instinctive first-time shot as the ball ran onto his right foot. This was evidence that, with less time to think — which leads to second thoughts and doubts — he could demonstrate his undoubted talent. It was a dark winter for the Frenchman, who was also questioned for assaulting his new wife.

When he seemed to have tested the manager's patience to the limit, with only that Everton goal to his name in a run of 23 games, he then showed nerves of steel to score a perfectly-placed penalty at St James' Park — having made a pig's ear of his previous attempt, three months earlier, at Luton. (With Gerrard having missed in the interim, he was back on spot-kick duties). Yet again, however, just when he was impressing, he showed his Jekyll and Hyde personality by getting booked for celebrating the goal — in itself understandable, after months of frustration — but compounding it by moments later running the risk of a red card by goading the Newcastle fans. Admittedly, he had a smile on his face but when your team is losing, a smiling opponent is not a particularly welcome sight.

He followed that with the 7th and final goal in the rout of Birmingham and, with his confidence suddenly returning, took Xabi Alonso's glorious pass into his stride at the Hawthorns, rounded the keeper and stroked the ball home for his 15th goal of the season. Suddenly he was looking more like the player Houllier had spent so long courting. Two strikes against West Ham at Upton Park when playing on the left wing edged him ever closer to the magical 20-mark that most strikers look to; the second of those goals against the Hammers, while going through the keeper's legs, was a fine finish on account of how early he took the shot, not allowing the keeper time to set himself. Cissé then repeated his feat of a year earlier by scoring the final goal of Liverpool's league campaign, this time the third in a win at Portsmouth. As with a lot of his goals, it passed very close to the goalkeeper, but in keeping so many of his shots hard and low he 'plays the percentages'. With his impressive end to the season he played his way into the manager's plans for the cup final one week later.

All sides of the player were on display in Cardiff, with a microcosm of his season distilled into one 120 minute game: anonymous spells, frustrating lapses in concentration, moments when he looked disinterested (admittedly following an injury) and arguments with opponents; sprinkled in amongst some moments of first-class control, a few bursts of pace, some good crosses, a willingness to accept playing in different positions, and a sublime finish followed by a manic celebration. Add in another intricate hairstyle and not one but two pairs of outlandish boots, and you had pretty much all he could offer.

The cup final goal took his tally to 19. A lot of strikers would be glad of such a 'disappointing' total, and it's made all the more impressive by how little time he actually spent as a centre-forward.

When his figures are adjusted to take into account only the minutes played, he averages six goals every ten full games. That much of his time was spent on the right wing shows those figures in an even more favourable light, although the figures are boosted by three goals against TNS and FBK Kaunas — fairly weak opposition — and by two penalties. It is also to his credit that he played the role on the right, which clearly wasn't ideal for him personally, without too much moaning.

For all Cissé's undoubted effectiveness in certain games, the overriding emotion where he is concerned remains frustration. He does some brilliant things: a great backheel, a stunning cross, a thumping shot, a burst of electric pace. But they are nearly always followed by a wayward pass, a simple error, a basic mis-control, a moment of switching-off. His instincts often seem at odds with his instructions. At times he appears so desperate to please and to fit in with what the manager wants, that he loses sight of his natural game, and is neither doing what Benítez requests nor what is best for him. You can see an uncertainty over whether to drive forward and push the full-back towards his own goal, or to hold his position; a kind of naivety in the role, which is understandable. When he runs at defenders he seems hesitant half the time, and too eager the other half, and the anxiety sees him overrun the ball by trying to rely solely on his pace, or he gets caught in two minds; but when he gets into position he delivers a surprising amount of dangerous crosses. Every time he plays, there's a sense that he feels on trial. It's his 'big chance'. While no player should be too relaxed or grow complacent, it's difficult for those who feel that one bad game will see them bombed from the squad. They have to fight for their place in the team, but too much anxiety leads to mistakes. They try too hard.

Emotional and temperamental, Cissé often seems frustrated with himself and with the world. Unlike a predator such as Michael Owen, Cissé doesn't have ice in his veins. The Frenchman wears his heart on his sleeve, and everything about him is a *display*: the daily differing hairstyles (his barber must be the second-richest man in Frodsham), the tattoos that spread across his skin like a contagious dermatological disease, and the multitude of facial expressions that leave you in no doubt as to what he's thinking and feeling: the scowls and screams to the heavens, or the biggest beam on earth when he's scored.

At times he looks like even he doesn't know what he's doing, whereas at Auxerre he fully understood his role in the side — namely to chase balls played over the top, score goals, and not worry about anything too complicated. He was the star man, there to put the icing on the cake. At Auxerre he had the full backing of the manager, Guy Roux. An unlikely and enduring friendship — Roux had been manager at the club for over 40 years — was highlighted when Roux, approaching 70, was best man at Cissé's wedding in June 2005.

When moving from the club where he had been gradually eased into the side as a teenager, Cissé found himself weighed down by a massive transfer fee, and had to contend with his compatriot, Gérard Houllier — the man who had pursued him for three years — receiving his P45 before the two had a chance to work together. Whereas Houllier would have been more patient and loving, and would probably have got more out of the striker with tactics more suited to his style, Benítez was more concerned with building a successful side based on his own principles. Cissé's reputation would probably have been boosted had Houllier remained; Liverpool's almost certainly would not, and that's the key factor. Benítez, far more stand-offish than Roux with his charges, has indirectly damaged the player's confidence. But his job is to get results, not to take on one player as his personal project.

With 24 goals in 43 starts for Liverpool (and a further 36 appearances as a sub), his record in England remains more impressive than he's given credit for, and his overall career record of 107 goals in 178 starts (and a further 65 appearances as a sub) stands comparison with most top strikers in the game.

Despite being written off all season long, Cissé remained defiant in May 2006, insisting his future lay at Anfield. He told *L'Equipe* "I still have three years remaining on my contract at Liverpool and my future, before anything, I imagine it will be here. Liverpool didn't want to let me leave for L'OM [Marseille] last winter and people have to understand it. Tottenham also showed interest too and Liverpool refused once again. I have stayed and fought, and I have took it on. I didn't want to leave after one year. That would have really been a failure. I am happy with my last season here. I have played in two or three different positions, so now I am a little more versatile — I defend a little better, even if there is still a lot of work to do, and I have also improved my crosses."

In some ways Cissé is like his compatriot, Thierry Henry, who suffered a similar fate while in Italy with Juventus: not quite trusted, and consigned to the flanks. Cissé is not in Henry's class (who is?), but he could be a lot closer than he often appears. Henry needed to find his perfect environment at Arsenal, under the guidance of his former boss, Arsene Wenger. It doesn't seem that Cissé has quite found such an environment at Anfield.

Chapter Thirteen

Most Improved

In stark contrast to Rafa Benítez's first season, there were precious few examples of players improving dramatically in 2005/06. No-one emerged from left-field; possibly because, with Benítez moulding his own squad and off–loading those he didn't want, there were no more of Gérard Houllier's 'duds' left to pleasantly surprise, while the Spaniard's own below-par signings were not given a full second season to turn things around; Josemi, Mauricio Pellegrino and Antonio Núñez were all culled without sentiment.

When the new manager arrived in 2004, he was able to inject new ideas into an ailing team and rejuvenate stale players, giving everyone a fresh starting point. Suddenly fringe players like Djimi Traoré and Igor Biščan were showing why Houllier invested in them in the first place, with the latter coming close to earning a future at the club. Darren Potter made a number of appearances, while Stephen Warnock made a mockery of the fact that, until Benítez arrived, he was due to be released. For half a season, Milan Baroš was a mobile, potent striker whose constant running put teams on the back foot; despite going off the boil in the second half of the season, and not ideally suiting Benítez's system, he still managed to double his original transfer value. Meanwhile, Steve Finnan emerged from a difficult first season — aided both by Benítez's extra organisational detailing and the added stability of having been at the club for a year. John Arne Riise rediscovered his vim, having apparently gone off the boil in Houllier's final season. Finally, Jamie Carragher was reborn with spectacular results as a centre back. Carragher had always been consistent; now he was consistently excellent.

In 2005/06 there was greater consistency across the board. Players like Carragher, Sami Hyypia and John Arne Riise maintained their high standards. Spaniards Luis Garcia and Xabi Alonso, while still proving hugely influential at crucial moments in games, were now judged against the very high standards they had set.

Steven Gerrard, with the Chelsea saga finally behind him, seemed happier in his football, enjoying his best-ever season for the Reds and winning the PFA Player of the Year in the process, but so impressive had he been for a number of seasons — bar the odd dip of a month or two — it was not a case of him upping his performances by a big percentage. Gerrard was playing in the best Liverpool side since he broke into the team in 1998, and it helped that he didn't have to do everything himself in order to excel; now he could also provide the finishing touches to the quality supplied by others.

The impetus came from the team gelling that bit better, the tactics being that much more understood, and from the players Benítez added to the spine: Pepe Reina, Momo Sissoko and Peter Crouch, all of whom added missing ingredients to the mix, in key central areas. In terms of radical improvement, only one existing Liverpool player stands out — not so much by improving as a player, but by finding the form a lot of people believed he remained capable of. That man was Harry Kewell.

It was a dark moment for the Australian when sections of the crowd in Istanbul booed him off after his groin snapped. With it snapped some fans' frustrations, but it remains a most un-Liverpool-like reaction from a crowd which tends to support those who play in red. Kewell had tested those fans' patience with 18 months of below-par performances, but in all that time he had struggled to find his fitness, and fitness always dictates form. For too long, the once-mercurial winger had been more like another Roman god: Janus, the god of doors (and *exits*).

Despite being tipped to be off–loaded, Benítez's faith in the player — which never seemed to waver — was finally repaid this season, with the Aussie providing consistent quality down the left flank. Rarely did he impress to the point where he was scintillating — although he was just that in the FA Cup semi-final against Chelsea — but he was offering a threat in every game. Whereas a year earlier opposing defenders had been in more danger of being hit by a stray piece of Kewell's disintegrating body, as yet another muscle disconnected itself from its mooring, he was now putting full-backs on the back foot.

"Without the support of the manager," said Kewell, "I'd have been left in a hole and probably faded away. If you don't have the backing of your manager and team-mates then you're lost. I went home to my family and they were supportive as well. I'm not a very nice person when I'm injured and I know that better than anyone. It was difficult but the people I care about the most stood behind me and I'm thankful for that."

Kewell was running at defenders again, getting past one and two at times, and hitting the byline to good effect. He is an intelligent footballer, who knows how to pick the right option. Even when he was struggling in 2004/05, more often than not he used the ball well, if unspectacularly. He fits into Benítez's plans as he is a versatile, passing footballer, with excellent control, who can take up different positions in the attacking third. His crossing — from which Peter Crouch definitely benefited — can be very dangerous, and he can thread a pass to a team-mate, understanding the geometry and movement involved.

What didn't follow in Kewell's improvement were the goals that had been such a big part of his game at Leeds, and which had flowed freely during his first five months at Anfield. At Leeds, he scored 63 goals in 240 appearances — better than one every four games; at Liverpool, his 15 goals have come at the rate of one every eight games. A header at Villa Park was his only strike in Benítez's first season, while a year later he ended the campaign with just three to his name, all coming at Anfield. When he did score, however, it was memorable and match-winning: the technically-perfect volley against Spurs as he lashed home Steve Finnan's cross with the kind of assurance that had been lacking for so long, giving Paul Robinson no chance to even sniff the shot; bursting onto Steven Gerrard's pass against Manchester City and, after two touches, striking low and hard past former Reds' keeper David James and into the far corner; and the 25-yard strike against Everton, to kill off the Blues' resistance, as he cut across the ball with little backlift, sending it into the top corner, and in so doing, beating Richard Wright to complete a 'hat-trick' against England goalkeepers.

"If I want to pay the manager back then I have to start scoring more goals for him and for the team," Kewell acknowledged. "I want to do the things I know I'm capable of doing. That's what is driving me on. I'm loving it at the moment. It's nice to be able to go out there on to the pitch and know you don't have to think about your groin all the time. I can concentrate on the football and that's great. I feel fitter and stronger than I have for a while so things are going well for me. Long may it continue."

He of course was tempting fate. A groin injury in the FA Cup semi-final kept him out of the next few league games, and the problem flared again in Cardiff to cause him to limp from his third consecutive cup final, with the muscle problem also jeopardising his participation in the World Cup.

Next season Kewell will face the added challenge of Mark Gonzalez — a man who makes even Michael Owen look slow; while Bolo Zenden will be fit again, and hoping to find a place in the starting XI. But Kewell, providing the latest injury problem clears up in time, will also hope to be bolstered by a full pre-season's training, going into what promises to be a crucial campaign for the Reds.

Part Three

Chapter Fourteen

The Team Behind the Team

When he arrived at Liverpool, Rafael Benítez not only had to search for the players who could form a formidable team, but he also needed to construct a backroom staff capable of assisting in the implementation of his every notion, as well as offering their own unique ideas. Getting the blend right off the pitch is important in ensuring it is correct on it. The famous 'boot room' had long gone, with what was essentially no more than a cupboard demolished during the Souness era. With the departure of Roy Evans in 1998 went its philosophies, developed over the previous 40 years. And yet in many ways the boot room is back, in spirit at least, in a modern Spanish incarnation; *El Cuarto Del Cargador*, if you will. Between 2004 and 2006, this was a collective that included Pako Ayesteran as assistant manager, Alex Miller as first team coach, Paco Herrera as reserve team manager, Jose Ochotorena as goalkeeping coach, and Hughie McAuley as reserve team coach, while legendary ex-centre-back Ron Yeats continued his long-held role as a key scout.

All managers need to trust and respect their assistants, but when a boss has such strong views and theories on football, and goes into such minute detail, it becomes all the more important. 'Old school' managers may adopt a less scientific approach: simple tactics, heavy on motivation (in other words: "I will throw the masseur's table at you Sonny, if you disappoint me"), and a desire to have the best footballers they can get their hands on — players who can make all the key decisions themselves. With Benítez, it's a much more involved process.

When assembling his back-room staff, Benítez was not looking for someone to collect the balls after training, or to trot out decades-old platitudes and clichés. The men in whom he has to put his trust cannot be merely competent, nor must their ideas be rooted in the past. It's a whole philosophy they need to share. It was no coincidence that, as with his first signings in the transfer market, Benítez went to Spain for most of his coaching staff. Pako Ayesteran, his assistant manager, was always going to follow him to Liverpool from Valencia. The two are a team.

"I met Pako in Osasuna nine years ago, when I signed him for the club" said Benítez. "He has always been a good worker, but also someone with understanding of the physical demands of the game. He's like me in that he is always thinking about football. He's always thinking about how to improve, reading about the game and talking to other people to learn more. This is the secret to being successful. It's impossible for a manager to control everything he needs at a club if he doesn't have good staff."

Paco Herrera, who was handed the role of reserve team coach (combined with senior scouting duties) was a slightly more surprising choice, although his friendship with the manager also dates back to the mid-'90s. Herrera had previously managed Spanish sides Meridia and Albacete during a long career in the game. Herrera announced he would be leaving the club in the summer of 2006, as did Yeats, who would be relinquishing what had been scaled-down scouting duties as he approached his 70th birthday. After so many years at the club in one role or another — playing throughout the '60s and scouting from the '80s onwards — 'Colossus' retires as one of the club's greatest servants.

Alex Miller was the one remaining 'Houllier man', having been employed as a scout in 1999, and later handed the additional responsibility of the reserves. Miller met Houllier when working for Uefa during Euro '96, and the two hit it off. Houllier later invited Miller to France to study youth development. Then, once Houllier was installed as Liverpool manager, he asked Miller to become the club's European scout. "At first I was reluctant to take up his offer," Miller explained, "because it involved no coaching as such, just scouting. I overcame that. Gérard wanted me to watch and assess the opposition and speak to him and the rest of the staff on their strengths and weaknesses and which strategies we should adopt, especially in Europe. If I wanted to speak to an individual player, Gérard would let me. Also I used to speak to the players on a Friday morning about the opposition."

Miller was retained by Benítez, and given yet another promotion. "It appears Rafa also felt a need for someone British who understood the mechanics of the game here," said Miller. "When he came, I was just about to go away with my family on holiday, travelling the west coast of America, and he wanted me to come back for a meeting. I came from San Francisco for just a day — and, on the morning pre-season training began, he told me he wanted me to be the first-team coach. I think he'd been out to see the Liverpool players with England at the European Championship in Portugal and asked them what they thought."

Benítez was in no doubt about the importance of his colleagues behind the scenes. "You can't win trophies or progress without all departments doing their job correctly," he said. "I'm the kind of person who likes to ask his staff about decisions, whether it's Paco, Alex, or Ocho. At the end, it's my decision, but I need these opinions, because they see the players every day. I'm not someone who will say, 'This is my decision, and I will not change it'. If we have a disagreement, I will listen to another point of view. There have been many times I've decided on eleven players to start a game, or thought about a change during a match, and I'll ask Pako or Alex for their opinion. Sometimes I will change my decision because of what they say."

This is one of Benítez's great strengths. True leaders are secure enough in their position to trust the views of those second and third in command. These underlings are not there to blindly follow orders, but to enhance the manager's capabilities. Loyal lieutenants must be able to speak their minds, not simply be yes-men. And yet, ultimately, the manager has to make the final decision.

The departure of Paco Herrera at the end of 2005/06 was a blow to Benítez, but the decision by the reserve team manager to return to Spain was made in time to allow a replacement to be sought. "We need to use Paco as much as we can before he leaves," said Benítez, shortly after the announcement was made. "He's been very important for us with his scouting and coaching. He is also a fantastic person, so it is a bad loss. But we must understand his reasons. He needs to be with his family. He has a wife and young daughter in Spain. The reasons for his leaving show the kind of person he is. I know he loves working here and is very grateful to the club, but you must always think about your family. We're thinking how we will change the structure but ensure we work in the same way. We're very happy with the work of Frank McParland, who works alongside Paco in the scouting. I have some ideas and the main thing is not to change what we're doing now too much, because there has been a lot of progression."

Gary McAllister's was a name mentioned as a potential successor. It's hard to think of too many other players taken so firmly to the Kop's heart during such a short period as their player. In return, during his two seasons at the club he took Liverpool to his heart, and has remained an astute commentator on the Reds. In the end McAllister, despite meeting with Benítez and Rick Parry, ruled himself out of the job, after the recent death of his wife, Denise.

"I should make it clear I was not offered the reserve team manager's job, but we spoke about it," McAllister told the *Liverpool Echo*'s Chris Bascombe. "I went to Liverpool to meet Rafa and Rick and we had a chat about the possibility of me returning. There is a vacancy on the coaching staff at the moment and we discussed it. I don't need to say how exciting and tempting an opportunity it was for me. Under any other circumstances I'd have jumped at the chance. But after we spoke I thought about the situation and realised the timing is just not quite right for me at this moment, so I told Rafa not to consider me for the job. I have two young boys and it's too early for me to start thinking about moving away from the Midlands so soon after Denise passed away. I'd never met Rafa before other than to say hello, but I thought he was an extremely impressive person."

Another ex-Red in the frame was Mauricio Pellegrino, the Argentine central defender Benítez had worked with at Valencia and then brought to Anfield for an ill-fated six months: a time when, while often failing to impress on the pitch, his influence and character were appreciated off it. As with McAllister, Pellegrino swiftly withdrew himself from the frame, choosing to instead spend another season as a player with Alaves.

Whoever the club end up appointing, it will be a key decision given the delicate stage of the team's development: as in 2002, Liverpool find themselves needing to push on and make that final step; the one that has proven elusive since 1990.

Delegation

Rafa Benítez, in an interview with former Scotland boss and current Uefa Technical Director Andy Roxburgh, went into detail about how he works with his staff: "I have a very good staff and every day we ask: Why this? Why that? We are always questioning, always looking for new solutions, new ways to proceed. We pay attention to all the details. Regarding football philosophy, in Spain there are two considerations: firstly, the short passing game or the long passing style? Secondly, to win or to perform well? I think you can play both styles of play, short and long. Our approach is to play well and win. It is important to have control over the situations in the game. If a team plays deep against you, you may need to circulate the ball; when you are being pressurised, sometimes the long ball is the answer. To know what to do in each situation is the key.

"In Spain, you must do your job on the pitch, coaching the players in tactical work or working with your physical trainer and other members of staff. You must be there every day on the field. In England, you can give responsibility to your people because you may have to deal with agents, the board or a player. You need to have confidence in your staff to carry out the general work, but I am always there to deal with the tactical training. Some members of my staff have been with me for eight or nine years and they know my philosophy and the way I work. But I also have an assistant, Alex Miller, who was at Liverpool before me and he knows the mentality of the players and the philosophy of the club."

Born in July 1949, Miller is the oldest member of the senior coaching squad, four years the elder of the departing Herrera. With Benítez and Ayesteran born in the 1960s, it seems sensible to have older, more experienced heads in the dugout. Not that Miller isn't open to new ideas; he has accumulated a wide range of experiences in the game: a coach at Rangers, where he'd been a player (and played a cup final with a broken jaw), and manager at St Mirren and Hibernian, before a spell as assistant to Craig Brown for the Scottish national side. Next followed a successful spell as Gordon Strachan's number two at Coventry, at a time when the midlands' club were a thorn in the side of a lot of teams, including Liverpool. He left Highfield Road to become manager at Aberdeen, where things didn't work out, and within a year he was sacked.

Craig Brown spoke highly of his former assistant. "I doubt there are many men in this game that Rafael Benítez could count on more than Alex to help him at Liverpool and it's a real credit to Rafael that he realises that. It would have been easy for things to change when Rafael came in. Alex had been doing a great job in his role of chief European scout for Gérard Houllier before Rafael came on the scene. He was the one who travelled to all the top European matches, spotted the best players and noted down the tactics of their European opponents. I don't think you can underestimate what effect that had on Liverpool winning the Uefa Cup [in 2001]. Because of Alex's knowledge, Liverpool knew exactly how to line up against teams. Now it's the same in the Champions League. I'm sure he's offering Rafael some fantastic advice and he only has to look through the team to see what impact he has had on the pitch."

Miller explained some of the thinking behind the preparation at Liverpool. "A lot has been said recently about the fact that many teams are playing 4-5-1 at the moment and even 4-4-1-1 where they can drop the second attacker into midfield. Other teams play with three central midfielders and two wide players who can drop back to make it a five when necessary. It depends on your personnel. If you have three really good midfield players then you can control the game. I don't think people should criticise what other teams do. It's almost become the norm now for people to make reference to what other teams are doing but I think you should just look after your own side. As a manager or a coach you should have only one interest and that's your own team.

"At Liverpool, we've got midfield players who can tackle, who can pass and who have good game intelligence. The passing expertise of our midfield players is excellent. In Rugby, if you control the scrums and the line-outs then you control the game. The same rule applies for central midfield. If your defence is getting a lot of possession and you have a poor midfield and a poor attack then you're not going to win too many games."

All right at the back?

The major improvement seen in the last two years has been in the defending, which is arguably as good as it has ever been in the club's history. Benítez: "The first priority is to improve defensive tactical play because this is less complicated than the attacking side and is important for success. The most important thing for me is to be organised. I work a lot on patterns of play and, of course, as the statistics prove, counter-attacks and set-plays are very important. When we talk about set-plays, I agree with Sir Alex Ferguson that delivery is everything."

Miller explained further. "We've definitely improved our defending structure. We're quicker to help each other and the players realise that when it comes to defending you need to have a team mentality.

"It's important to have a solid defence when you don't have possession of the ball. You need to have players who know how to deny space for the opposition to exploit. We're getting the message across to the players and they're working very hard in training. Everybody wants to see lots of goals in games but you're not going to see that nowadays because defending has improved greatly. Good defenders stay on their feet and look to close down the area the forwards want to operate in. We can't be critical of that, instead we should offer praise to the defenders for improving. For us, Jamie Carragher for the last eighteen months has been phenomenal. His performance level game after game has been exceptional."

With what appears to be the best defence in the country, the attacking side of the Reds' game remains the element in need of fine-tuning, which will include a number of additions. There are some special attacking players at the club, not to mention some unique talents. Key to the attacking side of the game will be getting Robbie Fowler, Fernando Morientes (if retained) and Harry Kewell — all of whom possess good game intelligence — to roll back the years on a consistent basis. And with younger, fitter and faster players certain to arrive and provide stiff competition for places, Benítez and his highly capable assistants will have the variety they crave in order to alter the tactics to suit the situation.

Chapter Fifteen

On the Defensive

The last-ditch tackle. The shoulder-to-shoulder ease-off. The arm in the air followed by a desperate look to the linesman. That annoying thing where a defender tries to let the ball run out of play for a goal-kick but the ball slows, and he ends up wrestling the striker to the ground in an advanced jujitsu move and still somehow manages to not concede a free-kick. All important parts of the game. All examples of the often under-appreciated art of defending.

In amongst the blood, sweat, tearing tackles and collision of crunching bones, beauty exists within the game of football. It may not always be evident throughout the course of a match, but it's there, bubbling beneath the surface. In the case of the current Liverpool side, it may be in an inch-perfect Xabi Alonso pass, or in Steven Gerrard's strike of a ball towards goal, or in a moment of Luis Garcia trickery as he bamboozles a defender twice his size.

In art, as in nature, symmetry and synchronicity are seen as being possessed of beauty. Over the course of 2005/06, there were ample examples of an almost telepathic unity among the Liverpool back-line. When watching a game from the stands, time cannot be paused; but re-watch on video, DVD or Sky+, and you can stop the action dead. In that split second, with reality frozen for an artificial moment of stillness that cannot be registered by the naked eye, there was the Liverpool defence, in the straightest of lines.

Getting people to think and act in unison is not easy. It's why, when it's done to perfection, it wins gold medals in the Olympic pool, and it's what makes the dancing in pop videos and musical productions something many marvel at. A group of people take a forward step on the same beat — has Benítez had the team down the community centre, attending evening classes in line dancing?

Defending is an art, of course. It can be a lot of things: gritty, ugly, desperate, essential. In recent years, think Stephane Henchoz's toe hooking away a shot by Steve Marlet at Craven Cottage in March 2002, where the Swiss' intervention left the Frenchman volleying nothing more than thin air; Igor Bišćan's superb recovery block at Goodison to deny Tomasz Radzinski in a 3-0 victory in August 2003; Djimi Traore denying a certain Watford goal with a remarkable interception with his amazing telescopic legs; Jamie Carragher's cramp-inducing efforts in Istanbul; Sami Hyypia rising high to fend off crosses from Barcelona, or Roma, or Chelsea, or AC Milan.

But it is only *beautiful* in perfection. Unlike the practised choreography of dancers, who follow set routines, footballers need to improvise in every situation. They need to anticipate when the pass will be made, and can never be sure how or when it will be played; however much they prepare on the training ground, every situation in a match is unique, especially as opposition players will think in their own idiosyncratic ways that cannot be replicated in practice situations. Improvising as a unit is an art-form.

Getting it right at the back is where any manager worth his salt starts. Unless inheriting a near-perfect defence, as did Arsene Wenger, a manager has to create some stability on which his plans can be constructed. In his first two seasons Benítez did not stray far from the personnel he inherited from Gérard Houllier: John Arne Riise, Sami Hyypia, Jamie Carragher and Steve Finnan were all at Anfield at the time the Spaniard took charge, although Carragher had not played at centre-back for a number of years. Djimi Traore also featured heavily at times, and had previously been seen as one of Houllier's worst buys.

Ignoring goalkeepers, Benítez's own defensive signings either failed to settle, were bought to bolster numbers, or were shrewd investments for the future. Spaniard Josemi came and went, having started brightly but tailed off badly, and Argentine Mauricio Pellegrino was an interesting experiment that didn't work. At least Pellegrino's presence allowed Sami Hyypia some respite in the second half 2004/05, when he was able to conserve his energy for the Champions League, where he excelled on the way to the Reds lifting the trophy. The following season, in the January transfer window, Villareal's Jan Kromkamp was swapped with Josemi to put pressure on Steve Finnan (rather than automatically replace him) and Daniel Agger, the 21-year-old Dane, is a great defender in the making, but one who needs time to bed in.

While the first-choice personnel were inherited, the style of defending changed: higher up the pitch, with the back four drilled in the art of the offside trap. Stephane Henchoz, an absolute master of defending the edge of the box, was sacrificed halfway through Benítez's inaugural season, having barely featured, due to his lack of assurance when forced to hold a higher line. And of course, behind them, Spanish international Pepe Reina replaced Jerzy Dudek, whose Anfield career looked over following the young keeper's arrival.

The most remarkable feature of Benítez's second season was how few goals the first choice defence of Reina, Finnan, Carragher, Hyypia and Riise (when playing at left-back) conceded. In fact, it did not include *one single goal* from open play until Didier Drogba's header in the FA Cup semi-final less than a month before the season's end, with the only two goals up to that point coming from set pieces late in games against Manchester United and Benfica. The obvious conclusion is that Benítez needs to play these five players more often, although there are myriad factors why it will not always be possible for him to field the team he wants. Also, it's impossible to say just how much their subsequent performances might have been helped by any games they sat out, especially if the fixtures arrived in quick succession.

Most interestingly, the one player whose inclusion in the defence made the most positive impact on results — with fewer goals conceded and more goals scored — was John Arne Riise. The Norwegian is not generally seen as one of the key components of the unit. Nonetheless, he and Jamie Carragher made the least number of costly mistakes, with just three each. The previous season, Carragher had made just four grave errors in 56 games, at a rate of 0.07 per game, while Riise was again impressive, with just two mistakes in 57 games (0.04 per game), although as he also played many times in midfield he was less likely to be making errors that proved directly expensive. Steve Finnan — the model of consistency — made just seven costly errors in his first 100 games since Benítez arrived, although six of these were in 2005/06.

The highest mistake rating in 2005/06 belonged to Josemi, who made goal-costing errors in exactly half of the games he played — although that totalled just six. In Benítez's first season, Josemi had already proven fairly costly over a larger number of games, with seven mistakes in 23 appearances (at a rate of 0.3 per game), plus a rash sending off at Fulham. Another much-maligned player, Djimi Traoré, took a backwards step in Benítez's second season, having done fairly well the year before (despite the most comical error of the entire campaign, perhaps the most comical error of *all time*). In 2004/05, Traoré had erred eight times in 42 matches, including that humdinger at Burnley, whereas a year later it was six in just 20 games — his error rating increasing from 0.19 to nearly one every three times he appeared. In his defence, he did not get an extended run in the side, so finding form and consistency was always going to be more difficult in those circumstances.

Stephen Warnock had the next highest ranking, with five errors costing goals in his 27 games, and a rate of 0.19 per game. Warnock had a disappointing second season, where he failed to build on his promising debut campaign. Of the midfielders, aside from Xabi Alonso with his chested own goal, only Steven Gerrard popped up, with three black marks to his name, the most obvious of which was when handing the winner to Thierry Henry on a plate at Highbury, in a repeat of his back-pass for England against France in Euro 2004.

Eradicating a large proportion of the individual errors played a big part in the overall defensive improvement. Upon his arrival in England, Rafa Benítez said he would work to make sure fewer and fewer errors occurred, and over time he has proven true to his word. In Benítez's first season, Chris Kirkland, Mauricio Pellegrino and Josemi were the main culprits, with 22 goal-costing errors between them; all were promptly loaned out, released or sold. Traoré took that total up to 30, and as a result in season two he featured less than half as often as the year before. They all made too many errors for the manager's liking. Of course, stats do not tell the whole story; someone like Sami Hyypia made a reasonable amount of mistakes — perhaps too many, in some people's eyes (sixteen, in just over 100 games) — but the amount of goals he saved does not appear on any record, as they cannot easily be quantified.

Starting point

When building a castle, medieval man learned to start with the ramparts and barricades; after all, you don't build something and, only afterwards, when it might be too late, seek to protect it. It needs to be protected while under construction. Making the defence the starting point does not necessarily make a team 'defensive', as much depends on where a team is in its development and evolution. In the early stages it's perfectly acceptable to win narrowly or even luckily; the key is to build on that, over time, to make the victories more comfortable. Obviously any victory has to be welcomed, but the earlier a game can be killed off, the more scope there is to rest players and conserve energy. (And of course, those people who insist on leaving games after 75 minutes can do so without worrying about missing too much.) Even though it was Benítez's second season, he knew he couldn't improve the attacking side of the Reds' game without first perfecting the defensive side, where some improvements had been made, but equally where just as many areas were still in need of attention.

It's also difficult to become an effective attacking force if you're constantly conceding goals. That's the paradox. One undermines the other. Strikers are under enormous pressure to score goals if, after 20 minutes, their team is already 2-0 down. And yet, if you are a strong attacking force, you can keep teams penned back for large periods of the game.

By the end of February, Liverpool had kept an incredible 28 clean sheets in all competitions. The problem at the time was that the Reds had not been scoring 'enough' goals; although, more often than not, one goal was proving sufficient to win games, just not sufficient to settle the nerves and let the traffic-worriers make their exit. While other teams had strikers approaching 28 goals, Liverpool had a defence with 28 clean sheets. It's not as glamorous to celebrate such facts — you don't see a 'most clean sheets' table in the newspapers — but where other teams had reliable goalscorers, Liverpool had a reliable defence. If a striker scores 28 goals, nothing *guarantees* that they will be worth a certain amount of points, especially if a defence is seriously deficient; 28 consolation goals are of no use to anyone. But keep 28 clean sheets, and that guarantees a minimum of 28 points in league football. (Of course, the ideal is to keep 28 clean sheets while a striker nets 28 match-winning goals, at a rate of one per game: then it's worth 84 points.)

The last Liverpool player to score 28 goals in a season was Michael Owen, in 2001/02. Clearly those goals were important, as the Reds made the quarter-finals of the Champions League, and finished 2nd, with 80 points, in the Premiership. Taking those goals in all competitions, and treating cup victories as three points for a win as in the league, those goals contributed towards 52 points. To highlight the importance of a sturdy defence, the first 28 clean sheets of 2005/06 contributed towards 72 points.

At Manchester United, Ruud van Nistelrooy has a phenomenal scoring record, with a ratio of three goals every four games. But Manchester United's fortunes since van Nistelrooy arrived have been in stark contrast to the years before the Dutchman was bought. In five seasons, van Nistelrooy's trophy haul stands at one league title and one FA Cup. (In United's most recent success — the Carling Cup victory at Cardiff — van Nistelrooy played no part, having not featured in the competition.) While scoring more freely than any other striker in the Champions League (Raul's record being over a longer period with Real Madrid), United's placings in the competition have actually declined year-on-year since the Dutchman joined, dipping to the point where this season United crashed out at the league stage for the first time in a decade. In each of the last three seasons, Chelsea have finished above United in the Premiership, and progressed further in the Champions League — without a striker anywhere near as prolific or fêted. This of course proves nothing, other than that a 25-goal striker, while every team wants one, is not the be-all and end-all. And with Alex Ferguson falling out with the striker in spectacular fashion at the end of this season, the Scot may end up sacrificing a regular source of 20-30 league goals. It will be interesting to see how it alters United's fortunes.

Norwegian wood

When it comes to Liverpool's defence, three players tend to get the most credit: Jamie Carragher, Sami Hyypia, and the 'unsung hero' Steve Finnan — who has so many mentions about being unsung, that actually he's positively rolling in plaudits! On top of this, Pepe Reina gets the most praise for keeping a clean sheet. Which leaves an odd man out.

John Arne Riise is still not really regarded for his defensive work, and remains a player revered primarily for his attacking instincts and ferocious shot (which is indeed potent, unless from a dead-ball situation, in which case only the opposition wall, and the child-craving wives of the men in it, need feel trepidation). And yet there is not a single statistic to prove that Riise is a liability; to the contrary, the defence does better when he is in it. The Reds have coped better with the absence of Carragher, Hyypia or Finnan than they have with the absence of Riise. Is this because the cover is better in the other positions? Possibly so. But then that just goes to show that, for the time being, Riise looks more indispensable than his more-lauded colleagues. On top of this, Riise did not pick up a single booking in 2005/06, and has just five in his five years at the club. This suggests that when he tackles, he gets it right more often than not, and that he is not prone to daft indiscretions that irk the referee.

Valencia's talented left-back, Fabio Aurelio, has been heavily linked with the Reds throughout the first half of 2006, and is of the kind of quality any manager would be interested in. But with Djimi Traoré and Stephen Warnock looking less assured in Benítez's sophomore season, any move for the classy Aurelio shouldn't necessarily mean an end to the option of Riise at left-back. With two top-class right backs, and indeed, with Benítez searching for such depth in all positions, Riise will be looking to continue his impressive form in the role. With Harry Kewell rejuvenated on the left wing, and left-sided knee-injury victims Bolo Zenden and Mark Gonzalez in the equation for next season, Riise's best chance of a game looks to be at left-back.

Now in his mid-twenties, he has matured, like all defenders, with age and experience. Attacking full-backs, by nature of their role, are likely to be caught out of position. You can't expect to bomb down the wing, then miraculously teleport back 80 yards in a nanosecond. Younger full-backs, who haven't yet amassed positional experience, risk even greater exposure. While Riise is not shy about bombing forward, he also shows responsibility with his attacking runs.

It was hard to not feel sympathy for John Barnes when playing for England, as Stuart Pearce — his monstrous thighs pumping like pistons in the most ill-fitting shorts in the history of the sport (allegedly stolen from a growth-stunted boy in the U11s) — was always haring past him. The more Pearce attacked, the more Barnes was forced to either hold his position and simply watch the attacking play unfold, or worse still, get back and cover. Some players — your more nominal 'wide midfielders', who tend to be more in the all-rounder mould — will be more adept at doing this; but you don't want someone like John Barnes having to worry about dropping back and marking for most of the 90 minutes. It's a waste of talent. A full-back needs to appreciate what's going on in front of him, and choose his moments. While Barnes was perhaps more inhibited and less proactive for England than he was at Liverpool (where he was given more responsibility and, frankly, more of the ball), his role in international football was made more difficult by a team-mate.

In the current Liverpool side, Riise seems to have developed a good understanding with Harry Kewell, with the Aussie having exhibited surprising defensive diligence during his return to fitness. There were games when Kewell didn't produce as much magic as he is capable of — and, bar the occasional game, he was rarely the mercurial winger he can still be — but he was always helping the team keep its shape, and covering for Riise when necessary. Kewell, who admittedly has a bit of John Barnes about him — certainly in his posture, and in the way he controls the ball — knew that unless he was putting in the type of barnstorming performances for which Barnes was famed, he had to offer a more rounded contribution.

What Riise offers is a bit of everything. He is fairly quick — although lacks the genuine pace of an Ashley Cole — and is tough in the tackle. He is a *solid* player, in all senses. He has phenomenal stamina, so he's not going to get caught out of breath upfield and find himself unable to get back. He's good on the ball and effective going forward, without being particularly skilful or subtle. At 6' 1" he's capable in the air — defensively, at least (he doesn't seem to get on the end of things in the opposing box). His long-throw has returned to being an effective option now that Peter Crouch is in the side. In five seasons he has made over 250 appearances for the Reds, so his durability is clear to see. In that time he has scored a goal approximately every ten games, the same as for the Norwegian national team. When he hits a ball, it stays hit: as seen most recently at St Andrews in the 7-0 thrashing of Birmingham.

Unlike the other left-backs used in 2005/06, Riise seemed in harmony with the other defenders, which is an essential part of being a unit. It's not just in holding a line for the offside trap, but the way he works the pitch width-wise as well. What a good full-back should always do is move to a more central position when the ball is on the opposite flank, and that's something Riise is very good at. When the ball is with the opposition on the Liverpool right, Finnan will be dealing with the situation, but Carragher has to move closer towards the Irishman to provide cover, and Hyypia then shuffles across.

In such a situation, the left full-back doesn't need to be anywhere near his flank, as there's no danger; if the ball is switched, with an almighty cross-field pass, he has time to get across to deal with the situation. You'll often find that when a cross comes in from the flank Finnan is defending, Riise will be in a central position in the box to head clear.

Hyypia endures

On 11th February the *Independent* ran a piece suggesting Sami Hyypia's days as a Premiership player were numbered. Coming swiftly after being given a torrid time by Darren Bent at Charlton, it was a not-unfamiliar sight of the last rites being administered to a player who, just months earlier, was playing his part in the club's record-breaking run of clean sheets. It also came when the club's overall defensive record remained outstanding, both in the Premiership and in Europe.

At the Valley, Hyypia was starting his 41st game of the season — out of 42 played by the club. He went on to play almost 60 games during the season, on the way to 372 appearances for the Reds in seven years — at an average of 52 per season. That is an incredible rate, considering the high standards the Finn has maintained for most of that time, and that he has also played 63 times for his country, the majority of which have come during his stay on Merseyside.

The most stunning testimony to Hyypia's consistency, both in terms of quality and durability, was when, in March 2006, he finally missed a European game. The away fixture against Chelsea on 6th December 2005 had seen Hyypia break Chris Lawler's club record for consecutive outfield appearances in European competition, when he started his 56th continental match in a row. But after just one more game — away at Benfica — Hyypia's amazing run came to an end. The Finn had played every minute of 57 consecutive European games for Liverpool from 20th November 2001 to 21st February 2006.

Hyypia makes mistakes, and when he does he often finds himself unable to rectify them if it comes to a foot race. But he still offers so many positive things to a defence — attributes that are hard to replace. Few defenders are as commanding in the air, or read the game so well. To dispose of him on account of his age and lack of pace would be to throw the baby out with the bath water. His positional sense will remain superb (defenders only get better in this regard), but every now and then a quick striker will give him the runaround — and it's seen as '*Fin*'. Of course, such occasional 'roastings' date back to 1999, when he arrived. With no pace to lose, and a stunning reliability with regards to fitness (he's not injury prone and carries not an ounce of excess weight), it would not be a surprise to see Hyypia still playing at the top until he is 36 or 37; whether or not it's at Liverpool remains to be seen, but Hyypia cannot be written off at 32.

Maybe Benítez will call time on Hyypia's career in the next year or two, but the manager has never been afraid of experience — a comforting euphemism for old age — at the back. By Valencia's standards, Hyypia is a relative spring chicken. The big Finn's future depends very much on how newcomers such as Daniel Agger and Gabriel Paletta fare, and the development of the teenage centre-backs at the club, but rather than new signings automatically marking the end of someone else's days, they can also represent cover, competition and alternatives. If the new signings don't prove better than Hyypia in the next year or two, then it need not necessarily be a bad thing — if it is because Hyypia, reacting to the competition, is continually excelling. The option to rest and rotate defenders will be there, although changing the back line every week is not always profitable. Against quicker strikers Benítez may opt for the more mobile Agger; he now has that choice. Football at the top has always been about getting in new players who have the potential to replace existing ones, but at the same time where the existing one is challenged to stay and prove he is deserving of the spot.

At just 21, and with little experience under his belt, Daniel Agger has to be given time to adjust. It could be that he replaces Hyypia for ten games next season, and Carragher for a further ten, giving the two key defenders an average of one game's rest per month. Those 20 appearances would almost double Agger's career total to date. He would get a chance to be eased in, all the while learning from his more experienced partners. On top of this, there will be competition from Gabriel Paletta, Jack Hobbs, Godwin Antwi and Miki Roque, all of whom will be looking to force themselves into the first team picture. It's an embarrassment of riches that any club would love to possess.

Chapter Sixteen

Young Guns Go For It

Rafa Benítez's second season at Liverpool was notable for the thoroughly dramatic restructuring of the reserve and youth team set-ups. The influx of promising new players was remarkable: a total of twelve new recruits aged twenty-one or under were signed, either to arrive immediately or for the start of 2006/07. Some were full internationals, others had represented their country at U21, U20 or U18 level. Of course, not all of these players are going to still be at Liverpool in three or four years' time — not all will fulfil their potential, naturally — but the better and broader the selection of younger players, the greater the chances of them surviving and prospering.

The odds are that at least some of these players will play a significant role in the full revival of Liverpool Football Club over the coming years. Without a billionaire's backing, getting the best young players is one distinct way of gaining an advantage over your rivals, even though it remains a highly competitive area, in which richer clubs can afford to offer greater 'incentives'. While Chelsea can afford to throw millions at players, they would of course still rather have the money in their bank than needlessly spend it; their avowed aim is to be self-sustaining within the next five to ten years, and youth development is an area they are aggressively targeting, as the battle with Manchester United for Norwegian-based Nigerian, John Obi Mikel — with accusations of coercion and kidnapping — would arguably suggest.

Liverpool Football Club, with its stellar global reputation and its esteemed manager, will always be able to compete in signing the best young players. But there are so many factors for any target to take into consideration, especially as it's almost certain a number of top clubs across Europe will be sniffing around: if a player is *that* good, he's hardly going to be the world's best-kept secret.

He may have to decide between a country that speaks his language (Spain or Portugal if he is from Latin America) and one that doesn't; he may have to choose somewhere where it's easier to return and visit family, or where the weather is more agreeable (again, if you are from a hot climate, the north of England can be a shock, as all Middlesborough's Brazilians have discovered over the years); he may, as happened with the large number of French youths who joined Arsenal and Liverpool in recent years (and is now happening with Spaniards at Anfield), opt for a team managed by a compatriot, or where fellow nationals ply their trade; he has to consider the level of effort the interested club puts in with regard to enticement, or making him feel valued or at home; he will consider the quality of the facilities; finally, he may take a look at those who play in the position he will be hoping to one day make his own, to see if he stands a realistic chance of making his way to the head of the queue.

Under Benítez, the Reds' reserves team stopped being a place where old players would go to die (metaphorically, of course, although for a while there were unsubstantiated rumours that Bernard Diomede had been buried there). Instead, it has become the breeding ground for the next generation of Liverpool players, with many of the younger new recruits going straight into the reserves ahead of far more experienced players currently out of the first team picture. The newly-formed second string experienced a good season, but at that level it is not about results (although winning is a useful habit to acquire) but grooming players so they can make the step up to the first team. Meanwhile, the greater the understanding built up by these players over the coming years, the better the chance of a number of them translating it to the first team. Consistency of selection — without experienced first-teamers constantly dropping in and out of the picture — creates a more secure environment in which the prospects can develop.

Meanwhile, the U18 side — which replaced the U17 and U19 sides — featured a lot of these same young lads. They performed exceptionally well, experiencing an excellent run in the FA Youth Cup — making it to the final for the first time since the Owen/Carragher vintage of 1996, and beating Manchester City 3-2 on aggregate.

Searching for the best

In the spring of 2005, Rafa Benítez announced that the club was going to be setting up scouting networks in Africa and South America, to cover areas not previously addressed by the club; an initiative that would first bear fruit with the signing of Argentine defender Gabriel Paletta from Atlético Banfield several months later. In April 2006, Independiente's Sergio Aguero, the latest 'new Maradona' to spring up in Argentina, was linked with a move to the Reds, although given his outrageous talent at the age of 17, it's one race in which the competition will be fierce, and the price driven increasingly high with every great goal he scores. "I have been a Liverpool fan for as long as I can remember and it would be a dream to play there," Aguero was reported as saying. "I watched the Champions League final and celebrated every goal as if it was for Independiente." He certainly remains a player to watch, and if he were to arrive at Anfield, it would confirm how serious the Reds are about South America. The smart money is on the player joining Atlético Madrid.

"We are constantly looking out for the best young players across the world," Paco Herrera, the Liverpool Reserve Team Manager, told Liverpool's official website in October 2005. "Part of my role as Chief Scout is to put together a database containing the names of all the most promising young players around the globe. We have freshened things up in the scouting department this season and we now have our people strategically placed in areas we believe to be the most important in terms of producing talented young players."

However, Herrera made it clear that the club wasn't just concentrating on these new continents, but also focusing its efforts much closer to home. "One area we are looking at in particular is England. This department now places a big emphasis on looking for young players in this country." This was backed up by the signings of Paul Anderson from Hull, Jack Hobbs from Lincoln, and David Martin from MK Dons — the second young English goalkeeper to arrive in a year, following Scott Carson, who is just four months his senior. Rushden and Diamonds striker Lee Tomlin, who made his league debut aged 16 in October 2005, was another invited to Melwood for a trial.

The signing of Martin — son of West Ham's Scouse stalwart Alvin — is perhaps one of the most symbolic of Benítez's reign. With Carson still only 20, and with some promising games under his belt, a goalkeeper of similar age and ability was brought in —almost unnecessarily so, you could argue, given that it would result in the Reds now possessing the current England U21 and U20 goalkeepers; you can still field only one keeper at a time. The result is that it becomes a long-term competition between Carson and Martin for the role of Pepe Reina's understudy. Whoever develops the faster can conceivably earn that right.

It's another case of Rafa bettering his odds. Should Carson fail, for whatever reason, there's now a fallback option; the law of averages suggests the chances of both Carson and Martin failing to become top class keepers are slimmer than of only one failing to do so. And ultimately, the shortcomings of either may not get to be tested, if Reina remains fit and avoids raising his hands near any more easy-falling Dutchmen. But the two young English keepers present an undeniably impressive insurance policy. In his limited games for the reserves up to now, Martin has shown he can dominate his area, in a manner similar to Reina.

In some ways it's a surprise to see someone like Martin choose to sign for Liverpool. It can't be easy face the challenge of usurping a peer like Carson, who has already been in a full England squad, and to face such a battle just for the position of first reserve (and indeed, even this position will only be up for grabs only when Jerzy Dudek makes his exit). Presumably Martin could have gone to another club and been instantly installed as second in command.

The message is clear: neither Reina nor Carson can rest on their laurels. In the summer of 2005 the club had also scouted Josh Mimms, son of former Everton and Spurs keeper Bobby. Mimms, who was just about to turn 16 at the time, became the youngest full-time scholar at the Academy: so the lineage continues.

Advanced scouting system

A thorough overhauling of the scouting system was one of Rafa Benítez's ways of ensuring a revival that endures, rather than one which quickly burns then equally quickly fades. Speaking on the club's official website, Paco Herrera explained how the new scouting system worked. "We have regular meetings with all of our scouts, all of whom have expertise in spotting young players, so they know what we are looking for. We have a structured report system that basically quantifies and details players' individual attributes. Obviously, each different position requires different qualities but what all potential new signings require is a good character, a good heart and determination.

"On a week-by-week basis we know exactly where all of our scouts are going, while on a monthly basis we'll have an idea of where we'll want them to be and who we want them to see. Within a few days of one of our scouts being sent on an assignment they will submit their report to us and we will then take it from there."

The club has any promising player watched on three separate occasions, by a different scout each time. These reports are fed back to the chief scouts; Herrera explained what happens if they are glowing: "Either Frank [McParland, the scouting co-ordinator] or myself will then go and take a look at him. If we agree with the scouts' reports then we'll recommend the player to Rafa. It is then up to him and Rick [Parry] as to whether we go on to close the case and buy the player."

It's about an holistic approach: getting things right in every area of a football club, in the short term, the medium term and the long term. It's no use aiming for just one of these targets, as too much planning for tomorrow, for example, can be undone by tomorrow's failure to arrive. A manager needs to have players ready for today, but also a collection with the potential to be ready at some point in the future. With Chelsea and Manchester United able to outbid the Reds on the biggest names, the club 'breeding' (or adopting) its own becomes all the more important.

High expectations

When young players are signed, there are expectations that they should be appearing in the side sooner rather than later. Any time a transfer fee is applied to a teenager, he is seen as a 'sure thing', when in truth, unless it's £20m being spent because he's already proved himself (as in the case of Wayne Rooney's move to Manchester United), then he's merely ahead of others in his age group.

Paul Anderson is a case in point. Following highly impressive displays for the youth team, so soon after his switch from Hull, he was immediately seized upon by some fans as a sure-fire hit for the future. Not only that, but the cliché, "If you're good enough, you're old enough," was trotted out. Where was the evidence that he was 'good enough'? While Anderson is certainly one of the most promising youngsters on the books, and deserved his place on the bench against Benfica in March (albeit also due to a shortage of numbers), for fans to start touting youngsters and demanding their inclusion is a dangerous path to go down. Unless of Michael Owen's calibre and, more importantly, possessing his steely temperament, it could be too much for them to handle, and do more harm than good. Fans often called for the introduction of Richie Partridge, and yet, all these years later, he's only a Championship player. Just because Partridge failed does not mean Anderson will fail; similarly, just because Owen succeeded, that does not mean Anderson will succeed; you cannot compare individuals in such a way. But you can hold them up as object lessons.

Being the best in your age group is suddenly no longer enough. The whole point about making it into the first team is that you are suddenly playing against the best from about 15-20 different age groups. Someone like ex-Arsenal captain Tony Adams, for example, was a star as a kid, but it was an older, more experienced Adams that young forwards faced at the start of this millennium; on top of that natural ability he had also acquired nearly 20 years of top-level experience by the time he reached his retirement season. As a young forward you may be used to getting the better of your age-group's equivalent to Tony Adams, but when suddenly faced with the real, mature player, it's a totally different prospect. That added experience makes it that much harder for a kid to come out on top, and that's why it takes time to adjust. It tends to be kids with blistering pace who make the most successful early breakthroughs, as even the most experienced players can struggle against raw speed; while experienced defenders can use their wiles to counteract a quick striker, there will be times when they are powerless if it comes down to a pure foot-race. In his first two seasons, Michael Owen often came unstuck against ageing centre backs like Dave Watson and Steve Bould, who would use their experience to nullify him; but there would be those one or two occasions when, if he got enough space, he could leave them for dead. By 2001, Owen had gained enough experience to know how to outfox them, rather than just outrun them: witness the way he flummoxed Adams by winning the FA Cup with a left-foot shot, the kind of thing he would never have attempted years before. Owen knew Adams was expecting him to turn onto his right foot, and that's how he found the space to angle a shot across David Seaman.

The new breed of youngsters — *Rafa's Rookies*, if you will — certainly doesn't need to be hyped to the heavens. But it's hard to not feel there are bright futures for at least a few of them. When discussing young players, all caveats have to be understood: it can go either way. There are no guarantees.

As usual there was a selection of promising Academy graduates. However, clearly Benítez and his staff didn't feel there was enough depth present, which isn't altogether surprising. When, at a tender age, a group of players start a programme at a club like Liverpool, there will be a gradual process of waste. As the years pass, fewer and fewer of the original intake will continue to excel. It could be that no promising 8 year-olds become outstanding 16 year-olds; so many changes take place between those ages, both physical and mental. Only rarely does a boy who looks a world-beater before his teenage years stay the course, and remain as gifted, dedicated and as physically capable of coping. Some boys fail to gain height, others fail to develop a suitable physique. Many lose their way, or their inspiration.

Paco Herrera explained the thinking behind widening the net for suitable young talent: "What we are trying to do is complement the work undertaken by the staff at our Academy, who tend to concentrate on finding young players based in Liverpool or the surrounding area. We too are searching for players between the ages of 16 and 18 but from a wider area. It's a very difficult task but our signing of Jack Hobbs from Lincoln is an example."

In the modern age, no youth system can survive on local products alone.

Obviously, the more outstanding locals the better, but there is no magic tap to turn on in order to deliver the area's next Robbie Fowler, Michael Owen, Steven Gerrard or Wayne Rooney. (Some areas of England will not produce that many world-class players in 50 years, let alone 15.) As with Arsenal — the team who patented the perfect modern youth system in England — Liverpool had to look further afield for additional quality. And in 2005, the Reds did so in dramatic fashion.

Athleticism plays such a big part of modern football. There can be no getting away from that fact, although the idea is to find tall, strong, quick but *skilful* players: Steven Gerrard and Thierry Henry can be looked at as paragons of the modern footballer. Brazilian football — the home of the most outrageously gifted ball players of all — is no different. In *Ginga: The Soul of Brazilian Football* (the film by Fernando Meirelles, director of *City of God* and *The Constant Gardener*) we see young boys rejected not because they're not good enough, but because they are not big enough; this, in the one country where you'd expect skill to be paramount, if not indeed the only thing that mattered. *Ginga* (not to be confused with the upcoming *John Arne Riise: The Soul of Norwegian Football*) is a heartbreaking story about the realities of the modern game, and how being too short or too skinny means failure; with malnourishment an issue in what remains a Third World country, you might expect more foreign clubs to sponsor the promising young players, and give them three square meals a day. In some ways it's hugely depressing for us, the spectators, but football is not an exhibition sport. It's a contest. It's about survival of the fittest, and not just the most talented.

The occasional small, slight Brazilian still makes the grade, if he is really outstanding, as is Real Madrid's Robinho; but it's no coincidence that Ronaldo, Adriano and Ronaldinho, the country's three top names, are all 'chunky' (although in the case of Ronaldo it's definitely more of a euphemism). While more of a defensive player, Arsenal's Gilberto Silva is 6'3" and approaching 13 stone. These days, if you have skill, you have to be able to look after yourself.

Of the new young players brought to Liverpool in 2005, a large number were imposing young men, with the appearance of having been weaned on raw steak rather than breast milk. The list of new arrivals included Momo Sissoko, 20 years old and 6'2"; Godwin Antwi, 18 and 6'1"; Miquel "Miki" Roque, 18 and 6'2"; Antonio Barragan, 17 and 6'1"; Besian Idrizaj 18 and 6'2"; and Jack Hobbs, 6'3" when he signed for the club on his 17th birthday. Indeed, the influx of giants continued in the winter transfer window, although admittedly this time with players intended for the first team squad: Daniel Agger (another youngster at just 21) standing 6'3", and Jan Kromkamp, who is 6'2". (All this talk of tall players, and, remarkably, no mention of the words Peter, Crouch and Beanpole.)

Excluding the more advanced and experienced Momo Sissoko, Antonio Barragan was the first to make the breakthrough, coming on as a substitute in the Champions League qualifier against CSKA Sofia in August 2005. Never having played for Sevilla's first team, he had all the same made a big impression at youth level as an attacking right-back, and turned down their offer of professional terms to join Liverpool. Torn cartilage in his knee hampered his initial progress with the Reds, but he made the bench for the crucial Champions League game against Benfica at Anfield, admittedly at a time of injuries, ineligibility and with other defenders loaned out, but it remained a vote of confidence all the same. Graceful on the ball, Barragan is quick and can beat a man, but like all new recruits from overseas, it's not just his development as a player that matters, but his adaptation to English football. To do so out of the spotlight, in the reserves, at a young age, gives him an advantage that other imports, such as Torben Piechnik and Bruno Cheyrou, never had the chance to experience.

One promising overseas recruit who struggled in his first season at the club was Austrian Young Player of the Year, Besian Idrizaj, who signed from Linzer ASK after a trial spell at Anfield. Given a two year deal and the squad number 32, he still has a year to impress, having been just 17 when he arrived. He was certainly keen upon his arrival: "I have always been a Liverpool fan and it is a dream come true to play for them. If you get a chance to go to Liverpool on trial then you have to take it. You cannot ignore a trial with the reigning Champions League winners. I would even have swum across the channel just to take part." He finally showed some real glimpses of class with a double for the reserves against West Brom, the first of which was a fine individual effort, having been out for a long while with an injury.

One of the more interesting signings was Welsh U21 striker Ramon Calliste, fresh from being released by Manchester United. While it may seem perverse taking on a rival's reject, a lot of it depends on what other options you have at your own club. Had Liverpool's Academy possessed young strikers with the potential of Fowler and Owen, then the staff would perhaps have ignored a player like Calliste. As it was, any player who is better than those you already have can only improve the pool even if, ultimately, it's perhaps unlikely he'll make the grade. There's not a lot to lose in testing his mettle. Paul Walker, the Press Association's correspondent for Merseyside and Wales, told the club's official site, "He's a player who showed great promise as a schoolboy and his talent has never been in question. He has tremendous skill, a great first touch and can boast electric pace." Walker admitted that many in the game were surprised when Calliste was released by United, even if his progress had slowed a little. Liverpool's scouting co-ordinator, Frank McParland, remembered trailing Calliste years earlier, and felt he was worth the gamble. Calliste did reasonably well in his first year, but seemed no closer to making the grade at Liverpool than he had at Manchester United. In May he was told he was being released.

Jack Hobbs was the youngest professional recruit in the summer of 2005, signed from Lincoln, where he'd played first team football as a 16-year-old, for £750,000. Hobbs had to wait until his 17th birthday to tie up formalities with the Reds, having already impressed on trial. A tall, imposing centre-half who'd tackle a tank, Hobbs went into the reserves initially as a central midfielder, with Herrera describing the thinking behind this strategy as ". . . preparing him for the future by playing him in a role which will test his speed, ball control and coordination much more at this stage of his development". If there's one thing the club no longer lacks, it's central defenders. The queue, in terms of the current hierarchy, reads something like: Carragher, Hyypia, Agger, Traore (for the time being), Paletta, Hobbs, Roque, Antwi and James Smith; plus Carl Medjani if he is recalled from France.

Of the local lads looking to make the grade, a couple stand out. Central midfielder Danny Guthrie, who turns 20 in April 2007, has been winning rave reviews for a while now. Excellent with both feet, he moved up to train full-time at Melwood in the summer of 2005, after coming through the Academy, and following a spell at Manchester United earlier in his youth. Not particularly quick or strong, he does have a genuine footballing brain; of course, he's looking to break through into what is currently the strongest area of the team, at the heart of the midfield. Can he realistically usurp Gerrard and Alonso? If he can, he will prove to be a very special player.

Adam Hammill is another youngster starting to make a name for himself. An extremely talented dribbler who moves the ball quickly, he's difficult to tackle when in full flow. Like a lot of tricky wingers, his final delivery can let him down, but along with defender Calum Woods, he moved to Melwood in February 2006. (Woods was released by the club three months later.) Elsewhere, Lee Peltier is another who was highly touted, as is 20-year-old David Mannix, whose progress hasn't been helped by a series of injuries. Craig Lindfield, a tall centre-forward, started to make a name for himself with his goals in the FA Youth Cup.

Success?

So what constitutes a success, concerning both young local Academy graduates and bought-in teenagers, when it comes to making the grade? Does a youngster have to become a superstar — an Owen or a Gerrard — or is it enough to become a handy squad player? Anthony Le Tallec and Florent Sinama-Pongolle have proved they can play at the top level, while still relatively young, but they were burdened by the levels of expectation placed on them upon their arrival, setting a very high level for them to attain merely to adequately satisfy fans. They've both become good players — better than some of those for whom the club paid twice as much money — but neither is yet at the level where he can expect to be a regular at a side like Liverpool; at 21, they still have plenty of time on their side. Sinama-Pongolle has done better in the Premiership, both for Liverpool and Blackburn, while Le Tallec is the preferred choice in the France U21 side, where he has recently excelled.

Are they worth retaining and showering with patience — providing they are patient enough to hang around — as their development progresses? Neither's future looks certain to be at Liverpool, with each at a crossroads that all players tend to reach as they hit their early twenties: the point when it becomes clearer if they will make it or not. Given the competition for places, the odds aren't exactly favourable for any young player.

Can it be said that these two players are 'failures', with a combined 200 first team games (for various clubs) under their belts by the age of 21? As footballers, they are clearly not failures, even if they don't yet reach the standards required by Liverpool. Will they be better players at the age of 26? Almost certainly. Of course, Liverpool cannot retain them until then, in the hope that they will 'come of age', if they are not featuring enough in the interim. Liverpool cannot put them on 15-year contracts and only bring them out of storage when they have matured, be it at 23 or 33.

As 21-year-olds, they need to be better than older, more experienced players to make headway at Anfield. If Sinama-Pongolle had not been signed at such a young age, the chances are he might have been sought by the Liverpool manager (whoever it may be) in 2011, after scoring 25 goals for Monaco or Lens; had he never been a Liverpool 'failure' (if that's what he turns out to be viewed as) we'd assess him more objectively. Did it matter that Sami Hyypia was rejected by Oldham in his early twenties, and didn't seem in any way special before the age of 24?

Compare the situation of Sinama-Pongolle to one of the new signings. It seems pretty certain that Jan Kromkamp was not good enough for Liverpool when he was 21. But at 25, after a couple of years of rapid development in Holland, he was good enough to be purchased (although even then it was without the guarantee of regular first team starts).

Then there is the example of promising young full-back David Raven, who went on loan to Tranmere in the second half of the season. At Liverpool he faced the prospect of trying to oust the consistently impressive Steve Finnan, only for the manager to then go out and buy Kromkamp — the current Dutch international right-back. If you are Raven, you'll feel pretty dispirited. But that's the nature of competition. Raven's job is to prove that he is better than those who bar his way. If he can't do that, he has little hope of progressing; if he can do that, he'll make his way at the club, as all any manager wants is the best players for his system, to guarantee results, regardless of whether they were free or they cost £10m. A manager's job is to have the best possible players at his club. It's then down to the players to force themselves into his plans.

What can we realistically expect from any young player? Look at Liverpool's squad, and you are talking about 25+ players who could play their part in the team, if asked. Twenty of them are full internationals. And yet they can't all play, can they? If an outstanding Premiership player costs £20m+, how bad an investment was it to pay a couple of million pounds each for two of the best young prospects in world football, such as Le Tallec and Sinama-Pongolle? Even players patently not good enough for the Premiership have cost far in excess of this amount: Ade Akinbiyi's £5m transfer to Leicester in 2000 is evidence of that. Even squad players for the top clubs don't come cheap; and yet all the top teams need their squad players.

Whatever their merits and failings, Le Tallec and Sinama-Pongolle are Premiership-standard players. The fact that their loans in 2005/06 took them to top-flight clubs shows that. Sinama-Pongolle has the pace and skill to worry defences, so his progress has been swifter; Le Tallec is a little more temperamental, and hasn't always helped himself, but is the kind of thinking forward who is likely to prosper later in his career. Sinama-Pongolle went on loan to Blackburn in January, immediately went into the starting XI, and stayed there for half a dozen games. At Liverpool he would have been close to making the bench, but being the player who narrowly misses out on the matchday squad of 16 is not going to help him improve at a key stage of his development. In terms of the player's education, it was a good move for all concerned.

The trouble with loaning players out for experience is that they get a taste for first team action, and so paradoxically returning to a bigger, better club at the end of the spell seems a backwards step: their careers almost feel put back into cold storage, as they give up playing in front of 20,000 people and return to a few men and their dogs in the reserve league. But if clubs don't loan them out, they can stagnate; they certainly won't be developing as well as is possible if they never get the chance to play and, in so doing, extend themselves.

Le Tallec's loan spell at Sunderland was always going to be trickier than his cousin's, given the type of player he is, and the season awaiting the Wearsiders. In a good side, in his true position, Le Tallec can be a real threat, as evidenced by his brilliant displays in the France U21 side this season. But because the top division's best teams obviously do not want another top team's raw talent (if the players still need experience, the other teams can't take that gamble either), it tends to be struggling teams who are willing to take the gamble; the same thing happened to Le Tallec when he went on loan to St Etienne. Again, it's good experience for the player — a tough education, if you will — but it's also not the best environment to see a 'ball player' like Le Tallec flourish and exhibit his skills. The Sunderland goalkeeper was always a lot busier than their centre-forwards.

John Welsh was another bright talent in his teens who just didn't prove good enough when push came to shove. All youth team graduates have to prove they are better than those established players ahead of them; if they are not better, how can they deserve to replace them?

And that's the thing about Academy graduates: just to make Premiership or Championship football is an achievement. Take the best 20 15-year-old players from one part of the country, and how many of them can you expect to become professionals in the top division? You'd be lucky to get one or two. Since 2000, the only undoubted star to emerge on Merseyside has been Wayne Rooney, while you have Kevin Nolan and Joey Barton looking like very fine Premiership players, and after them, good steady players like Stephen Warnock at Liverpool and Tony Hibbert at Everton.

So many promising young players vanish off the face of the Earth. Ten years ago, the equivalent of John Welsh would not have had the tremendous competition ahead of him in Liverpool's central midfield: John Barnes, Jamie Redknapp and Michael Thomas were the only real options, and a tenacious battler like Welsh might have found himself in the team on account of his aggression. In 1996, a John Welsh would also not have had to face the best, and most athletic, central midfielders from all over the world, but mostly just those from Britain and Ireland. Indeed, that was the year Patrick Vieira arrived, and set the new standard for the position. At the age of 21, Welsh is not even close to Steven Gerrard's level at that age; nowhere near as good as Xabi Alonso, who is just two years his elder, and who was excelling in Spain at the age of 19; and, most pertinently, not as good as Momo Sissoko, who is several months younger. When even Didi Hamann cannot get a regular start, you have to concede that you are not good enough. That is not to say that an outstanding product of the Academy stands no chance of making the team; just that merely *very good* players stand far less chance.

FA Youth Cup –– winners then and now

Liverpool and cup finals: rarely a dull moment, is there? In recent times there has been the dramatic late comeback against Arsenal in the FA Cup, courtesy of Michael Owen; the thrilling 5-4 victory against Alaves in the Uefa Cup; and, of course, the most amazing and significant reversal of fortune the club has ever seen, against AC Milan in Istanbul.

In 2006, weeks before the senior team had added yet another remarkable final to the list with the defeat of West Ham, it was the kids' turn to provide a nail-biting conclusion to a final, spread across two legs of the FA Youth Cup final, when the Reds faced a strong Manchester City unit. Liverpool's kids emulated their elders by making hard work of the biggest club final they can possibly play in at that level, although they took on the role of AC Milan by racing into a three goal lead and enduring nervous moments in the face of a spirited comeback. But unlike the Italians, the young Liverpool side held on, to win the tie 3-2, having won the first leg at Anfield 3-0 and lost the second leg by a two goal margin.

Mentally speaking, it was always going to be difficult to prepare for the second leg, having run up a comfortable — but not emphatic — lead in the first leg. In a strange way the pressure was on: the team, perhaps consciously, perhaps subconsciously, will have felt like it had 'won' the cup; so, in the second leg, it could only possibly lose it. City, with nothing to lose themselves, threw caution to the wind, as witnessed by the way they kept three men forward for every Liverpool corner. It was a game of defence against attack, and the attack won: just not by the required margin. Some of the players still looked like boys, their shirts hanging off waifish frames as they skipped across the turf. Others, like Godwin Antwi and Jack Hobbs, looked like nightclub bouncers. At the final whistle they ran as one to the travelling Liverpool support, which was in Manchester in great number for the following day's senior semi-final against Chelsea, and threw themselves into the crowd. They donned black permed wigs and moustaches, and danced jigs. To them, it meant the world. Alas, for some it will be as good as it gets.

In the first leg, in front of 12,744 at Anfield, Manchester City's powerful front two of Etutu and schoolboy Daniel Sturridge (who, at just 16, can still be signed by other clubs) were easily dealt with by Godwin Antwi and Jack Hobbs, whose dominance was rarely called into question. Charlie Barnett's delivery from set pieces was the key, as he whipped in almost unstoppable crosses that curled and dipped, and it was from his corners that two of the three goals came, courtesy of Robbie Threlfall, who smashed home a loose ball from close range, and Miki Roque, who headed the third goal. While the Liverpool youth team followed the methods of the senior team and marked zonally, suffering no panic as a result, City conceded two goals when man-to-man marking. In between, Ryan Flynn guided home a precise low shot after good work from Paul Anderson. Anderson came close to scoring on a number of occasions, forcing the City keeper into some fantastic saves as well as hitting the bar with an acrobatic bicycle kick.

Liverpool named the same team for both games, as well as the same five substitutes, while the same two subs were introduced each time. The teamsheet read: David Roberts, Stephen Darby (capt.), Jack Hobbs, Godwin Antwi, Robbie Threlfall, Paul Anderson, Charlie Barnett, Ryan Flynn, Paul Barratt, Craig Lindfield, Adam Hammill. The used subs were Miki Roque and Jay Spearing, and the unused subs were Josh Mimms, Michael Nardiello, Jimmy Ryan. Nine of the squad were in their first year at the Academy, and can return next season to defend their trophy.

Close call

The Reds made heavy weather of the second leg, coming close to throwing away such a healthy advantage. Jack Hobbs was particularly excellent in the second leg, playing with a lot of authority and making some outstanding interceptions. Not the quickest, the bulky centre-back was first to most loose balls, reading the play well and getting across to snuff out any danger. Both he and Antwi, whose best work was in the air, were a lot busier than in the first leg, and needed to be at their best as City launched a series of attacks. Craig

Lindfield barely got a touch up front, while Paul Anderson was struggling to get on the ball to affect the game. Adam Hammill's tricks were leading him nowhere, as City swamped the Reds.

None of the defenders could do anything about the goal that brought City back into the tie. Daniel Sturridge picked the ball up 25 yards from goal, and in one movement turned and hit an unstoppable curling shot into the top corner. Having hit the post in the first leg, Sturridge was showing a lot of quality and strength for a mere 16-year-old. Early in the second half of the second leg, he controlled a ball in space in the area, and fired a low shot past Roberts to bring City within one goal of levelling the tie. Steve Heighway sent on Miki Roque at half-time, to help steady the midfield, and after Sturridge's second, replaced Adam Hammill with Jay Spearing in an attempt to stem the ceaseless flow of attacks. And it worked, with Liverpool finally getting some kind of foothold in the game. Hammill, who'd been trying his best to work some magic as the team's most gifted individual, was none too impressed, with a show of frustration more familiar to senior prima donnas, although to his credit he quickly calmed down.

The Reds held on, and a handful of Benítez's new signings were already having an impact at the club. But what can be read into the success, with respect to players possibly going on to represent the first team?

Quite feasibly, doing well in the Youth Cup could be down to a well-organised, solid team that lacks the great individuals capable of making the grade; and players making the grade is what the youth team is there for. However, there are almost always top-class individuals graduating from teams that win the Youth Cup: the Manchester United kids of the mid-'90s, then Owen and Carragher at Liverpool, and more recently, Wayne Rooney from the successful Everton youth team, Luke Moore from the Aston Villa side, and a number of Arsenal players now in the senior team picture at Ashburton Grove. And yet ultimately, Liverpool could have had the worst set of kids in its history in 1996 but Michael Owen would still have made the grade.

Ten years on

Ten years on, only three of Liverpool's cup-winning team of 1996 are still Premiership players — Jamie Carragher, Michael Owen and David Thompson — while only a further three are professionals at football league clubs: Jon Newby, the only other player to make the senior team at Anfield, albeit very briefly, is plying his trade at Bury, Gareth Roberts at Tranmere, and Andy Parkinson at Grimsby. In the West Ham side beaten 4-1 over two legs were Rio Ferdinand and Frank Lampard, before he'd sufficiently escaped his father's shadow to drop the suffix 'Jnr'. It was a game that provided the first glimpses of four players who would become England's finest, but the majority of the rest would disappear, almost without trace.

David Larmour, the striker who scored in the first leg of the final, was released by the Reds in the summer of '96 and signed for Doncaster Rovers. In 20 appearances in the Third Division he failed to score, and was released. He returned to his native Northern Ireland to sign for Linfield in September 1997 and it was only then that his career took off. Larmour scored more than 20 goals in each of his first four seasons with Linfield, and was called up to the Northern Ireland squad in August 2000.

Jamie Cassidy had been one of those hottest-tipped to succeed. Having battled back to overcome serious injury before playing his part in the youth cup success, he was awarded a squad number during the 1996/97 season. A promising career beckoned. And yet injury struck again, and by 1999 he was in Division Two with Cambridge United; a year later, he was at non-League Northwich Victoria, where once again he failed to shine. Future Liverpool star to footballing nonentity in four years. It's a sad tale, but not an uncommon one.

Jamie Carragher explained the strength of the side: "There was Roy Naylor in goal; Lee Prior was at right back, left-back Gareth Roberts. Big Eddie Turk [Turkington] at the back with Phil Brazier. Me and 'Little Thommo' [David Thompson] were in central midfield. Stuart Quinn on the right and Michael [Owen] played up front with Parky [Andy Parkinson] and John Newby, who moved to Bury, and a good friend of mine Jamie Cassidy played on the left hand side. It was a good side; we were very tough to beat. I think we bullied our way to that!"

Carragher was in no doubt who the star was: "Michael was a latecomer to the team, but you've got to hold your hand up and say he virtually won us the cup that year. The other lads did a lot of work in the early rounds. I think Michael came in for the Manchester United game and I think that was when the press started getting on to how well we were doing and he scored a hattrick in that game."

In 2016, who will be the household names, representing their countries with distinction having contributed considerably to the Liverpool cause? The early favourites are the non-Liverpudlians, brought in by Benítez having already started excelling elsewhere. But Adam Hammill has the skill to succeed, and plenty of the others have the character to make the breakthrough if they develop to their full potential.

Chapter Seventeen

A Deep, Dark Winter

Whatever philosophy a manager adopts, he has to have the conviction to stick to his principles. Without exception, everything in football has pros and cons. All players, all systems, all formations have good days and bad. Nothing is immune to bad luck and human error. Sometimes it's a collective off-day at the office, or individual mistakes that undermine the best-laid plans; other times it might be the opposition, in Scissors/Paper/Stone-style, whose overall inferiority is made irrelevant by possessing the one playing style that troubles yours (as Liverpool found with Wimbledon in the 1980s). It's about finding the methods that, on the whole, have more benefits than drawbacks. The drawbacks will be magnified during a bad spell, and while the aim should be to eradicate all faults, it's how something works over the full course of a season that counts. A manager has to ride out the rough patches with beliefs intact; unless of course, he reaches a point where the failures become so pronounced that a failure to adopt a new approach becomes pigheadedness. (Team loses its 100th consecutive game; manager finally thinks *Hmm, maybe the 0-0-11 formation needs revising. And perhaps the circus midget in goal wasn't such a good idea.*)

If you operate a rotation system you create competition, keep legs fresher, and everyone feels he is in with a chance of getting at least the occasional game; but you also risk disturbing harmony and rhythm, and may end up 'resting' a player whose confidence is sky-high. Djibril Cissé arguably suffered from being dropped after some of his better games; although at other times, he followed a great game with an anonymous or infuriating performance. It's hard to tell if he was inconsistent because he wasn't selected consistently, or if he wasn't selected consistently because he was inconsistent. What came first: *le poulet ou l'oeuf?* It's harder to reward a player's good performances with a place in the side if, for tactical reasons, he doesn't fit in with the requirements for the next game.

Rafa Benítez picks his team on account of the opposition's strengths and weaknesses, and how best to overcome them. Inevitably there will be times when it will look more sensible for him to just pick his strongest XI, and to let the opposition worry about his side; the way of the 'old' Liverpool. But that's a simplistic view, that fails to take a lot of other factors into account. The days of using just 15 players all season, and barely deviating from the strongest XI, are long gone; no team can sustain such efforts in the faster pace of today's game.

Clearly rotation isn't perfect. Equally, keeping the same players every week, when competing on numerous fronts, isn't perfect either. Where to strike the balance? One week a certain option may look the only way forward; the next week, an alternative is a better plan. But you cannot keep chopping and changing your beliefs on an issue like rotation; you can switch formations and alternate tactics, but a philosophy like rotation only works if you stick with it for a prolonged period of time. Rotation normally reaps its greatest rewards in the final months of the season, so it can be disingenuous to assess it in the winter months. It's like a long-distance runner pacing himself, saving a sprint finish, rather than going gung-ho from the start.

As happened a year earlier, the English teams not used to competing in Europe came unstuck. Bolton, a consistently well-organised and difficult side to play against, were less of a threat in the league in what was their inaugural season in Europe. Middlesborough, as with their first appearance in the Uefa Cup a season earlier, struggled in the Premiership; this season they progressed even further in continental competition, with a remarkable 4-1 victory over Basle in the quarter-final from a position of 3-0 down on aggregate, and a similar jaw-dropping comeback in the semi-final against Steaua Bucharest taking them to their first European final. But all the while they were in danger of being dragged into a relegation battle, and ended in 14th place, with just 45 points.

And of course, Everton were spectacularly undermined by their efforts to play games midweek and at weekends. They propped up the Premiership in the early weeks of the season, until they lost — albeit a little unluckily — to Villarreal in the Champions League qualifiers (which made David Moyes' appearance on Sky in May 2005, sipping champagne and claiming his side were the best on Merseyside, all the more premature). On top of this, the Toffees' league form continued to falter during their equally brief Uefa Cup run, with league defeats following both of their midweek games against Dinamo Bucharest, and with their elimination duly confirmed following the shocking 5-1 mauling in the first leg. It was only once they were out of Europe — crashing out of two competitions by mid-September, with an almost masochistic intention to self-harm — that they managed to start climbing the Premiership, except by now with mid-table the newly revised height of their ambition (when many of their fans would have been expecting another Champions League push). The organisation and preparation that went into their success in 2004/05 was aided by not having to plan for — and expend energy during — two games each week. Meanwhile, Arsenal, who were used to such demands, found themselves with a more threadbare squad than in recent years; as a result, they had by far their worst Premiership campaign in a decade whilst experiencing by far their best campaign in Europe. Like Liverpool a year earlier, they just couldn't juggle both.

Maybe the problem at Liverpool in January and February 2006 was that key players like Carragher, Hyypia and Gerrard had been rested less than was ideal. Then again, perhaps the impressive results in the autumn wouldn't have been achieved had those players been taking it in turns to sit out games at that time. Who knows? It's impossible to judge: you cannot play out the season in two parallel universes and compare the results of alternate methods. Use a player sparingly in the early months of a season, so that he has energy left for the second half of the campaign, and it will all prove pointless if he suffers a serious injury in December or January.

In 2004/05, the run-in was actually aided by injuries; or rather, players returning from enforced lay-offs. The inspiring sight of Djibril Cissé overcoming such a horrific injury and getting fit in double-quick time will have given his teammates a boost, even if he didn't contribute too much before the final league game against Aston Villa, while Xabi Alonso's influence, after nearly four months out, had a more direct impact on the play. The winter months had seen Milan Baroš and Luis Garcia miss a number of weeks with hamstring injuries, while Steven Gerrard's broken metatarsal allowed him to split the season into two halves. The following season, Momo Sissoko's career-threatening eye injury, which at the very least seemed certain to curtail his inaugural season, acted more like a welcome break, with the midfielder missing just one month of football. But Bolo Zenden, who injured his knee in November, did not manage to return to add fresh legs to the season's finale.

Mid-season slump

Liverpool's season had been going unbelievably well. Too well, if anything. Sometimes when a team has a spell when nothing goes wrong, even if it is not playing particularly well, it hits doubly hard when the impregnability suddenly vanishes. Every goal against, every point dropped, suddenly feels like a hammer blow to the players. The Reds' run of ten wins and a draw from eleven games at the back end of 2005, at a time when they seemed incapable of conceding a single goal, provided the players with confidence, but could also have also generated a false sense of security.

By the start of February 2006, the highs of 2005 seemed a distant memory. With one win in six games going into the away match at Wigan on 11th February, Rafa Benítez was experiencing his worst run as the Reds' manager. Unlike earlier difficult spells during his stewardship, Rafa had both the Champions League success and the run of ten wins in eleven games under his belt to buy him some respite. A scrappy 1-0 win at the JJB stadium, secured courtesy of a Sami Hyypia left-foot volley that just about crept over the line, ensured the Reds avoided racking up three consecutive away defeats in a week.

Downward spirals in football usually require something remarkable to arrest the decline. In this case, paradoxically, it was a piece of uncharacteristically poor play which *precipitated* the slump: Xabi Alonso's chested own-goal in the last minute against Birmingham was such a cheap way to lose two valuable points against a struggling ten-man side. Had Robbie

Fowler's spectacular overhead kick in injury time stood, then the momentum may have miraculously reappeared — especially as it was Fowler on his comeback, it was spectacular, and it was last-gasp. But it was disallowed, and Alonso's own goal became a kind of turning point, compounding Rio Ferdinand's undeserved last-minute winner at Old Trafford in the previous league fixture.

With the winter enduring well into March, Liverpool stayed locked in darkness. A big game lifted the Reds, albeit too momentarily. The performance against Chelsea at Stamford Bridge was excellent for 30 minutes. Until the killer blow of the first goal, carelessly conceded against the run of play, the Reds looked the better team. But as soon as that goal went in, the life was sucked out of the team. They battled on, but lacked that necessary extra bit of vim, and the frustrating inability to score when dominating games put pressure on the whole team. When it was going well, as it was in the first 40 minutes at Charlton, tiredness was not noticeable, but when up against it there was less raw energy to call upon, as confidence dropped away. Any setback seemed to signal the end of the resistance.

Players were tired. Not exhausted, but enough key men were clearly heavy-legged. A little flat, a little jaded. Mentally, as well as physically. Between the penultimate day of November 2005 and the second day of January 2006, the Reds played a staggering ten games. Four of those were Premiership away games, while two were on the other side of the world. This followed a fairly heavy schedule early in the season, and led straight into another intensely busy period: eight games between the 1st and the 26th of February. January was no cakewalk either. Mistakes were creeping into the play, and were often the result of tiredness. Goals were being conceded at the end of the first half, or at the end of the 90 minutes — which suggested problems with concentration; a further hint at tiredness.

Apart from Steven Gerrard, it was hard to pick too many other players in top form in January. Harry Kewell had his best spell in a red shirt since Benítez arrived, but he was one key player who was only a couple of months into his season. He found a rhythm to his game, and was fresh. Many of the first team had already played more games by the end of January than they had throughout the previous season. Xabi Alonso had an enforced mid-season rest in 2004/05, playing a total of 32 games, 27 of which were starts. By the end of January 2006 he had already played 34, starting 30. By mid-April that figure stood at 49 games. Approximately one-quarter of his total career appearances came in 2005/06, despite his club career stretching back to 1999. Meanwhile, two of the new players were not used to full seasons that involved almost constant midweek games. Peter Crouch effectively only played half a season at Southampton in 2004/05, and had been in and out of the teams he played for before joining the Saints. Momo Sissoko, while one of the fittest players at the club, wasn't used to regular football at Valencia, and virtually doubled his career-games tally once playing in the more demanding English game. Meanwhile at the other extreme, Sami Hyypia and Jamie Carragher had been playing football almost incessantly since the start of 2004/05. Hyypia, his 33rd birthday approaching, had played almost 110 games in two seasons.

Cup demands

The FA Cup wasn't helping. The previous season a half-strength Liverpool crashed out to Burnley and that was it, all over and neatly out of the way (albeit amid near-hysteria from some quarters of the press). In February 2006, there was the Benfica tie to worry about, with the all-important first leg in Portugal taking place just three days after facing Manchester United in the FA Cup — which itself was never going to be a casual stroll at pre-season friendly pace. Then, during six days in March, shortly after the second leg of the Benfica tie, the Reds faced away trips to Newcastle and Birmingham (in the FA Cup) and the Anfield Mersey derby. That's the price of success — extra games. But it also makes it more difficult to focus equally on all the competitions when they start to overlap.

The early start to the season — which so quickly followed the late-May end to the previous one — along with the trip to Japan in December, had taken its toll. All this was compounded by the heavy Christmas programme and the demanding New Year schedule, which now included a run of difficult FA Cup games: an away tie at Luton Town, a combative side in the top half of the Championship, followed by an unenviable trip to Fratton Park, which may as well have been constructed within a wind tunnel. Next came Manchester United, who hadn't been beaten by the Reds in the competition for 85 years, and then yet another away trip, to Birmingham: the one Premiership team Benítez had yet to get the better of, with two draws and two defeats in the four games up to that point. On paper, it was a tricky tie — although two goals in the first four minutes ended any Birmingham resistance, and the game became totally one-sided. Reward for victory was yet another meeting with Chelsea.

It wasn't a coincidence that Manchester United opted out of the FA Cup in 2000, when presented with a similar schedule after their Champions League success a year earlier. With the Reds facing Chelsea in the semi-final at Old Trafford, a week after third place in the Premiership was secured, there could be no major regrets about the cup progress; the Reds' semi-final opponents, just one point away from securing back-to-back league titles, would not have been caught even without the complications of those extra games, but the game's hosts — Manchester United — might have been overhauled.

Pitch imperfect

Also adding to the demands in January and February was the unusually poor quality of the pitches. Liverpool seemed to be facing teams with the worst playing surfaces at the precise time those pitches were falling apart. For a while the games resembled the kickabouts on the wasteland that surrounded the Atatürk stadium in Istanbul. Portsmouth's newly-laid patchwork of a pitch was more like an old jigsaw with the corners of the pieces curling upwards; whoever had lain it had forgotten to flatten it down with a roller. Stamford Bridge was a colossal bog, while at Wigan the pitch looked like it had been used to film 'Attack of the Giant Moles'. All it needed was an away tie at Hackney Marshes to complete the list of substandard surfaces. Perhaps pitches up and down the country had decided to 'go retro' and imitate those of the 1970s. Thankfully Anfield, while not at its best, was still in pretty good shape.

Despite all this, it's credit to Benítez, Pako Ayesteran and the other staff members that, as winter belatedly turned to spring, the Reds were suddenly full of running again. At a time when the players should have been on their last legs, crawling on hands and knees through games, there was a bounce in the step. A run of 12 straight victories, nine of them in the league, in the final 12 fixtures of the season provided a remarkable conclusion to the campaign. After such a monumentally gruelling season, it does offer evidence that the rotation system was reaping dividends.

Chapter Eighteen

Retaining the Champions League

Winning the Champions League was the Impossible Dream. The unbeatable foe was despatched; the unbearable sorrow borne by AC Milan. But what of the attempts to retain the title won in such unbelievable circumstances?

The reality was that while the fans could still dream, those dreams weren't helped by the fact that the English FA did their best to make it Mission Impossible. While it was not the sole reason behind the Reds' failure to retain the trophy — which was always going to be a long shot — the fact that Liverpool were not chosen by the English FA in the row over the final Champions League qualification spot only made the task all the more difficult.

When most Champions League holders successfully navigate twelve fixtures in the defence of their title, they feel the satisfaction of having reached another final. In Liverpool's case, the Reds began at -6 games: a bit like starting the London Marathon in Ealing. Six extra games at the start of the campaign added a significant amount of mileage to the season and, more than anything, were a test of the Reds' endurance as much as their ability. These games were obviously not as tough as standard Champions League encounters, especially the initial tie with Total Network Solutions. But the early start, so soon after the belated end to 2004/05, meant legs were wearier when it came to the knockout stage. The summer, which should have been spent recharging batteries, was instead spent playing competitive football; as a result, the pressure the players were under was extended, and the season became more mentally tiring too.

Someone was always going to lose out when Liverpool were belatedly included in the competition, having originally been told that the club would be playing in the Uefa Cup. In order to make it as uncomplicated as possible, and to avoid being unfair to other clubs with equally genuine claims, Uefa installed Liverpool at the very first stage of the competition, along with all the minnows. Given the English FA had effectively abandoned Liverpool, the club were not handed 'English' status; instead, in yet another handicap, the Reds were treated without nationality. Having come so close to being denied the right to compete at all, everyone at Liverpool was just happy to be involved in the main event — and as such, not inclined to complain. However, it was still a decision that had major consequences for the team's forthcoming season. Qualification for the group stages — and nothing short of that — should have been guaranteed by the result in Istanbul.

The English FA's decision to hand the country's fourth spot to Everton, rather than Liverpool, was farcical. Without a doubt it was fudged. The FA should have been proud of the achievement of an English club on the continent and reflected that in its decision; instead it was keen on making a big deal of its own self-importance by basing the reward on its own league, and not Uefa's. The FA should also have accepted that one of the reasons the 4th-placed Premiership team qualified for the competition in the first place — when, for a number of seasons, it was open to just the first three places — was down to Liverpool's good record in Europe since 2001, with the previous five years' worth of results going towards giving the country such a healthy coefficient. In that time, Liverpool were the top-ranked English club. Victory in Istanbul helped safeguard that 4th-place reward for seasons to come.

That it was Everton and Liverpool vying for the remaining spot made it all the more difficult, and threatened to make the issue too emotive. Had Liverpool lost to AC Milan, Everton would indubitably have earned the right to represent England in the competition. No-one could have disputed that. But the Reds *didn't* lose. They won. Irrespective of the manner of the victory — which just happened to catch the public's imagination — the correct decision was to submit the European Champions. It has to trump all other achievements, with the exception of becoming the national champions, with which it rates on a par. The Champions League should, above all others, contain the champions of all countries and the champions of that very competition.

The Spanish FA thought so, when faced with the same decision in 2000; and Uefa clearly assumed any country would do the same (and for which they deserve a fair share of the blame). As soon as the English FA plumped for the more mediocre achievement, in the process ignoring the Spanish precedent, Uefa immediately acted to ensure such a miscarriage of justice could not be repeated. It meant changing its rules in a rather desperate (but necessary) act to allow *its own champions* into the *Champions* League. What kind of credibility would any competition (especially one with that name) have if the winners were not allowed to defend their crown? (The World Cup, which recently altered its qualification rules, is different, given it's every four years; a team can change dramatically in that time, and qualification for the event is usually welcomed by the winners, as friendlies are far from beneficial.)

League consistency was the key, said the FA. But in whose currency and in what language does finishing 4th, 34 points behind the champions, make for more of an achievement than winning the very competition that everyone wants so desperately to be involved with in the first place? It's akin to relegating the Premiership Champions when promoting the Championship's play-off winners.

Why wasn't the Reds' Herculean effort in Europe, and the toll it took, taken into account by the FA? Competing in the Champions League in midweek makes playing league football on a Saturday or Sunday all the more demanding. It is like expecting the England team to win the World Cup when at the same time it is forced to play the old Home International fixtures against Scotland, Northern Ireland and Wales; travelling to and fro between Britain to Germany in between each game, and in so doing, leaving the Three Lions with a far more demanding schedule than the teams they would be competing with. Remember: Everton were playing one tough game every week; Liverpool were playing two. That's the price of success that everyone wants: more games. But it shouldn't be punished by self-serving administrative decisions.

A year on, the situation was still simmering in an amazing repeat of the inter-city showdown. Spurs, so affronted by the rule change made by Uefa in the wake of the Liverpool/Everton farce, were threatening to sue the European governing body, as they looked set to secure 4th place in the league at the same time that Arsenal were reaching the Champions League final; success for the Gunners would mean that they, and not Spurs, would be the team to go into the 2006/07 competition. Not only would Arsenal qualify by beating Barcelona, they would go straight into the group stages, and not have to endure six unwelcome games in the middle of summer.

Spurs, like Everton and the FA a year earlier, were basing their argument on misinformation — like the notion that the outside lane on the motorway is the 'fast lane' when in reality it's only there for overtaking, it becomes the received wisdom — but that does not make it right. Nowhere in any ruling has it ever said that finishing 4th *guarantees* Champions League football; the proviso was always in place that meant the claims of the 4th placed team could be negated if the European Champions came from the same country and finished outside the qualification places — people just ignored it. As it transpired, many of Spurs' players fell ill with food poisoning on the day of the deciding game, and they were pipped at the post by Arsenal.

While Liverpool could have obviated any argument in 2005 by finishing above Everton, the Reds — victims of their own success — had a hectic run-in undermining their domestic efforts. Was it realistic for any team to win Premiership matches against Middlesborough and away at Arsenal just days after each of the two gargantuan tussles with Chelsea in the semi-final?

If the team let itself down in any way, in struggling with two demanding competitions, there is also no doubt that the game's administrators were at least as culpable in reply.

Wenger's changed tune

While happy to have at last taken an Arsenal team to a Champions League final, Arsene Wenger risked becoming somewhat of a hypocrite in the midst of the achievement. (Not that he will have cared). In 2005, when commenting on Liverpool's Champions League success at the expense of league form, he made the kind of remarks that would come back to haunt him. "You could argue that four places in the Champions League is already quite a big share — and that if you are good enough to win the Champions League, you should be in the top four of your country." Twelve months later, Arsenal were sitting 5th in the league, 24 points behind Chelsea (and indeed, 15 behind Liverpool) and preparing to face Barcelona in Paris.

In his own best interests, Wenger obviously did not want Liverpool in the Champions League in 2005/06. It would help close rivals earn more money as well as the kind of kudos that attracts the best players. While omission from the Champions League allows teams to concentrate on their Premiership form, it also damages the club's credibility and makes signing the best players all the more difficult. Back in May 2005, Wenger added: "If you call it the Champions League, basically you should only have the league champions there." This was a slightly strange comment given that at the time Arsenal could finish no higher than 2nd, with Chelsea confirmed as Champions; at least Liverpool could claim to be the champions of *Europe*. It also seemed a little late to be making such a point, given the competition was changed as far back as 1993, along with the fact that, under the Frenchman, Arsenal had enjoyed entry as Premiership runners-up on no less than five occasions. In reaching the final in 2006 — and deservedly so, especially given the injuries they suffered — Arsenal became the third English club to reach that stage since the competition changed from the Champions Cup. None of those clubs — Manchester United, Liverpool and Arsenal — had been domestic champions the previous season. When Arsenal were by far the best team in England, in 2003/04, they could not also manage a fully-focused European challenge.

What really sticks in the craw about Wenger's sniping in 2005 was how he unnecessarily disrespected the Reds' achievement by comparing the team to Coventry City. Perhaps they were the words of a man who knew his own greatness would not be confirmed until he could match the achievements of Rafa Benítez and Jose Mourinho, both of whom had won the Champions League — as well as top European leagues — at a time when Wenger had a right to believe he was presiding over his strongest-ever team at Highbury, a team that should have been doing better on the continent than it had been. "The championship has to be our absolute priority as you cannot make the Champions League the priority," he insisted, a year before fielding hugely weakened teams in the Premiership ahead of the key games against Real Madrid and Villarreal, when the Gunners were trailing Spurs by a handful of points in the hunt for 4th place.

"The Champions League has now completely become a cup competition", added Wenger. Which begs the question: at what point was it not a cup competition? Before 2006, Wenger's previous best showing in the competition came in 1994, with Monaco. Which came — you guessed it — after his team had finished 2nd in *Ligue Une*. "Everybody can win it," Wenger continued. "It's like last year, when Millwall were in the FA Cup final. Next year, you could have Coventry."

Coventry did not make the FA Cup final — although Liverpool did. And at long last Arsenal tested themselves on the biggest stage in Europe. Not that Wenger was comparing his latest achievement to that of a lower league side.

The long campaign

Despite it being a monumental inconvenience, Liverpool's passage into the group stage of the Champions League came without too many hiccups. Steven Gerrard, who had come so close to leaving the club a matter of weeks earlier scored the Reds' first, second and third goals of the season as he smashed home a hugely impressive hat-trick against TNS of the Welsh League. It was important that he showed the fans he was fully committed to the cause, but no-one expected him to lay down such an impressive marker. While the other Reds huffed and puffed against lowly opposition, Gerrard charged through the Welsh ranks and made the second leg a formality. Not that he would see it as such. With Djibril Cissé's first-half goal in the second leg putting the tie beyond all doubt, the captain came off the bench with 20 minutes to go and took his tally to five goals in one-and-a-bit games with two swift strikes.

FBK Kaunas were up next. There was a scare in Lithuania as FBK took an unexpected early lead, but the Reds hit back with three goals to win the game. Gerrard was again on the scoresheet, as was Cissé — while the same two players scored the goals in a 2-0 win in the return leg at Anfield. The main story in Lithuania was that, after a six year wait, Jamie Carragher finally scored another goal for the Reds.

CSKA Sofia presented the final hurdle in the quest to reach the point that should have been the start. Yet again the away tie came first. Cissé, who had just scored a brace against Bayer Leverkusen in one of two friendlies shoe-horned into the fixture list, continued his impressive early-season form with his fourth goal in the qualifiers, while Fernando Morientes finally got in on the goalscoring act, with a well-taken double, the second of which came after the Bulgarians had pulled a goal back just before half-time. With ten minutes remaining, Benítez felt comfortable enough to send on 18-year-old Spaniard Antonio Barragan for his debut. In the return leg at Anfield the manager rested several key players, as he had a year earlier against AK Graz. In came Scott Carson, Stephen Warnock, Josemi and Darren Potter. As with the Graz game the Reds lost 1-0, but the manager's trust in a weakened team was rewarded for the second year running with an aggregate victory, and a place in Group G.

Yet again the FA's decision to include Everton — who by this point had crashed out — impacted on Liverpool. While the Reds were in the top tier of seeds, the club was not awarded country protection in the draw, given that England's quota had been taken, and as such, all that could be granted was a 'wildcard' entry. The result was inclusion in a tough group that pitted the Reds again Chelsea, arguably the best team in the second tier of seeds, and whom Liverpool would not have met had they entered the competition as England's entrants; a re-draw would have taken place. Being drawn with a team from Spain — in this case, Real Betis — never represents the best of luck, and again they presented one of the toughest possible opponents left in the draw at that stage. Completing the group were the Belgians, Anderlecht, who possessed a better reputation in European football than their current side merited.

It all started so well. Within two minutes of the first match kicking off in Betis, Florent Sinama-Pongolle had scored a fabulously-executed goal. Reina's kick fell out of the skies towards Peter Crouch. The two Betis centre-backs visibly panicked, unsure of what to do about the big Englishman. So intent were they on stopping Crouch they ignored the ball, which fell to Sinama-Pongolle who lofted a shot heavy with backspin over the keeper. It was inch-perfect, and a finish that would not be bettered by any Liverpool player for the rest of the season. Crouch was again involved ten minutes later when he played an excellent disguised reversed pass to Bolo Zenden, whose cross was turned in by last season's Champions League hero, Luis Garcia, to double the advantage. Early in the second half the Spaniards pulled a goal back, as a pass dissected the Reds' defence and Arzu raced through to slip the ball under the advancing Pepe Reina. It was the only goal the Reds conceded in the entire group phase, as they held out to consign Betis to only their second home defeat in Europe in 14 matches.

Both games against Chelsea — match days two and six — finished goalless despite the hype, with Michael Essien's horror tackle on Didi Hamann and William Gallas' unpunished handball from a Jamie Carragher header the only distinctly memorable moments from either. The fifth game, at home to Betis, was another 0-0 draw, although it was one of those nights when the Reds peppered the opposition goal to no avail. Crouch, still searching for his first goal in a red shirt, had almost a dozen attempts. Which just left the two games against Anderlecht, where six easy points were picked up. Cissé scored a stunning goal in Belgium, volleying home a corner on the turn. He also completed a 3-0 stroll in the second leg, notching his 8th European goal of the season in the last minute (having also scored two in the European Super Cup final). By then the game had been won by a clinical strike from Morientes, followed by an excellent long-range glancing header by Luis Garcia.

Chelsea's defeat to Betis in Spain, having also taken six points off the Belgians, meant that Liverpool topped the group — and would therefore avoid the mighty Barcelona. Being drawn against Benfica, conquerors of Manchester United, looked a favourable tie on paper, but the reality would prove rather different.

For 84 minutes of the first leg in Portugal it was as comfortable as expected. The main concern was the serious injury to Momo Sissoko, who it was feared might lose the sight in his damaged eye. Without creating a chance of note, the Reds controlled the game and restricted Benfica to speculative efforts. But then a free-kick was drifted into the area and Sami Hyypia lost out to Luisao, who headed home from close range. With both Hyypia and John Arne Riise injured for the second leg, and with new defenders Daniel Agger and Jan Kromkamp cup-tied, Liverpool's hopes of keeping a clean sheet — essential without an away goal in Portugal — were severely diminished. The goal would prove costly.

The anticipated initial Anfield onslaught saw the Reds miss a string of chances in the first half and hit the woodwork twice; in reply, Benfica also hit the crossbar from distance. Crouch was booked for diving when another referee could easily have given a penalty after clear contact. The wind was then promptly ripped from the Reds' sails as Simão, so close to joining Liverpool six months earlier, curled in a sublime shot from outside the area. Proof that it would not be Benítez's night arrived when Robbie Fowler's goal, after the Benfica keeper failed to gather a corner, was ruled out for the ball having gone out of play first — a decision not vindicated by video evidence. As Liverpool chased the game, throwing men forward, Miccoli finished off the tie with a late goal on the counter-attack. While 3-0 on aggregate was no reflection of the two games, which were fairly even, it was also true that Liverpool did not do enough to warrant a win in either match. Benfica deserved their place in the next round, to face Chelsea's conquerors, Barcelona.

Implications

Failure to emerge from Group G would have represented failure in the defence of the crown. Going out a round later, while far from satisfactory, was also far from disastrous. It didn't help that the Benfica games came at a time when the Reds were in their worst form of the season. Had the tie taken place a couple of weeks later, when the Reds suddenly couldn't stop scoring, it might have been a different story; but then that's life — you can't pick and choose when you play important games. Timing plays a big part in football.

Reaching the last 16 helped Liverpool maintain its impressive standing in the continental ranking system. The Reds' coefficient for the season was 17.76, down almost 14 points on the previous year's total. Having been ranked 5th after the success in Istanbul, the team slipped just one place a year later. Now ranked 6th, the Reds are guaranteed seeding for the group stages of 2006/07, should the qualifying round be successfully navigated; Arsenal could not overtake Liverpool even with success in Paris, while Barcelona were already ahead, in 2nd place. Based on a rolling five-year period, Liverpool's overall coefficient dropped from 115.86 to 105.95, due mainly to the results from the 2000/01 season — when the Reds won the Uefa Cup — dropping from the equation, as the 05/06 figures took their place.

It's testament to the work of Gérard Houllier and Rafa Benítez — as well as long-serving players such as Hyypia, Carragher and Gerrard, and the one coaching constant, Alex Miller — that Liverpool are ranked so high in Europe based on the results of the last five years. In fact, if the coefficient was based on a six-year period, to take into account the entire 21st Century, the Reds would be ranked 4th, behind only AC Milan, Barcelona and Real Madrid. Juventus, who are currently 5th, had a very poor season in 00/01, while Inter Milan, currently sitting 4th, fared only marginally better. Both teams would drop below Liverpool when considering the millennium.

A lot of people in football would have been surprised if told at the end of 1999 that by 2006 the Reds would be the 4th-best team in European competition based on results during the new millennium, especially with Manchester United having just won the Champions League at the time. Again, it shows how far the Reds have come, and how unexpectedly close the club has got in recent years to tallying the great continental success of the past with the present. While the club, unlike Chelsea, Arsenal and Manchester United — who have won two titles apiece in that time — has yet to get its hands back on the league trophy, it stands above all three in continental competition since the year 2000. Two European trophies, and two European Super Cups, tell their own story.

Chapter Nineteen

Progression: Linking Past and Present

Linking the past with the present remains the unwritten stipulation for any Liverpool manager. Exceeding the past is a virtual impossibility; getting close, a pipe dream. But having the two eras at least relate to one another is not beyond realistic expectation.

No Liverpool manager will ever be able to top the achievements of the past — at least not in terms of quantity of silverware. Bob Paisley's three triumphs leaves him out on his own as the master of Europe — no other man has won the trophy three times in the history of the competition — and his six league titles in nine years easily eclipses Sir Alex Ferguson's haul in terms of titles per season. No Liverpool manager will be able to rebuild Liverpool from lower-league mediocrity, as did Bill Shankly; nor will anyone ever be as large as life or as deft with a soundbite (in the days when it was just a great quote). No future Liverpool manager can ever hope to deliver a league title every other season, as did Kenny Dalglish, with a double thrown in, *having previously been the greatest player in the club's history*.

It's no wonder Gérard Houllier grew frustrated, feeling that the great strides the club made during the first half of his tenure (between 1998 and 2002) were not granting him more respect from certain quarters. Had Houllier taken Newcastle — who in 1998 were in a comparable position to the Reds, and who would spend a similar amount of money in the coming years — to the honours to which he took Liverpool, he'd have been granted the freedom of Tyneside. As it was, his final two years were dire, despite another trophy secured at the expense of Manchester United, and his reputation, for many on Merseyside at least, was tarnished beyond redemption. Houllier answered some of his critics with his success at Lyon, but this was a side that had won the French title on each of the previous four years; it would take a very good manager to keep that run going, but it's not a sign of greatness to keep a smooth and steady ship on course. He did well to recover from the sale of Michael Essien, but the £24m the club received offset the loss.

What Benítez did at Anfield, in his first attempt, was to lead the club to its *most thrilling* win. He also went one better than both Bill Shankly and Kenny Dalglish by winning the European Cup, although the latter never got the chance to lead his side out in continental competition, and the former was denied at the semi-final stage by some outrageous refereeing against Inter Milan. One of the great regrets of the 1980s, in footballing terms, is that the awesome team of 1987/88 never had a tilt at the European title.

In the Reds' halcyon years, rather than rebuild, the Liverpool manager would merely add an 'extension' every season: one, maybe two players, to raise the level of what was already a superb team. Joe Fagan deserves a lot of credit for his treble in 1984 — the finest season in the club's history — but his task was made all the easier by inheriting by far the best team in England and, as it would prove, the best team in Europe as well. Fagan added a mixed bunch of players, with Michael Robinson failing to impress on a consistent basis, while John Wark was more impressive, even if he never quite displayed the form he had at Ipswich. But the framework was already in place.

It must have been a dream to inherit that 1983/84 team, although the pressure of following in the footsteps of not just Bob Paisley, but Bill Shankly before him, will have been huge. By 1983/84, youngsters like Ian Rush (with 47 goals that season), Ronnie Whelan and Steve Nicol were starting to excel, while older players like Graeme Souness, Alan Hansen and Mark Lawrenson were at their peak. And of course, there was Kenny Dalglish, who, at 32, was at the perfect age: legs still mobile, and the great footballing brain replete with experience and canny know-how.

Benítez's task was never so simple. Just as Bill Shankly quickly demolished what he inherited in 1959 and totally rebuilt his side (which took four seasons to come together), Rafa had a sizeable task on his hands, if not one that required quite such a total revamp. But Benítez still had to take half of his house all the way back down to the foundations (carefully storing the sofa and the table lamp for safekeeping), in order to rebuild it in a new style.

What Benítez's first season provided was the most amazing high, but without the bedrock of consistency. His second season delivered the latter, but even though the Reds undoubtedly progressed, there was nothing more significant than the FA Cup to parade through the streets of Liverpool to jubilant fans.

Definite signs of progression
You can judge a team's progression in a number of ways: with your own two eyes, in terms of your subjective assessment of performances; in terms of league position, or the number of trophies won, and their importance; or with statistics. These can include myriad factors, from the more tenuous, nay desperate act — as Gérard Houllier discovered — of counting corners, through to the most important statistics of all: points, and games won.

In Rafa Benítez's second season, progression could not be measured purely in terms of success in competitions; while the team did significantly better in the Premiership and the FA Cup — the two pillars of English football — it fared worse in Europe and in the less-consequential Carling Cup. By March 19th, Liverpool were already on 61 points, three more than the entire total the previous season; it was the club's best points tally at that stage of a season since the Premiership came into play, and the Reds would keep winning, hitting the 70 point mark on April 9th, having defeated an obdurate Bolton side. And 3rd place — and with it, qualification for the final Champions League preliminary round — was secured on April 17th, the day after a hard-fought 1-0 victory at Blackburn, when Spurs lost at home to Manchester United. At the same time, any remaining hopes of finishing 2nd were dented by the result.

There were also some areas where the team regressed, most notably in its ability to convert a satisfactory amount of chances for much of the season. The problem was especially evident in the early months of 2006, although the balance was then dramatically redressed with a run of 20 goals in five games. Picking up Robbie Fowler on a free transfer started to look inspired after the returning fans' favourite scored four goals in four starts, following on from two unfairly disallowed efforts in earlier games. The strikes allowed by the referee were in each case the first — and therefore, most crucial — goal of the game, and the mistakenly overruled last-minute effort against Charlton would have won the match 1-0. Fowler's goal against Fulham on 15th March proved the catalyst for the team to go on a scoring spree, and the forwards, having not managed a league goal between them for the Reds since the turn of the year, then managed twelve in six games.

Plenty of observers felt the sparkling football seen in the first few months of Benítez's reign had been replaced by a more pragmatic style, although part of this may be attributable to the initial excitement at the newness, in the autumn of 2004, of Xabi Alonso's passing and Luis Garcia's trickery, coupled with a return to more of a pass-and-move pattern of play. It may also be a case of remembering those early home games against West Brom and Norwich as being representative of the season; they weren't. There was precious little football played on the road, despite some sparkling home displays. The away form was what most needed remedying.

It didn't help Benítez that the arrival of one of his most exciting transfers — the ultra-quick Chilean winger Mark Gonzalez, another signing from *La Liga* — was delayed by both injury and work permit problems. Gonzalez's pace would have given the team a lot more penetration from wide areas. Bolo Zenden, another clever creative player — if not exactly a 'Zidane' — ended up missing most of the season. So two attempts by the manager to take the attacking side of Liverpool's play to the next level was thwarted, although a fit Harry Kewell finally appeared — and performed consistently — in the second half of the season.

Improvement

While the Spanish-influenced style of football was a definite improvement on Houllier's increasingly one-dimensional tactics, it was not without its drawbacks. Benítez realised that the defence needed tightening, and that became his number one priority in his second season.

At Valencia he was able to perfect the defensive part of the team in his first year, and won the La Liga title on the strength of it; in many ways, a sound defence in Europe helped Liverpool win the Champions League in his first year in England, although the team's defending was not consistent, as witnessed in many Premiership away games, and in Istanbul. It was in Benítez's third season at the Mestalla that the defence was at its strongest, but by then it was also offset with a thrilling attacking sextet.

In Benítez's sophomore year at Liverpool, the attacking football wasn't compromised to the degree where no chances were being created — clearly, they were — but neither was there an overabundance of flair and swagger; not that Benítez was keen on showboating players, but he'd clearly prefer to be winning games more comfortably. Of course, flair and panache become easier to exhibit once an unassailable lead has been run up, and the Reds' wayward finishing, from all players, often stopped the team entering the comfort zone. Results were secured, but often not without nervous moments. The thrilling football, when on display, tended to come from the team as a whole, in incisive pass-and-move attacks, rather than audacious individual brilliance.

Statistical proof
Statistics in football are important. More and more managers use technology to monitor every detail of a player's performance, relying on technical aids like Prozone to assess the distance covered and the passes and movements made. Statistics can receive a bad press — "There are three kinds of lies: lies, damned lies, and statistics" — but they can only arise from what takes place on the field. The figures themselves cannot be invented, merely inventive use of them undertaken. The more detailed the statistics, the greater the depth of insight they can provide. Used well they can give a true indication of form, but no amount of statistics will alter someone's perceptions of what they've seen.

Possession is an interesting statistic, as it can mean so much and yet ultimately count for so little. What matters is where you have the ball, and *what you do with it.* The only time possession is the only thing that matters in football — the be-all and end-all — is in a keep-ball session on the training ground, when no goal posts are involved. There may be periods during any given game when it's crucial, such as keeping the ball to ward off an opponent's comeback, but as 100% possession is not a possibility, even for the most gifted sides, there is always the risk of conceding a goal in the limited time spent without the ball. Proponents of the more direct game, such as the much-derided Charles Hughes, note that it usually only takes a handful of passes to score a goal — therefore, why bother passing more times than is necessary? Cut out the fannying around, and get it in the mixer. Hughes, who was partly responsible for taking English football into the dark ages, was taking things to the extreme. More often than not, five passes strung together will not end up resulting in a goal. While it may only take a few passes to score the majority of goals, it can involve all kinds of situations — not just being long and direct. For example, a 15-pass move could break down with the opposition winning the ball deep in their own half, but then promptly giving it away while under pressure, from which point it takes only a couple of passes to score. Statisticians may point out that it only took two passes to score, but much will be owed to the precise passing that worked the dangerous situation in the first place. Football is full of pithy sayings and 'truisms' that, while sometimes accurate, are often wide of the mark. Brian Clough said that it only takes a second to score a goal — but that does not mean it's possible to score 5,400 times in a match. It only takes a second to score when the ball is running loose in the box, but in reality it can take a lot longer to fashion the chance. Possession is important when working teams across the pitch, trying to drag defenders out of position to find the opening for the killer pass. But possession for the sake of it — possession that goes nowhere, especially when drawing or losing — is not something to be celebrated. All these different scenarios are bound-up in one statistic, which doesn't take into account the state of the game (although Sky's assessment of the action areas, and the two combined, can be more revealing).

Under Gérard Houllier, the Reds started doing something unusual after decades of pass-and-move: the team was having far less of the ball, and were apparently happy about it, knowing it could quickly counter-attack when the opposition had been drawn out. An instant change made by Benítez was to have the Reds keeping the ball. The problem with possession football is that keeping the ball for too long — without moving it quickly and incisively — can simply allow the opposition to gather its ranks. So which is better? To have the ball and risk over-playing, or to not have the ball and to look to break quickly the moment you finally win it?

Clearly most coaches would prefer that their teams have more possession of the ball, as then their side is essentially in control. A team like Barcelona can enjoy such potent possession that there's never a blind alley or the worry about momentum draining from the move: individuals like Ronaldinho, Samuel Eto'o, Deco and Lionel Messi can inject pace, movement and invention at any given moment.

Of course, Barcelona are the apotheosis: a collection of players against whom, in terms of individual flair, any side will pale in comparison; and who, crucially, also work hard. Liverpool look to keep the ball, but cannot hope to play with such élan; however, unlike Barcelona, the Reds have the option of knocking the ball high into the box if, once an attack reaches the final third, no passing option is on, and if players like Harry Kewell, Steven Gerrard, Xabi Alonso, Robbie Fowler, Fernando Morientes and Luis Garcia cannot work space and drag players out of position with individual skill or movement. While this may seem a rudimentary approach, it is an effective way of making sure moves don't run aground upon good marking and rigid banks of defenders. Benítez had to find ways of making Liverpool effective, not beautiful, and it is better to have the option of a high ball into the box than to be faced with working the ball back. There has to be some end product to the possession, and Peter Crouch offers a perfect alternative, especially as he can be as involved as anyone when the ball is on the ground, and so isn't only there for an aerial threat.

Liverpool's possession football, while not as devastating as Barcelona's, was still capable of ripping through teams in its own way, but it wasn't backed up by enough rippling of the net, especially in the period after New Year. Somehow, creating chances isn't deemed attractive or exciting unless a goal results; an opposition goalkeeper can make 30 saves in a 1-0 victory, but if you judge the game on its scoreline alone, a 3-0 with three shots will always look more attractive.

The failure to convert chances eventually had an inevitable adverse effect on the team's performances, with heart and confidence lost; for a while it seemed that no matter what the players did, they could not get the ball to cross the white line. A familiar quote from Benítez during 2005/06 was that his side had "controlled the game". This often came at the end of a slender win that should have been more convincing, or after dropped points when, by rights, the Reds should have put the game to bed by half-time. For a while it wasn't an unfamiliar sight to see the Reds batter teams 0-1.

Winning margins

An interesting comparison with past and present teams is in the win percentage over the course of a season. Liverpool may not have won the league in 2006, but it was winning more football matches than during almost any period of its history — including most of the seasons when league titles ended up on display.

It wasn't asking too much for Benítez to improve on the win ratio between 2002 and 2005. In each of the two seasons before the Spaniard arrived, Liverpool's overall win record stood at less than 50%, and in Gérard Houllier's final season, 2003/04, it was just 44.2% (although to put that into context, under Graeme Souness it had been as low as 37%). Despite winning the Champions League and reaching the League Cup final, Liverpool's win rate in Benítez's first season was just 48.3%, with the Reds losing 19 of 60 games, and drawing a further 12.

So what has been the high-water mark in recent years? In the treble season of 2000/01 — when every possible fixture was fulfilled for the first time in the club's history, with not one single cup exit — the side won 61.3% of its matches, but only 52.6% in the Premiership when securing third place on the final day of the season. The following year, when the Reds amassed 80 points in the league in finishing 2nd behind Arsenal, the league win rate was a hugely impressive 63.2%, but the overall win rate, despite a run to the quarter-finals of the Champions League, was reduced to 57.6%, largely down to 15 drawn games.

The win-rate for 2005/06 was 66.1% in all competitions, and 65.8 in the Premiership (which also shows an incredible consistency between cup and league form). To put that into context, the club's overall record in the top division, over 90 seasons, is 46.98%. Times have changed, of course. It's indicative of how the goalposts have been moved (metaphorically, of course) that, remarkably, the 2005/06 win ratio was far higher than the average across the 18 title-winning season, which stands at 60.2%.

In fact, the most recent season's Premiership win percentage is higher than in 17 of those title-winning seasons, with only one exceptional season — 1978/79 (with an incredible 71.4% of league games won) — ranking above the current season. The 2006 vintage even outstripped the amazing 1987/88 team, which went 29 games at the start of the season without defeat, and won 65% of its league matches with some of the best football the country had ever seen. Amazingly, 16 of the 18 league titles were won with less than a 62.5% win rate. This could be connected to the change in the points system in 1981, when a win, which was previously worth two points, was subsequently rewarded with three. With a draw devalued as a result, winning games became more important. The modern game, while more demanding in so many respects, also includes the insurance policy provided by large squads. In recent seasons, the number of defeats suffered by the teams winning the Premiership has dwindled, with Arsenal going unbeaten in 2003/04, and Chelsea suffering just one defeat the following season. (This season it was five, although the final two games were not taken seriously by the Londoners, with its players already focusing their minds on the World Cup.) The English game is full of teams replete with internationals, including those in the relegation zone, but the squads of the top teams have sufficient depth that bad days at the office are kept to a minimum.

Of course, teams are ultimately judged on silverware and on league position, and no statistical analysis will alter that. But you cannot skip a stage in evolution. You have to become a very good side before you can become a truly great side.

Chapter Twenty

The Big Four

One of the aims of Rafa Benítez during his second season was to firmly secure Liverpool's place in the domestic top four — alongside Chelsea, Manchester United and Arsenal — and in so doing qualify for the Champions League with plenty of room to spare. Benítez had to match in his second season what Houllier managed in his fourth. Of four Champions League campaigns since the turn of the millennium, only one had not been secured at the wire; while, of course, in 2005 it went well past the wire, and down to a (Uefa) steward's enquiry weeks after the end of the season.

To achieve this first aim, the gap between Liverpool and the previous season's top three had to be significantly narrowed. The distances of 37 points behind Chelsea, 25 behind Arsenal and 18 behind Manchester United had to be at least halved within twelve months. Overtaking all three clubs in just a year, especially considering that they would likewise be looking to improve, was always going to be impossible, but such great points deficits had to be eaten into.

The second aim had to be a satisfactory defence of the Champions League title, even if retaining it was a long shot. Unbeaten in topping a group that included Chelsea, with only one goal conceded in six games, was certainly a good start. But timing was not on the Reds' side this time around, with the tie against Benfica coming when Benítez's team were looking fatigued and out of sorts, with some key personnel absent, and a confidence crisis engulfing the strikers that would abate only once it was too late for Europe. The withdrawal of Sami Hyypia and John Arne Riise from the second leg, combined with the ineligibility of Jan Kromkamp and Daniel Agger, left a defence short on the required quality — it was not the ideal time for Djimi Traore's first appearance at centre back during the season — and Momo Sissoko's eye injury from the first leg left less defensive protection higher up the field. Once Benfica scored, 36 minutes into the game, the tie was killed. Add in the six extra qualifying games, the European Super Cup final and the World Club Championship, all of which would eventually take their toll, and the size of the task of the title defence becomes all the more clear.

Chelsea -- blocking the path

Before Chelsea changed the Premiership landscape with their über-squad, an average of two points per game was often enough to get a team within touching distance of the league title (in the 1990s, the title was won with 78 and 79 points, while in 1997 Manchester United won it with just 75 points — less than two points a game).

In 2004/05, Liverpool managed 1.5 points per game, meaning the Reds dropped as many points as they won. A year later, and the average was up above two gained out of every three available.

Unfortunately, there can be no talk of Liverpool's progress without monitoring the enduring, possibly even increasing strength of Chelsea. The West London club now dominates every aspect of English football. You can only become league champions if you can beat the competition, and when the competition has so much stacked in its favour, it becomes an even tougher task. Chelsea are the apparently immovable object blocking the Reds' path.

When most teams spend heavily, there quickly and inevitably follows a period of frugality. A cash injection, like the one Jack Walker gave Blackburn, is usually just that: a temporary boost that quickly wears off. Chelsea's situation involves less of a cash injection, more an intravenous drip. The supply need never be turned off, as the resources are unlimited. It is the club that faces no consequences; the equivalent of the alcoholic who can drink all day and face no hangover. English football may indeed start to take on a *Groundhog Day* feel — with Chelsea repeatedly successful — because, much like the character Bill Murray plays in the film, there is no tomorrow to worry about. They can perform what would be certain acts of suicide by other clubs, and wake up the next morning as if nothing has happened (although presumably without Cher singing 'I Got You Babe'). Yes, their aim is to become financially self-sufficient in time, to become a viable business in their own right. But that's easier to achieve if you can first spend ten years investing unlimited funds in the team and the infrastructure, as they plan to.

Were Liverpool in the same financial shape as Chelsea, Benítez could have bought Michael Owen in the summer of 2005, and perhaps the goals-for column would have been a lot healthier — and the points tally healthier still. It's conjecture, but it's certainly true that Owen was sought, and his fee was too much. As a point of comparison, the fee Liverpool balked at to secure Owen's return was a fraction of the sum written off by Abramovich in the wake of the Adrian Mutu scandal. As it was, Benítez had an entire team to reshape, leaving the field clear for Newcastle to buy Owen, even though the player wanted to return to Anfield. Budgetary limitations constrained Benítez, and stopped him building precisely the squad he wanted; they do not constrain Mourinho. It is certainly true that the extra £3m Benfica demanded for Simão would not have proved a stumbling block had the club not had to worry about finding the cash.

Liverpool FC cannot necessarily afford the players it would like; Chelsea can afford those it *doesn't even need*. Shaun Wright-Phillips went from Manchester City's star player to a Chelsea afterthought, having to wait months before he played a full 90 minutes; this from a player establishing an exciting reputation at international level, and who would stroll into the right side of the Anfield midfield. Which begs the question, where's the 'sport' in that? Other teams may say the same about Liverpool's might in the past — and teams like Charlton may say that now — but Liverpool is still accountable for its spending, as it always has been. If the club fails to qualify for the Champions League, there are serious implications. Historically speaking, as with most teams at some point or other, the Reds have been given financial support (in its case, by the Moores family), but never completely bankrolled. There has always been a business to manage, an accountability. When observers claim that the game has always been the same, they ignore that Chelsea are the first club in the history of football to exist outside of any financial responsibility, so great is the wealth of their multi-billionaire Russian backer. Rich clubs are part of the sport; unfeasibly rich clubs are not.

Until 2003, Chelsea was like any other club. Ken Bates, having bought the club for just a single pound note in 1982 (taking on debts of £1.5m), invested a significant amount of money in the team in the '90s, on a scale similar to that seen at other clubs; but in making Chelsea relatively successful — qualifying for the Champions League and winning a handful of cups — he left the club in massive debt (reportedly £80m).

By rights that overspending should have resulted in dire consequences but even that financial mismanagement was obviated by Abramovich's takeover, the debts disappearing at the stroke of a pen. Abramovich's money therefore not only invested in a brighter future for Chelsea but also 'justified' the overspending of several years before his arrival, spending which had allowed Chelsea to compete for Champions League places with Liverpool, Arsenal, Manchester United, Leeds and Newcastle United, rather than languish and falter.

So Chelsea didn't even have to pay the consequences of the overstretching in the years before the Russian arrived; overstretching that meant they pipped Liverpool for the Champions League spot at the end of 2002/03, which in turn meant Abramovich was buying into a 'Champions League' team. Imagine how nice it would be for Liverpool to maintain its place at the top of the table by running up huge debts, and just at the point when those debts were about to seriously bite, find an investor who not only wiped out those debts — rendering them irrelevant — but then invested an incredible £300m in the team? It wouldn't guarantee any success; but it would certainly stack the cards in your favour.

Teams like Liverpool, Manchester United and Arsenal became 'superpowers' in English football first and foremost from activities on the pitch; a rich and lengthy history of success adding glamour, and as such, opening up revenue streams to cash in on that popularity. They became big clubs via evolution. In Manchester United's case, success after 26 years of mediocrity coincided with the sport's boom years, and the financial aspect of the club changed dramatically, as they became the first team to really cash in on the available rewards, having also become a PLC.

Financial management has always played a part in the success of football teams. But gross and spectacular overspending has almost always been punished by swift financial ruin; Leeds United's spectacular fall from grace is the perfect example. Having overstretched, Leeds had no option but to sell its best players and, soon enough, face relegation. Of course, Chelsea have Abramovich's money, so they are not technically spending what they don't have. But they are spending what they have not earned.

Chelsea's hierarchy consistently cries foul over a lack of respect for their achievements. But what does the club expect? No one forced them to spend £300m+ on the team. Without a league title for 50 years, Abramovich turned up and two landed on the doorstep within 36 months. Coincidence?

Of course, it also coincided with the arrival of Jose Mourinho, and clearly he played a big part in turning that wealth into consistent results. He bought the right players (although inherited key new arrivals like Petr Cech and Arjen Robben), and got them playing without their egos. But even before Mourinho arrived, Chelsea had made the semi-finals of the Champions League and recorded its best league position for 50 years, after the first wave of Abramovich's spending. In fact, Claudio Ranieri had just overseen Chelsea's most successful ever season in terms of points recorded, with an impressive tally of 79; their title-winning team of 1955 would have recorded just 72 points under the current three points for a win system, and that was from four extra games. In his entire history as a manager in European football, Ranieri had never finished above fourth place (and subsequently made a terrible mess of Valencia); once Abramovich arrived with his open chequebook, he instantly took a team to second. So how can money *not* be a significant factor?

If Jose Mourinho had as much faith in his ability as he claims, he may have chosen against spending so extravagantly. Of course, you can't blame him for spending the money at his disposal, but at the same time it's like buying a Ferrari and then claiming it wasn't money that helped you accelerate faster at the lights than the man in the Fiat Cinquecento. You may indeed be the better driver, but you are also relying on an 'unfair' advantage. It's undeniable that Mourinho is a great manager, possibly even as brilliant as his hype insists after his success with Porto, but unlike all other managers he now has the insurance policy of never being able to make a mistake in the transfer market. He spent £21m on Shaun Wright-Phillips, but barely played him. What does it matter? The player was not able to join one of Chelsea's rivals in 2005, as the Stamford Bridge club offered Manchester City the most money — effectively making it a one horse race. All managers make duff signings, but Mourinho can sign so many players if he wants to, he has no worries about those who don't work out. Should Chelsea's top brass wish to sell Wright-Phillips in the future, they can do so to whomever they please; they don't need to look to recoup his market value (which might only be offered by their rivals) or even close to it; in fact, they could sell him for a box of old tracksuit tops to an 'unthreatening' mid-table team if they so wished.

The history of football is full of teams with more money than other teams; someone always has to have the most, and someone else the least. But never before has one team been outside the financial implications of the sport. Benítez could do an utterly remarkable job with Liverpool in his first three years — a better job than any other man alive could possibly do — and find it still not enough, given where Chelsea were when Mourinho arrived (on a large upward curve), and where his ability and Abramovich's money have taken them. At the time of writing, Chelsea are almost certain to sign Michael Ballack on a free transfer from Bayern Munich (but of course, they can afford the reported £6m a year in wages), while rumours about Andriy Shevchenko refuse to go away. While their competitors need to put wage ceilings in place, as part of a pay structure based on income, Chelsea can go that extra mile to line a player's pockets.

In winning the league title for the first time in fifty years in 2005, Chelsea recorded staggering losses of £140m, far and away the biggest in football history. The previous year's loss of £88m looked obscene enough, but a year later it was almost doubled. Compare this to Liverpool's situation. The club's annual report revealed a profit before tax of £9.5 million (£7.53 million after tax) for the year ending July 31st, 2005. That figure compares with the previous year's loss of £21.9m. Turnover at the club rose by 32% to £121.05m compared with £91.57m the previous year, with the Champions League success bringing in £28.8m. The different ways the two clubs are run could not be more stark.

Chelsea's success is not all down to money. In fact, it's impossible to say precisely how much of it is down to the Russian's roubles; it cannot be quantified by a percentage. But clearly, it's enough to make it hugely relevant. Abramovich lured the great manager and the majority of the quality players. Any team that gets success the way Chelsea have need simply enjoy it and try not to care what anyone else thinks, because whatever they now do to try an win over 'floating voters', it won't win the kind of respect neutrals reserved for Arsene Wenger's Arsenal, where a fantastic team was assembled on a very shrewd business plan. Successful teams will always be resented to some degree, partly down to sour grapes and jealousy. And Liverpool, Manchester United and Arsenal are certainly envious of the current domestic domination of the Blues: who wouldn't be? But with Chelsea there are the extra layers: the way they wield their financial muscle; the arrogance of their manager, who, deep into his second season, was alienating more and more people; and a 'win at all costs' mentality — diving, blatant handballs — that, while understandable, wasn't going to win the friends they crave (to become a more powerful world 'brand', they need to win lots of new fans).

What would have been more interesting for the game of football would have been to see Jose Mourinho work on a budget more in keeping with his rivals. Had he still been successful, then it would have been without caveats, and all the unreserved praise in the world would be his.

But he made his bed . . .

Bad blood

A lot of bad blood arose between Liverpool and Chelsea during 2005, spilling over into 2006. Familiarity breeds contempt, and after nine meetings in sixteen months, the contempt was positively overflowing, before yet another meeting, in the FA Cup semi-final, made it ten: each season throwing up two league encounters, two in the Champions League, and one in the latter stages of a domestic cup. Chelsea won all four Premiership matches, plus the Carling Cup final. Liverpool won the two semi-finals — Champions League and FA Cup — and, after two draws, topped Group G of the 2005/06 Champions League. An 11th meeting awaits in the Community Shield in August 2006.

The dislike between the two camps never quite reached the almost war-like levels aroused between Arsenal and Manchester United in the earlier part of the decade. Chelsea were also entering into slanging matches with Arsenal, as Jose Mourinho and Arsene Wenger went head-to-head in an extreme personality clash, while, as voyeurs, we watched with fascination. There was no love lost between Benítez and Mourinho, but any enmity between the two was contained. *Just* . . .

There were a number of flash points, both on and off the field. Michael Essien's tackle on Dietmar Hamann in the Champions League group game at Stamford Bridge was as bad as any seen all season — the studs of his boot were lifted well over the ball, and a couple of feet to the right of it as well: straight into Didi Hamann's kneecap. Momo Sissoko also put in a poor tackle in the match, although his foot bounced off the top of the ball; Essien's tackle alone was later reviewed by Uefa, who imposed a two-match ban on the Ghanaian. Six months earlier, Eidur Gudjohnsen had riled the Reds with his blatant 'simulation' to get Xabi Alonso suspended from the semi-final second leg.

It didn't end there. Arjen Robben's collapse in the face of the merest brush from Pepe Reina's glove was another example of the kind of gamesmanship that left a sour taste in the mouth. While Reina was technically wrong to raise his hand, it was not done in an aggressive manner. The laws seem to make no mention of hand-raising being punishable in itself, merely when connected to the threat or intent of violent conduct; the assumption being that if a player raises his hands, he makes it harder for the referee to determine that no contact took place. If the referee sees hands go up and a player go down, he can be forgiven for drawing the obvious conclusion, whatever the replays subsequently reveal to the watching world. As a result, along came the unwritten rule that to raise a hand is asking for trouble. If Reina was technically wrong to touch Robben's cheek in what is a common Spanish gesture, then Robben was morally wrong to act like he'd received a pair of Glasgow kisses from Duncan Ferguson and Colin Hendry.

Jose Mourinho was always happy to weigh in with inflammatory comments. Of course, Mourinho often cuts through the crap and says exactly what's on his mind, making great headlines along the way, as he gets to the heart of the matter; at other times he goes too far, and only further invites contempt. It's hard to warm to someone who predicted, just a day after chief executive Peter Kenyon claimed in a Guardian interview that Chelsea want to be loved, that his team would be crowned Champions by the start of April. (It transpired that, by the start of April, Chelsea's wobbles invited widespread belief that Manchester United were back in with a chance, however slim.) It's easy to mistake confidence for arrogance, as the line between the two can be fine; arrogance is often a case of saying what confident people merely think and opt to keep to themselves. Confidence is thinking you'll be Champions by April; arrogance is *stating* it. There was almost national hysteria when Chelsea promptly lost 3-0 at Middlesborough, but the defeat also highlighted how consistent the Stamford Bridge outfit had been since Mourinho's arrival.

In the early part of 2005/06, with the Reds due to meet the Blues, Jose Mourinho made comments in the press that he wouldn't leave transfers to the last minute — saying such acts were 'desperate', with the implication that Liverpool and Benítez, who had lost out on some last-minute deals in the summer, were precisely that. Of course, when you have the money to pay the asking price of *any* player, and millions more if subsequently demanded, you need never be desperate in your life. Again, this brings us back to the ease with which Chelsea can conduct their transfer business: fees and wages are never an issue. It's almost certain that, because of their wealth, they are forced to pay more than any other club would for the players they pursue. But it never reaches a point where they feel scared off by a hiked fee. Didier Drogba might have cost another club £15m; Marseilles asked Chelsea for £24m — and they paid.

Although the Reds would ultimately prove unable to sustain a title challenge, Mourinho was clearly worried by Liverpool's progress under Benítez. Ever since the Reds defeated the Blues in the Champions League semi-final in May 2005, there were scores to settle. Even well into the following season, Chelsea refused to accept the validity of Liverpool's winning goal, conveniently overlooking how the referee later confirmed he was going to award Liverpool a penalty and send off Petr Cech had the advantage not fallen the Reds' way.

Meanwhile, Liverpool's progress in the Premiership, especially over the autumn months, coupled with the two teams being paired together in the group stages of the 2005/06 Champions League, made the Reds the Blues closest rivals for much of the season. In a reversal of their usual fortunes, Arsenal were going exceptionally well in Europe but, until the Spring, struggling massively in the league. Manchester United were doing increasingly well in the league, but crashed out of the Champions League at the group stage for the first time in a decade. In fact, they ended up bottom of their group, and as such, didn't even make the Uefa Cup as consolation; leaving them free, and fresh, for the Premiership.

Of the strongest four clubs in the land, only Liverpool and Chelsea occupied both the Champions League qualification spots in the Premiership while simultaneously progressing to the Champions League knock-out stages. (Arsenal made a late push for 4th spot, but spent much of the season off the pace). Only Chelsea and Liverpool looked consistent, and Chelsea especially so.

Chelsea had the upper hand over the Reds in the Premiership, completing a back-to-back double with a 4-1 victory at Anfield and a 2-0 win at Stamford Bridge. Neither scoreline was a fair reflection of the games (2-1 and 1-0 would have been more fitting), with Chelsea scoring against the run of play in each, but the Reds still contributed to their own downfall, missing chances and making mistakes at the back. Defensive errors allowed the Blues to open the scoring on each occasion: a clumsy tackle by Djimi Traore on Didier Drogba in the first game resulting in a penalty, and poor application of the zonal marking system from a corner allowing William Gallas to score in the second. At Anfield, Liverpool were pressing for an equaliser with the score at 2-1 to the Londoners when two mis-hit shots by Chelsea players fell to unmarked colleagues to tap into an empty net; although fortuitous, praise must go to those players for getting ahead of play in the first place. If you are going to hit teams on the break, as Chelsea do, then getting men forward quickly and in numbers is an essential part of the plan.

In the Champions League, the Reds retained the upper hand, even though both games in the group stage ended goalless. Chelsea's defeat in Spain to Real Betis meant Liverpool topped the group, consigning the Londoners to a tie against Barcelona, while Liverpool faced Benfica, conquerors of Manchester United.

In the league game at Stamford Bridge in February 2006, a playing surface part lunar, part marshland, didn't help the quality of football on display. Mourinho, ignoring his team's ability to bypass midfield when aiming for Drogba, claimed the pitch didn't affect Liverpool as "they play the game in the air"; an assertion following on from earlier claims that Liverpool were a long ball team. This was an accusation repeated and added to by Alex Ferguson after United's cup defeat at Anfield: namely that Liverpool knock it long and "only play for five minutes" to win games. (Which begs the question: why not out-play and out-score Liverpool for the other 85 minutes?)

Neither's claims were backed up by the possession statistics. A team can do a lot with a long-ball game — such as create chances by getting the ball into the 'mixer' time and time again and hoping to prod home a loose ball in the confusion — but one thing it cannot hope to do is have a decent share of the possession. And it is this that made a lie of the accusations. The long-ball game is essentially *anti*-possession. It says 'we'll have the ball for a third of a second before either creating a chance on goal or letting you have the ball back'. In each of the four big late-winter games — against Manchester United (one home, one away), Chelsea and Arsenal — Liverpool had the lion's share of the possession. On top of this, in each of these games, the Reds had the most corners (against Arsenal at Anfield it was to farcical proportions, while United only forced their first at Old Trafford in the 87th minute), and while corners don't mean anything on their own, they do reflect the balance of play.

The mere presence of Peter Crouch enabled other managers to denigrate Liverpool's ability to pass the ball on the deck. Not every opposing manager will be looking to speak the truth, either before or after a match; part of their job is to spin their own deficiencies with understandable acts of propaganda, while another part of their remit is to put pressure on their rivals.

Before the Champions League clash with Chelsea at Anfield, just five days before the league encounter, Mourinho made his first accusation about Livepool's 'direct' style. If anything, once the game began, Liverpool appeared too intent on keeping the ball on the deck at all times, perhaps to prove there was more skill at hand than the opposing manager had credited them with. If that was the case, Mourinho clearly won that particular 'mind game'. (The trouble with modern football and 'mind games' is that, since Alex Ferguson started going head-to-head with rival managers in the press, literally every comment gets grouped into this bracket. Also, even if a manager is attempting mind games, the success or failure of these psychological ploys isn't always 100% apparent; sometimes it's a purely footballing reason that determines a result.)

Then Arsenal's Freddie Ljungberg made a series of baffling comments, following the most one-sided game between the two teams in a long time, as Liverpool finally comprehensively outplayed the Gunners, in a 1-0 win at Anfield, after several years of being on the receiving end of harsh football lessons. His comments included a suggestion that Arsenal had been dragged down to Liverpool's level in terms of rudimentary football. "We probably both deserved one point", Ljungberg said, after his team was so inferior on the night that the only Gunner to emerge with any credit was their goalkeeper, who kept the score respectable.

This is not to say that Liverpool don't use the long ball. Clearly they do. Sometimes it's a beautiful long pass from Xabi Alonso or Steven Gerrard (with new signing, Daniel Agger, also exhibiting a sweet left foot), sometimes it's a more rudimentary 'out' ball from the back to clear the lines. After all, no team should be ashamed to 'hit and hope' occasionally, especially if it possesses a striker capable of turning the situation to the team's favour. Football should be about amassing as many beneficial skills as possible, not about concentrating solely on one method. Under Benítez, one thing the

Reds do not lack is variety (although, with Cissé often out of the picture, or out on the right, pace has been absent from the striking positions; a problem that will surely be rectified).

This is clearly not the best, nor the most 'beautiful' Liverpool side ever, but it's one of the most varied in terms of its approach, and it involves a healthy dose of skill. Benítez's side can play a number of different ways, and often does so during a single game. It can break up and destroy, but with Harry Kewell and Steven Gerrard on the flanks and Alonso in the centre, not to mention Luis Garcia popping up all over the attacking third, it can illuminate with creative inspiration. Up front, Peter Crouch gives the team a number of options, and one of those is the opportunity to go more direct. But he is equally happy — perhaps even happier — with the ball played into his feet. Luis Garcia and Robbie Fowler don't want the ball in the air. Fernando Morientes, like Crouch, is a technical player who, despite being an aerial threat, is more comfortable in open play with the ball at his feet.

Every perfectly accurate ball knocked long to a striker makes it, at best, a 50-50 chance of retaining possession as he battles the centre-back — who has two advantages: first, that he is facing play, and as such, can run forwards to attack the ball; and second, he is only trying to get the ball out of the danger — precisely *where* it goes is not crucial, providing it gets enough distance. A striker looking to win a header is also looking for the flick to be accurate, while most headers flicked on towards goal will favour the goalkeeper, by virtue of the fact that flick-ons can never have many targets, since most of the players are behind the target-man who is trying to win the header (although you may get one runner going beyond him, as did Luis Garcia for the second goal against Everton at Anfield). Often the best-case scenario is a fight for the 'second ball'. So retaining possession is not easy. But that's just with *accurate* passes; how many extra long passes go straight through to the goalkeeper or out for a goal kick?

No matter how tall or how good his control, Peter Crouch cannot win everything — and he would need to do just that in order to give Liverpool decent possession statistics, if indeed all the Reds did was hit it long to him. The truth is that the claims of Mourinho, Ljungberg and Ferguson were not backed up by the facts of what actually took place.

Famously, Bob Paisley said that the game of football is not about the long ball, or the short ball, but the right ball. So having the correct personnel to play (and receive) the long ball, when it is the *right* ball, makes perfect sense.

Arsenal

The major shock of 2005/06 was the inconsistency of Arsenal: a team that fell clearly, and swiftly, into transition. For the first time in a decade — in fact, since Arsene Wenger arrived in 1996 — Arsenal finished outside the top two. It was also, therefore, the first time that the Reds had finished above the

Gunners in that period. As with Liverpool and Everton the season before, Arsenal had to endure their local rivals, Spurs, looking down on them for much of the campaign. And like Liverpool in 2005, Arsenal's league form bore no resemblance to the team that took to the field in Europe, where they, like the Reds, beat Juventus (now with Patrick Vieira in the side) in the quarter-finals of the Champions League, before winning the semi-final 1-0 on aggregate. After leading Barcelona for much of the final, the Gunners finally capitulated, losing 2-1 to two goals in the final 15 minutes.

Perhaps this yet again highlights just how difficult it is, with the pace of ferocity of the English league, to fight on more than one front. The domestic cup competitions don't pose too much of an added burden, especially with the earlier rounds of the FA Cup taking place on weekends set aside for that purpose, but difficult midweek games in the Champions League, on top of Premiership fixtures, make for an incredibly tight schedule to juggle. In the first season in a decade in which Arsenal were below par domestically, they could finally summon the energy — and perhaps freedom (with lower expectations) — to do themselves justice on the continent. The one trophy Chelsea, the new English kings, dearly wanted was the one that continues to elude them, despite their increasing spending. Arsenal, meanwhile, were no longer the 'Invincibles' of 2004, who swept all English teams before them, but were suddenly beating Real Madrid and Juventus. As champions of a country, there comes a desperation to translate that success into the highest honour: winning the European Cup becomes an obsession, the next Holy Grail. When you are not reigning national champions, and not getting close, European campaigns can be seen as a bit of a bonus (as indeed they should be: in years gone by, only the best team in the land qualified). It's interesting to note that Manchester United's domestic dominance came to an end when Alex Ferguson seemed most intent on winning a second European Cup — the league title alone was no longer enough to appease him (and now they win neither). With the signing of Juan Sebastian Veron, and the experimentation with more continental formations, Ferguson could still get no closer to repeating the feat of 1999, and in the process, confused United's domestic tactics.

Unless a change of manager has occurred within the past two or three years, a successful club should not really be in transition. If one occurs, it means the manager has lost a little control and let things slide; no team can remain at the top of its game season in, season out, but any necessary change should be gradual, so as to retain as much momentum and understanding as possible. All players' careers are finite in length, and some lose their hunger earlier than others; at that point they will need replacing. But if too many reach that point at once, and leave noticeable gaps, it can allow other teams to nip in and overtake. The aim is to continually prune and hone the team and the wider squad.

Where Liverpool's 25-year domination effectively died, back in 1991, was in Kenny Dalglish's failure to keep on top of updating an ageing squad. Dalglish's signings in 1987 were pure perfection: John Barnes, John Aldridge and Peter Beardsley, with Ray Houghton following shortly after, while a year later the return of Ian Rush was a no-brainer. There was the right amount of talent, experience and longevity present with the purchase of each. But subsequent signings were either of inferior quality, or too old to offer long-term solutions to what was already an ageing squad. In the aftermath of Hillsborough, and the stress it caused Dalglish, it would be incredibly churlish to blame one of the club's legendary servants — both on the pitch, and as manager — for taking his eye off the ball. Who didn't? But had the right young players been bought in to supplement players like Rush, Beardsley, McMahon, Whelan *et al*, then what was clearly not the greatest Arsenal side would not have been able to muscle in during 1990/91, once Dalglish stepped down. It didn't help that injury had forced Mark Lawrenson into early retirement in 1988, but Alan Hansen calling it a day in 1990/91 season, at the age of 36, was less of a surprise, given his knees had been creaking for some time. In some ways, there are two Dalglish eras: pre-Hillsborough, and post-Hillsborough, just as there are two distinct Gérard Houllier eras: pre-heart operation, and post-heart operation. Dalglish did sign Jamie Redknapp, while Steve McManaman had made an appearance in the first team, but neither was yet ready to excel in the starting XI. Then along came Graeme Souness as his successor, and instead of rectifying the problems, got it all badly wrong.

One of Bob Paisley's secrets was in the way his teams silently evolved, without fuss or panic; shedding a star player here and there, and making sure there was a ready-made replacement already groomed in the reserves. Players like Terry McDermott were sold at an age when still able to offer something to the team. At no point did Paisley have to commit to any radical work in the transfer market. He made it appear seamless.

It is the logical process of maintenance, but is of course easier said that done. You don't leave a leaky roof and dampness in the walls until the house collapses; you fix them as you go along. Looking at Arsenal in 2005/06, it seems that after nine years — the same time that Paisley managed Liverpool — Arsene Wenger finally lost control of the evolution of his team; not completely, but just enough to leave them well off the pace in the Premiership. And yet it's impossible to write them off, such is the potential still at the club, and such is Wenger's record since arriving in England. The way they ended the season went a long way to proving that quality is still in abundance in North London.

The future

When looking at the future that faces Liverpool, the situation at Arsenal means they remain an interesting comparison to draw. Financial concerns clearly contributed to Arsenal's dip — with the move to the new stadium at Ashburton Grove, and no wealthy benefactors, the books had to be balanced somehow. The sale of Patrick Vieira led to a hole in the middle of the Gunners' midfield, and in the overall character of the side, and they weren't able to buy big to replace him. Bought for £4m nine years earlier, Vieira was sold for £13.75m — at a time when he looked fractionally past his best, and when he was fast approaching his thirties. For much of the season, the highly-touted youngsters who'd been gaining valuable experience in the League Cup and in league cameos looked too raw to handle the pressure of regular Premiership and Champions League football, especially in the absence (or lack of form) of some of the more senior players.

However, by the end of the season it appeared that players such as Cesc Fabregas, Phillipe Senderos, Mathieu Flamini, Antonio Reyes, Robin Van Persie and Emmanuel Eboue were coming of age, as individuals and as a unit. Patience is a virtue, and Arsenal's resurgence at the end of 2005/06 proved its worth. The disappointing league campaign during the final year of their Highbury tenure does not changed the fact that Arsenal remain the unofficial blueprint for the Reds' future: a very canny manager in place, to be charged with investing in the long-term success of the club by procuring a string of highly-rated younger players, while off the pitch the club looks to relocate down the road without jeopardising investment in the team.

In terms of securing, and settling in, the next generation of players, Arsenal had a distinct head-start, with Wenger having been steadily doing just that for a number of years; Benítez, meanwhile, found himself under-stocked in the youth department by his predecessor, Gérard Houllier, who developed his reputation largely due to his involvement in the French national youth system, and yet hadn't managed to buy enough teenagers able to make the breakthrough. At Arsenal, with Vieira gone (and Henry possibly going), Sol Campbell often looking twice his age, and with Robert Pires, Jens Lehmann and Dennis Bergkamp in the twilight of their careers, they are now clearly behind Liverpool in terms of key players at, or approaching, their peak years. Of the Reds' main players, only Sami Hyypia and Didi Hamann, both at 32, are approaching the end of their excellent careers (although Hyypia, as someone who never relied on pace, should be able to eke out a few more years at the top; yet again he has played over 50 games in a season for Liverpool).

In Hamann's case, the German has already been edged into a more auxiliary role, following the arrival and impressive form of Momo Sissoko. Meanwhile, if he is kept on, Robbie Fowler, at 31, still has some life left in him, especially if he can continue to adapt his game in the style of Bergkamp, and is used as sparingly as the Dutchman was at the same age. Liverpool's strength can be seen in the fact that Steven Gerrard, Pepe Reina, Xabi Alonso, Jamie Carragher, Harry Kewell, Luis Garcia, Boudewijn Zenden and Peter Crouch are all aged between 23 and 29, while the ever-reliable Steve Finnan has just turned 30. The core of the Liverpool side is now at a very good age, and will allow youngsters like Daniel Agger to come into the team without having too much of a burden to carry.

Manchester United

Manchester United have become the most baffling side in the country. It's hard to say if they are in decline, on the rise again, or in transition. For much of 2005/06 they looked like an fading threat, with a quite awful Champions League campaign — their worst in over a decade. With the poorest and least-balanced midfield they've possessed in that time, they looked ill-prepared to protect a defence containing fine individuals, and finally a top goalkeeper to replace Peter Schmeichel, but lacking a real sense of unity.

And yet, in terms of points, they secured more than in some of their more recent title-winning vintages, and they did win a trophy, albeit the League Cup. This was done with long-term injuries to Gabriel Heinze and Paul Scholes, although the latter hasn't looked at his best for a couple of seasons. Roy Keane finally bade the club farewell, in typically rancorous style, but his effectiveness had been on the wane for a long time; in fact, his departure coincided with an upturn in the club's fortunes on the pitch.

It's undeniable that they have the best collection of strikers in the Premiership — although none of Wayne Rooney, Ruud van Nistelrooy and Luis Saha came cheap — while Christiano Ronaldo, for all his often-needless tricks, is turning into a dangerous wide player. But the youth team is throwing forth no remarkable graduates, and the original 'Fergie's Fledgelings' are now all well into their thirties.

How will the Glazers, the Americans who now own the club and who reportedly have no interest in football (or *sawker*) as a sport, treat Manchester United in the coming years? They have plunged the club into debt by virtue of their takeover, but they also know that success on the pitch is the main factor to making profit. The Glazer factor makes predicting how United will fare in the coming years all the more difficult, as does the age of Alex Ferguson, who has to reach the end of the line sooner rather than later.

Chelsea's successful translation of silver into silverware seemed to violently knock both United and Arsenal out of their strides. For the best part of a decade these two sides were battling it out for the Premiership crown, sharing every title between 1996 and 2004, and with the other usually the runner-up (Liverpool got in on the act only once, finishing 2nd in 2002). Then, all of a sudden, Chelsea just blew them out of the water. Since then, United have recovered better than Arsenal, domestically at least, although the Salford club have spent pretty heavily themselves in recent years.

As with Chelsea, you can see the level of investment at Old Trafford: Rio Ferdinand, Wayne Rooney, Ruud van Nistelrooy, Christiano Ronaldo and Luis Saha account for approximately £100m, at an average of £20m each. Chelsea's five most expensive players (Michael Essien, Didier Drogba, Shaun Wright-Phillips, Damien Duff and Ricardo Carvalho) total just a fraction more, averaging out at £21m.

Take the five most expensive signings from Liverpool's squad (Cissé, Alonso, Hamann, Crouch and Morientes), and the average is just £9m apiece. Of course, Liverpool spent in excess of that amount on Emile Heskey and El Hadji Diouf, two £10m players no longer at the club; of course, Manchester United famously spent £28m on Juan Seba Veron. But the majority of the regular starters at Liverpool are either Academy graduates or players who cost no more than £7m.

Arsenal's average spend on its five most expensive current players is far closer to — but still in excess of — Liverpool's: Antonio Reyes, Theo Walcott, Thierry Henry, Aleksander Hleb and Robert Pires average out at £11m each. But more than any other manager at a top club, Arsene Wenger has sold on players for far in excess of what he paid for them; his only expensive 'flop' being £13m Sylvain Wiltord, who left for nothing. As is becoming the norm, deals like those involving Reyes and Walcott are very much dependent on future appearances for the club, but a club has to make sure it can afford to pay the upper ceiling, should the stipulations be met.

Of course, all of this is not to say that the more you pay for someone, the more successful they will automatically be; just that the odds are better, usually because they've proved more in their career or have outstanding potential. You don't always get what you pay for, but players like Rooney are almost certain to strengthen a team.

Title races

What's clear is that any realistic title challenge from Liverpool in the coming years also depends on what these three clubs do to strengthen their teams. While investment in the team at Anfield is almost certainly required to meet the club's ultimate ambitions, the competition will always have their say. On top of these sides, you can usually expect one club to emerge from the pack, as did Everton in 2004/05 and Spurs a year later, while Newcastle always seem to be an unlit powder keg of potential. But such teams tend to find it hard to sustain their momentum, and are often undone by the added demands of European football — the very thing they crave. And unlike Liverpool, these teams are competing for 4th place at best.

Chapter Twenty-One

FA Cup: the Road to Cardiff

The FA Cup has proved the most elusive trophy in Liverpool's long and illustrious history. While the club has won fewer European Cups (five) and fewer Uefa Cups (three), these are trophies that have only been competed for in certain seasons, dating back to the early '60s. The FA Cup has been an annual feature in the Reds' calendar for well over 100 years. It took until 1965 to win it for the first time, and remained the one trophy never to be procured by Bob Paisley, the man whose immortalising statue, should it ever be commissioned, will need to be made not of bronze but silver or gold. Paisley was left out of the team that lost to Arsenal in the 1950 final, having scored the winner in the semi-final, and he had no more luck during his nine years as manager.

It's hard to think that there could have been many more difficult runs to the final than the journey to Cardiff in 2006. There was not one easy game on paper. A start away at Luton Town was a potential banana skin, at a time when opponents from far lower down the league structure would have been more easily dismissed. In the five games leading to the final, four were against Premiership opposition. Two of those were away at teams in the basement, but both Portsmouth and Birmingham had proved particularly difficult opposition in recent seasons. Birmingham were the only top-division team Benítez had yet to get the better of, and the ease with which they were despatched could not have been expected.

In fact, Benítez has had an unusually difficult run in domestic cup competitions: not one opponent from below the Championship in two seasons and four cup runs encompassing 14 games: Millwall, Middlesborough, Spurs, Watford (twice), Chelsea, Burnley, Crystal Palace, Luton Town, Portsmouth, Manchester United, Birmingham, Chelsea again, and West Ham. With the exception of the Anfield match from the two legs against Watford, all of the Championship teams have been met only at their grounds. These have all been difficult games. You can usually expect at least one 'easy' game per season in each domestic cup competition; as an example, in the treble season five years ago, the Reds faced Stoke City away in the League Cup, and Rotherham at home in the FA Cup. As another example, Manchester United played non-league opposition in the 3rd round of the FA Cup in each of the past two seasons.

Benítez's win-rate in domestic cup matches is 79%, spread over 14 games. It's a fantastic record, given that these have often been closer to Premiership-type matches (especially when taking into consideration teams like Crystal Palace, who were only recently relegated and looking to bounce back up via the play-offs). For a man who, after his first game in the FA Cup, was scorned for his failure to understand and respect the traditions of English cup football, the overall picture took on a far different complexion.

Run to the final

The FA Cup run got under way at Kenilworth Road, in the kind of remarkable game that leads supporters to think 'this could be our year'. In much the same way that victory over Olympiakos in the Champions League the previous season sparked belief, as the Reds scored the necessary three goals, the comeback from 3-1 down to Luton to win 5-3 had an important psychological impact.

The game had started so well, with Steven Gerrard curling in yet another fine goal in his personal crusade to prove he could outscore most centre-forwards in the country. But Luton showed the plucky resistance typical of lower division teams in these situations, where there's nothing to lose. However, if they expected to get back in the game, they surely didn't expect to race into a 3-1 lead so early in the second half. The third goal was from a harsh penalty, as the Luton striker stepped on Scott Carson's ankle before falling over, but the scoreline was no more than the Hatters deserved.

Benítez reacted quickly, shifting Djibril Cissé — who had earlier missed a penalty with the score at 1-2 — out to the right wing, as he introduced Florent Sinama-Pongolle, the catalyst of the Olympiakos comeback, to play up alongside Peter Crouch. It reaped instant dividends as the little Frenchman latched onto the Gerrard's through-ball and finished with a low hard drive to bring the score back to 2-3, and then Xabi Alonso, in another nod to the Champions League run the previous season, made the score 3-3, as he had in Istanbul. This time it was from a dipping 40-yard volley. Sinama-Pongolle then headed the Reds into the lead, meeting Steve Finnan's inch-perfect cross. A remarkable game was then rewarded with a fitting denouement. With the score at 4-3 as the game headed into injury time, Luton's goalkeeper Marlon Beresford ran forward to attack a corner; the ball broke to the Reds, and Xabi Alonso, from fully 65 yards, passed the ball into the unguarded net with his wrong foot (a lesson to all those players who can't pass it five yards with their less-favoured side), to complete a brace of goals whose combined distance exceeded the length of the pitch (a first in the history of the sport?) For his second, Gerrard was unmarked and facing an unchallenged run to goal; he began to berate his Spanish colleague for not passing, his arms raised in disgust, before watching the ball trickle into the empty net and joining in the celebrations.

Next up was Portsmouth, at Fratton Park, which is never the most hospitable of places in mid-winter. In a distinctly forgettable game, the Reds raced into a two goal lead, courtesy of a Steven Gerrard penalty and a fine strike by John Arne Riise. Portsmouth pulled one back from a free-kick, but that was as far as the excitement stretched. Reward for the victory was a home tie against Manchester United, whom the Reds had not beaten in the competition for 85 years.

United will have been reasonably confident travelling to Anfield, having not been beaten by Benítez's Liverpool in the previous four league encounters either. The FA Cup proved different, and just seconds after Harry Kewell forced a brilliant save from Edwin van der Sar, the Reds took the lead. A short corner routine between Gerrard and Steve Finnan looked to have caught United off guard, but then the ball was shifted again and the advantage looked lost. Finnan eventually delivered an inviting cross for Peter Crouch, who stooped to head home off the post. United rarely troubled the Liverpool goal in the remaining 70 minutes, and it proved a surprisingly comfortable victory.

The game ended with a serious injury to Alan Smith as he jumped to block a Riise free-kick, and fell awkwardly. "When I looked, the leg was lying one way and my ankle was pointing towards Hong Kong so I knew I was in serious trouble," Smith admitted afterwards, having been diagnosed with a broken leg and dislocated ankle. A section of Liverpool fans did themselves no favours by altering the lyrics of Riise's song, created after a free-kick goal against United five years earlier, to "I wanna know how you broke Smith's leg", although the majority clapped the injured player from the field.

Next up were Birmingham, another side Benítez had yet to get the better of during his time in English football. Any thoughts of a torrid evening, coming just 48 hours after an away game at Newcastle, were banished within four minutes, by which time both Sami Hyypia and Peter Crouch had nodded home easy goals when unmarked (perhaps Birmingham didn't see them as aerial threats?). Seven minutes before the break it was 3-0, as Crouch — roundly booed as an ex-Aston Villa player — side-footed home after excellent work from Luis Garcia, who in turn benefited from Gerrard's efforts by the touchline, as he somehow not only rescued a ball that appeared to be going out, but turned it into an incisive pass. A minute later Crouch came close to scoring his first professional hat-trick, and at long last Birmingham were roused: finally there was a Blue going beyond Liverpool players and finding space — although the man in question was a disgruntled Brummie who ran onto the pitch to remonstrate with manager Steve Bruce. Unfortunately Bruce's players were showing less pace and failing to exhibit as much character, and if 3-0 at half-time seemed bad, 7-0 at full-time can only have felt like a disaster.

The rout was completed by goals from Fernando Morientes, Riise (with a real howitzer), an Oliver Tebily own goal, and a Djibril Cissé shot that Maik Taylor woefully mishandled and allowed to creep over the line shortly before the final whistle sounded. That Bruce was an ex-Manchester United stalwart only added to the away fans' enjoyment. It wasn't even the best performance of the season by the Reds; the team had arguably created more clear-cut chances in drawing 0-0, as they had at home to Real Betis, and away at Middlesborough. But a little more composure in the finishing — allied to bigger slices of luck — made all the difference.

Semi-final: Chelsea *again*

Luis Garcia and the winning goal in a semi-final against Chelsea. So, did this one cross the line? The semi-final against Chelsea on April 22nd at Old Trafford had the feel of a final about it, courtesy of the ever-intensifying rivalry between the two clubs and their increasingly hostile managers, and the fact that 'only' Middlesborough or West Ham awaited the winners. This was the biggest test the Reds could possibly face, even if the final would be the bigger occasion.

It proved a rather magnificent weekend for Liverpool in Manchester: a cup final won the previous day by the youth team, and less than 24 hours later, another cup final reached, as the senior side recorded its eight successive victory. Harry Kewell was the Man of the Match, in his best showing in a red shirt. He was sensational. Yet again he limped out of a big game, but this time he'd been match-fit and sharp at the start (even if a muscle problem was worrying him), and this time he left the pitch having shown what a special player he can be. He must have been delighted to see that he was facing Geremi, and that Chelsea's narrowness gave him space to run into. But he made the most of it, even when Chelsea double-banked him. He had been consistently good since returning the side in the autumn, but at Old Trafford he was simply electric.

A lot was made before the game about the growing enmity between Jose Mourinho and Rafa Benítez. The Spaniard angered his Iberian counterpart with the announcement that Roman Abramovich was the real star at Chelsea; that his money was the key factor in their success. While it could perhaps have been left unsaid, it is clearly true: Mourinho is achieving nothing that Benítez, Arsene Wenger and Alex Ferguson couldn't were they also to have such a tremendous war chest (although Ferguson has had a very healthy amount to spend this decade).

Mourinho, as is his style, had seemed to cause most of the friction with his fractious comments in the press over the previous 18 months, finally rousing a response from the more mild-mannered Benítez. Mourinho's comments before the game centred around how 'easy' his team found playing the Reds. After the match, he refused to shake Benítez's hand, and, as he had in the defeat in the Champions League semi-final in May 2005, and in the defeat to Barcelona in March 2006, he claimed his side had not been beaten but lost due to the referee. There was a distinct lack of class to his comments, and being such a distinctly bad loser does him no favours. "I can't wish Liverpool all the best for the final but I wish them good luck for the Champions League qualifier at the start of next season," added the Chelsea boss, through a sarcastic sneer. "I am not worried at all about Liverpool and they have no chance of winning the Premiership title next season. We are 45 points ahead of Liverpool in the Premiership over the last two seasons and they have only beaten us twice in ten games."

On the day, Jose Mourinho's tactics were baffling. The team he put out was a dream for Liverpool, playing straight into Benítez's hands. Mourinho changed radically from the pattern and personnel that gave Liverpool so many problems in the five previous domestic games, and left out Joe Cole, his club's big lucky charm against Liverpool. Frank Lampard was deployed on the left of a midfield diamond, at the apex of which was Michael Essien, the more defensive-minded midfielder. Paulo Ferreira, a right back, was played on the right of midfield, while Geremi, predominantly a right midfielder, was played at right back.

Chelsea's four quick and tricky wingers presented the one area where the Londoners clearly had more quality. And yet not one of Cole, Damien Duff, Arjen Robben and Shaun Wright-Phillips even started the game. Instead, Mourinho tried to pack the centre of the park, where the Reds are always at their strongest. Was Mourinho trying to be too clever? Or was he more worried about negating Liverpool than forcing the issue himself? Chelsea's tactics meant Xabi Alonso didn't have much time on the ball, but he didn't need a lot in order to spread play out to Harry Kewell; by lining up in such a narrow formation, the Reds' playmaker was given a constant outlet. With the ball arriving regularly, Kewell had Geremi on a skewer: twisted, turned, and thoroughly roasted (modern parlance prohibits the use of 'spit-roasted', which could be mistaken for something *very* different).

The game itself was surprisingly comfortable for Liverpool for 60 minutes. Chelsea had a great early chance, when Didier Drogba side-footed wide with just Pepe Reina to beat. At no stage in the move was Drogba onside, but the flag did not go up. The Reds then won a free-kick 19 yards from goal for John Terry's high foot on Luis Garcia, a decision that angered Mourinho. While it may have been fractionally harsh, it was still a fairly dangerous challenge, and the defender forced the referee into a judgement call. Terry's studs were showing as he launched his full weight into the challenge. It was argued by many pundits that he had to go for the ball and that the size of Luis Garcia made it look worse, but Crouch had only just been penalised near the touchline for a high foot on Terry; if Crouch was not excused for being taller than Terry, Terry could not be let off for being taller than the little Spaniard. Luis Garcia's boot was high too, but not quite as far off the ground, and nor were his studs showing. From the resulting free-kick, Riise yet again demonstrated that, when confronted by a wall, placement beats power, as he curled a shot into the bottom corner.

Terry was aggrieved once again early in the second half, this time after being penalised for pushing down on Riise. Replays confirmed it was the correct decision, as the Chelsea centre-back used the Norwegian for leverage in his jump. Almost immediately after, two wayward defensive headers — by Ferreira and William Gallas — presented Luis Garcia with a clean run on goal, albeit with John Terry thundering across. Just over 20 yards out, and with the option to take the ball further negated by Terry's proximity, the Spaniard struck a sublime left-footed half-volley into the top corner. Carlo Cudicini did not move a muscle. Having missed two far easier chances, Luis Garcia was yet again the hero in the big game. It's a nice habit to have.

Chelsea caused a scare when Riise's wayward header fell to Drogba, 12 yards out. Pepe Reina made a decision to go for the ball that was there to be won as it hung in the air, and was a fraction late. Drogba headed home, setting up a frantic finale, during which Joe Cole volleyed over with just Reina to beat, as the last seconds of injury time ebbed away.

Hammer time
West Ham would provide the opposition in the 2006 FA Cup final. The Hammers were the surprise package of the season, finishing 9th in the Premiership with 55 points a year after being promoted via the play-offs, having previously finished only 6th in the Championship. (As a side note, yet again the lowest-placed team in the play-offs went on to be the team that gained promotion: there has to be a connection to the pressure of the occasion, with a team like Ipswich, which finished 3rd and 12 points ahead of the Hammers, disappointed to not gain automatic promotion, while the team that scraped in — in this case, West Ham — sees the whole thing as a big bonus.) Whatever their credentials in the more physical lower division, West Ham adapted brilliantly to top flight football, eventually overtaking Wigan, who had been amazing all and sundry with their early season form. Alan Pardew had assembled a young, fast and fit side at Upton Park, with Teddy Sheringham, who turned 40 in 2006, providing the brains.

The Reds had won both league games, 2-0 and 2-1 respectively, but in the latter Sheringham had posed a number of problems for the Liverpool offside trap. The more recent game was notable mostly for the spat between Luis Garcia and Hayden Mullins, with each receiving a red card that meant suspension from the final. While the referee might have used his discretion, given the harsher than normal punishment that would automatically result — still a three game ban, but one of those being more than an 'ordinary' match — it was hard to argue that the incident wasn't worthy of the two red cards. While no one was likely to be injured by what was only technically 'violent conduct' — although someone's eye could have been taken out by a flying handbag — Pepe Reina could testify that players have been sent off for far less. Luis Garcia's dig into the back of Mullins was unnecessary, and the timing could not have been worse. He could comfort himself with the knowledge that his season wasn't completely over; he had been included in

Spain's World Cup squad for the summer.

West Ham had not beaten Liverpool in the FA Cup, with their best result a draw at home in 1914; then again, Liverpool had not beaten Manchester United in a similar length of time until 2006. Liverpool won the replay in 1914, and the other three meetings between the sides in the competition, although the most recent meeting was way back in 1976. Form can hardly be a guide in such circumstances; the teams the managers fielded 30 years later would be *slightly* different.

A week before the final, in the concluding Premiership fixture, Xabi Alonso went over awkwardly on his right ankle. As the stretcher bearers lifted him from the pitch it looked serious; another break, it was first feared, a season on from the same injury following a clumsy Frank Lampard tackle (the injury that ruled Alonso out of the Carling Cup final in February 2005, but which thankfully didn't prohibit his participation in Istanbul). If that was the case, not only would it mean the Reds would be without their playmaker for the FA Cup final, but such a likeable, dedicated and talented professional would lose his first chance to play on the highest stage in football — the World Cup — having been selected for the Spanish squad.

The good news was that it turned out to merely be a sprain, but it became a race against time to fit for his first Cardiff final. One player who would be absent, though, was Robbie Fowler, who was cup-tied after earlier representing Manchester City in the competition.

Cardiff farewell

Having won the first English final to be held in Cardiff's Millennium Stadium in 2001, Liverpool were looking to complete the symmetry by winning the last to be held there. (Assuming Wembley is finally finished.) The build-up to the occasion was marred by the theft of up to 1,600 tickets from a Royal Mail van parked outside Goodison Park. (Not that any famous theatre impresarios were witnessed at the scene.) The Millennium Stadium refused to issue duplicates, due to security concerns, and while the fans who lost tickets were issued replacements, these came from the allocation reserved for a ballot of fancard holders. It was not the ideal to start to the week.

Chapter Twenty-Two

Cardiff, You Were Kind

Those Cardiff Arms: how Liverpool fans will miss their warm and welcoming embrace. The old Cardiff Arms Park, rebuilt as the Millennium Stadium, was the best hunting ground any Red could have hoped for. If the 1990s were a decade Liverpool fans were glad to see the back of, the new millennium had an apt venue for the club's rebirth as a trophy-winning force.

If getting into Cardiff on the day of a final was always a logistical nightmare for the fans, then at least their team managed to emerge with the prize they sought more often than not. Four times in five cup finals it was a Liverpool captain hoisting aloft the trophy before it left Wales on its way to the Anfield display cabinet.

Both sets of supporters mixed well, something epitomised throughout the day as, across the city, impromptu kickabouts took place on the streets; if not quite the symbolic laying down of arms that took place in the trenches of WWI on Christmas Eve in 1914, it was as friendly as two sets of fans can be.

The largest shadow

All cup finals now live in the shadow of Istanbul — not just those involving Liverpool. How do you top that? was the question asked one year earlier. The answer? Nothing possibly could.

However, the team had a damned good go! With arguably the most exciting ever Uefa Cup and Champions League finals already graced — and won — by the Reds in recent years, it was only a matter of time before the FA Cup was added to the roll of unforgettable honour. The 2001 final was dominated by Arsenal, but won for Liverpool in ultra-dramatic fashion by two late Michael Owen goals. But the 2006 final had everything.

What was achieved on Saturday 13th May, 2006 ranks far lower than Istanbul in the grand scheme of things, given the FA Cup is not the European Cup (quite obviously), and that West Ham are not AC Milan by any stretch of the imagination. Add that Cardiff is most definitely not Istanbul, no matter how much Efes you've drunk, and that 2-0 down after 30 minutes (before quickly pulling back a goal) to a good side is not the same as being 3-0 down at half-time to a superb one, and you have a list of reasons why this game could not come close to matching the events of 12 months earlier.

But in the more limited context and situated in less exotic surroundings, there could have been nothing more in terms of excitement and spectacle. The excitement was often the result of mistakes, but that is not to say that technical excellence wasn't present: Gerrard's passing and stunning goals, Momo Sissoko's jinking runs, Cissé's fabulous volley; all these set in opposition to the incisive spells of pass-and-move by West Ham, for whom Nigel Reo-Coker, Dean Ashton and Yossi Benayoun were all showing both work-rate and excellent touch.

As one West Ham fan remarked later in the evening, in a pub flanking the River Taff: 'Football was the winner'. Which is of course something no one ever says if his or her team has just won. For the record, 'football' wasn't delicately engraved onto the FA Cup on the 125th line — 'Liverpool Football Club' was.

Alan Pardew's West Ham, in their naivety, did something rather foolish: they turned themselves into the favourites to win the cup with more than 60 minutes remaining. Having been such massive underdogs — which of course was daft, given their quality and the confidence they had gained — they put themselves in a position where it was their trophy to lose. And they duly lost it.

The suggestion that West Ham would freeze on the big occasion proved unfounded. Liverpool, weighed down with the pressure of being firm favourites, were the team that started nervously. The Hammers repeated their excellent (and worrying) unlocking of the Reds' offside trap previously seen at Upton Park a few weeks earlier, when Teddy Sheringham had linked with runners from deep. This time it was Dean Ashton performing the role to good effect.

West Ham's strikers were often happy to stand offside in the early stages of moves, as a runner from deep — such as Lionel Scaloni for the first goal — was picked out in another area of the pitch, thus avoiding the linesman's flag. Eventually Carragher and Hyypia were unsure of just what to do, and the uncertainty helped cause the general unease seen throughout the team in the first half.

Yet this is no one-dimensional Liverpool outfit, capable only of defending. When the team's back line is having a rare bad day at the office, its attacking players come to the fore. West Ham ended up as the fourth team to take a two goal lead against Benítez's Liverpool — the fifth if you include Olympiakos, whose early away goal at Anfield instantly counted 'double' — only to find themselves on the losing side. The manager will certainly not have been happy to see his team need to come from behind on these occasions, but all teams have games where they concede an unexpected number of goals, for a variety of reasons. Not many can pull a rabbit out of the hat so consistently.

Two of Liverpool's most reliable players were the surprising culprits in forming yet another mountain to climb. Going into the 125th FA Cup final, you could count the mistakes made by Carragher and Reina on one hand. By 3.30pm on the day of the game, eight fingers were required to count their errors, with 25% of their entire season's costly mistakes coming in the final's first 28 minutes.

After 20 fairly sedate minutes in the intermittent Cardiff sunshine, West

Ham broke down the Liverpool left. Lionel Scaloni's underhit cross put the ball into a dangerous area, but it was food and drink for Carragher and Reina. As the keeper spread himself to gather the ball, his centre-back got to it first and stabbed it into the net at the near post. At first it looked like Carragher had meant to turn the ball behind for a corner and sliced it into his own goal, but it later became clear that he was withdrawing his foot to let the ball roll to Reina, who had presumably given a call — only for it to strike Carragher's standing leg.

While the move took place in a wider area, it was almost identical to the goal Reo-Coker had scored against the Reds at Upton Park. On that occasion it was Marlon Harewood on the edge of the six-yard box, in a central area, anticipating the squared cross; whereas Dudek was given no chance at Upton Park, Reina would have gathered the cross, had Carragher not inadvertently turned the ball past him.

Seven minutes later it got far worse for the Reds. This time Reina was able to get his hands on the ball, as Matthew Etherington's under-hit shot skipped under the despairing lunges of Carragher and Gerrard, but it should have caused the Spanish keeper no problems. Instead the ball slipped just inches from his grasp, which was enough for Dean Ashton to pounce and prod the loose ball over the line. The Liverpool of the previous 61 games were nowhere to be seen. In their stead were Hartlepool United's reserves.

Cometh the half-hour, cometh the man. A quickly taken Gerrard free-kick played in Peter Crouch, whose feet were level with the last defender's, but whose arm was offside. Crouch side-footed a controlled volley past Shaka Hislop. The harsh decision to disallow the goal did not affect the flow of the game. Just moments later, Gerrard sent an almost identical pass into the box, this time to Djibril Cissé, who had an even more difficult volley to contend with. The Frenchman hared forward as the ball came over his right shoulder. He cleverly adjusted his feet to take a slightly shorter stride just ahead of making the strike, to make sure he wasn't too far ahead of the pass, and executed a very difficult technique to perfection in sending the ball flashing past a helpless Hislop. The momentum was suddenly with Liverpool.

Half-time was an unwelcome interruption for Benítez's team, disrupting the Reds' flow. Straight from the restart West Ham were foraging down Liverpool's right flank, with Etherington pulling back a cross with which Harewood connected firmly, but whose effort Reina saved with his feet; the ball broke to Benayoun, who danced past Carragher's frantic 'all or nothing' lunge, but yet again Reina stood big and blocked with his feet; in doing so starting the process of atonement for his earlier error.

The game ebbed and flowed at pace, but with Liverpool struggling to create anything resembling a gilt-edged chance. That was until a free-kick routine was well and truly botched, but quickly rescued by Xabi Alonso, who floated a ball to the back post. Fernando Morientes, only just on as a sub, jumped, but it was Peter Crouch who headed the ball back in the direction of Sami Hyypia. The big Finn thankfully heard Gerrard's call, and left the ball as his captain burst forward and unleashed a superb rising half-volley that was as controlled as it was powerful. West Ham's dream, to quote their song, was fading and dying. Their bubble had well and truly burst. Or so it seemed.

Yet again the Happy Hammers had an ally in Lady Luck — whose name should have been the 12th on their teamsheet — as in the 64th minute Paul Konchesky's intended cross looped over Reina and into the far corner of the net. In many ways their performance merited the good fortune going their way, but even so, this was an outrageous fluke. It was reminiscent of Cissé's effort against Portsmouth at Anfield earlier in the season, and sometimes they happen. It was not easily saveable, given that all keepers have to take a starting position that anticipates the cross — which 99 times out of 100 was exactly what Konchesky's effort would have remained. If keepers started taking up positions at the back post on the extremely rare off-chance that one might loop in, they'd concede 50 goals per game at their near post.

It would have been a terrible way to lose a cup final, but if it's your team that scores it, any goal is a great goal to win it, especially if it comes in your first major final for 25 years. By this time Harry Kewell had limped from his third consecutive final, distraught that another last-minute fitness battle in the build-up to the game had been lost before the 50 minute mark, having again failed to make an impression on the big occasion. Soon to follow was Xabi Alonso, whose sprained ankle was the main talking point in the days before the game; he was passed fit, but was clearly not feeling 100% confident about the injury, with his performance severely inhibited. Two minutes after West Ham again took the lead he asked to be removed.

Liverpool were a spent force. Gerrard and Finnan were limping, and in the final minute of normal time, with West Ham still leading 3-2, Cissé fell to the floor in agony holding his foot (possibly as the result of radiation seeping from his radioactive boots). Scaloni knocked the ball out of play so the Frenchman could receive treatment, but the Hammers failed to sufficiently clear their lines once Liverpool returned the ball. Riise lofted it hopefully into the West Ham box, and Anton Ferdinand's header sent the ball back out. It bounced once, on its way to a distance of 35 yards, before a weary Gerrard — who had earlier skied a free-kick with an air of resignation that suggested even he felt the game was up — strode forward and thumped the most thunderous half-volley that did not even touch the ground before hitting the back of Hislop's net. It was surely the best strike of all the 125 finals. If West Ham felt it was going to be their day given the luck involved in each of their goals, they surely lost that belief in that moment. Steven Gerrard was playing in a different stratosphere. He would not accept defeat.

Extra time, by which stage all substitutions had been made, threw up scenes more reminiscent of a war zone than a football match, with players strewn supine across the pitch with muscles in spasm, as physios and teammates attempted to alleviate their pain. If Liverpool had been disappointing over the course of 90 minutes, there could be no doubt about the character and determination of the players in the final two periods of the game, given that fully five Reds were stricken with cramp and hobbling. Despite this, it was Liverpool who controlled the final 30 minutes of play, with Didi Hamann, one of the fresher players on display at the time, immense in the Reds' midfield.

It was the 62nd game of a long season, and it showed. Rather than run, Finnan had to walk straight-legged into a 50-50 and still he emerged with the ball. West Ham's players were less troubled with cramp, but clearly tired. Harewood went over after a superb Sissoko tackle, in which the Malian hooked the ball away; it left the Hammer writhing in agony, and suddenly Harewood was in possession of the booby prize for Least Able To Walk. After having his ankle strapped he managed to get himself back onto the pitch, but hopping about on his 'good' leg was his only option.

As penalties beckoned, Liverpool broke away, only for Cissé's cross to leave Ferdinand the fractional favourite against Morientes, who was inches from winning the game. It appeared to be the last chance, but the game had one more magical moment. West Ham won a free-kick on the right of Liverpool's area in the 120th minute. The delivery was dangerous, but no one could get a head to it, as heavy legs refused to leave the ground; instead it hit Reo-Coker on the back, and looped up over Reina and — it seemed certain — into the top corner for the fourth fortunate goal for the Londoners.

Reina now appeared to find a sixth, maybe seventh or eighth finger on his left hand, as he somehow managed to claw a ball that was already past him back from the goal-line and onto the inside of the post. A stunning, world-class save, but one which left the keeper in the back of the net as the ball bounced across his six-yard box. Sami Hyypia swung at it, but only presented the ball to Harewood, who had started the game like a hare on amphetamines but finished it like a tortoise on tranquillisers. With an open goal beckoning, he could not summon the simple finish required as he hopped, swung and winced in pain. The ball span harmlessly wide. As with in Istanbul, Liverpool survived thanks to a miraculous last-gasp save and the failure of a striker to score from a distance of six yards. As with Istanbul, it went to penalties. And as with Istanbul, Liverpool's goalkeeper would prove the hero.

If penalties aren't the fairest way to decide things, then this was a game where no other is redundant alternative could have been possible: playing until one team scored the 'next goal's the winner' could have resulted in the goalkeepers being the only players left on their feet. Deciding it with free runs at goal from the halfway line would have been equally pointless as few players would have made it as far as the area before collapsing.

Penalties are often won by the team that is happiest still to be in with a shout of winning the match. The team that feels it should have had the game won in normal time is usually the one that feels the pressure. In this instance, Liverpool were clearly the happier with spot kicks, given their injuries and the fact that West Ham had never been behind in the game. The Hammers were the team who twice thought they had the final won.

Didi Hamann, who had scored in the Champions League shoot-out but had missed against Birmingham in the first final in this stadium, was the first player up. As he approached the ball he slowed to see if Hislop would dive early; he didn't. Rather than sending the keeper the wrong way, the German had to rely on accurate placement, which he coolly achieved. Bobby Zamora was the first Hammer to step forward, but his firmly-struck and well-placed penalty was pawed away by Reina in a brilliant moment of goalkeeping.

Sami Hyypia, almost certainly only taking a penalty as he was one of the few players still relatively fit, did not make the cleanest of contacts and it was an easy save for Hislop; Sheringham, who must have taken 50 more penalties than Hyypia in their respective careers, made no such mistake, and suddenly it was level once more. Gerrard, who had missed penalties in the past, thumped his effort into the top corner with supreme confidence; after the two earlier goals, he must have felt invincible. Konchesky's luck, however, had run out, and Reina saved his effort with an outstretched boot. John Arne Riise, who had seen his well-taken penalty saved by Dida a year earlier, opted instead for the eyes-closed-blast-down-the-middle, as Hislop dived to his left. Despite it being an easier penalty to save, the ball hit the back of the net.

So it came down to Ferdinand versus Reina. The young Hammer's more famous brother had beaten the Spaniard from around the penalty spot with a header in January. Anton might have had more luck getting on his knees and heading his spot kick, as his tame shot left Reina with his easiest save of the afternoon. Cue delirium in the red half of the stadium, and a collection of half-fit players running towards their goalkeeping hero. It was the Reds ninth success in ten penalty shoot-outs over the years. And Benítez had the piece of silverware his team's season merited.

Chapter Twenty-Three

Conclusions, and Looking Ahead

It was a season that seemed to endure longer than the gestation period of an obdurately overdue elephant. And yet, come May, as the team took its run of consecutive wins into double figures, things could only end too soon for Liverpool. In amassing a points tally that would have won the league on a handful of occasions in the last 20 years, the Reds ended the Premiership season in imperious form but no higher in the table than 3rd place. For all the improvement, it still wasn't enough to force Chelsea to break sweat.

The biggest room for improvement was against the two teams that finished above the Reds. Liverpool took just one point from the four fixtures against Chelsea and Manchester United. Theoretically Liverpool would have been crowned champions had they won the two head-to-heads with the Londoners; with Chelsea subsequently six points worse off, and Liverpool six points to the better, the 12 point swing would have wiped out the nine point differential. Admittedly, this does not account for the fact that Chelsea coasted their final two fixtures, losing both; had they needed to win, the results might have been very different. And doing the double over Chelsea is easier said than done.

If only . . .

As expected, the *if only*s were trotted out at the season's conclusion, in relation to the strikers and the chances not taken earlier in the campaign. There may be some truth to them, but *if only*s are all too easy to fall back on. By the same token, Manchester United could say 'if only we'd defended better, we'd be champions', and Arsenal could say 'if only we'd not had so many injuries/if only we'd repeated our European form...' — and so on. Even Chelsea will think there were games they lost or drew which they should have won; *if only* this and that, and they could have ended up with 114 points after winning all 38 fixtures.

Liverpool had the biggest gap to close on the champions, and it was the Reds who made the most progress; *if only*s seem churlish in the circumstances, as to expect progress beyond the addition of 24 points in just one season (while in the process hitting an 18-year high in terms of points won) would have been unrealistic. Manchester United, themselves in need of improvement, added just six points to their league total, while Chelsea 'regressed' by four points and Arsenal went into free-fall.

It's arguable that, as things stood at the end of 2005/06, Benítez had more holes in his squad to fill than Jose Mourinho, whose extra funds had allowed him to solve all problems within his first two years. The right side of

Liverpool's midfield is one such area the manager will need to address; while far from ideal to play the world's best all-round central midfielder on the right wing, as Benítez did with Steven Gerrard, it's also true that the Reds looked at their best when the side also contained Momo Sissoko and Xabi Alonso. The only other viable way to get all three into the starting XI is to play three central midfielders, with Gerrard at the tip of a triangle, as a semi-striker. Doing so, however, leaves room for only one other forward, which will bring its inevitable criticisms.

A fairly substantial part of Benítez's rebuilding programme took place in the winter of '05/06, and those new players — Jan Kromkamp, Daniel Agger, Robbie Fowler and Paul Anderson — will almost certainly be more settled, fit, and adapted to the demands of the league and to the manager's methods by the start of next season. Where Mourinho has been dealing with the finished article, Benítez's players arguably have more scope for improvement. While the Spaniard's side is clearly on the up, the Portuguese's looked to be fractionally on the wane: fewer league points, no domestic cup success to add gloss to the season, and a worse performance in Europe.

There have also been signs of an impending implosion in the Chelsea camp. Mourinho admitted he had twice come close to quitting during his second season, and that he wasn't enjoying the job as much. It's difficult to stay at the top, and 2007 could be the year Chelsea slip from their perch as a result of the strain and the pressure, although it would be a fool who suggests they would not return to the summit at some point soon after, as their resources mean they can freshen things up at any time. Adding players of the calibre of Michael Ballack will obviously strengthen his squad, but where will Mourinho find room for a player who performs an identical role to Frank Lampard? The challenge is to reshape a successful team, without sacrificing the elements that made it successful in the first place.

Liverpool's ability to challenge for the 2007 crown hinges on the two key issues this summer: the quality of the squad after the new signings, and the fitness and freshness of the key players following the World Cup. It's anyone's guess as to which teams' players will return from Germany in good shape; to stand a realistic chance of becoming the English champions, Liverpool needs its strongest players available over the course of the campaign. An advantage can also be gained if other clubs lose their star men.

Unlike a year earlier, the Reds did not suffer any major injuries during 2005/06. Players missed the odd game here and there, but there was no hint of the type of injury crisis that made the manager's inaugural season such an extra challenge. In 2004/05 Benítez had seen the team shorn of key players: Steven Gerrard, Xabi Alonso and Djibril Cissé all broke limbs (as did Didi Hamann, but in the last game of the season), while Milan Baroš and Luis Garcia had fairly serious hamstring injuries. To list Harry Kewell's ailments would need another book in itself, while Chris Kirkland was laid up more times than a Thai hooker. As had been the case since his arrival, Vladimir Šmicer was unable to show his undoubted class due to yet more fitness problems, and he barely appeared before his 11th-hour contribution in Istanbul.

Beyond these important players, emerging strikers Florent Sinama-Pongolle and Neil Mellor both had very serious knee injuries that curtained their seasons at the halfway point, just as they started to score important goals. Antonio Núñez, a good if unspectacular player, stood little chance of making an impact once his knee ligaments were severely damaged in only his second training session. Any new arrivals in 2006 need to have more luck than the hapless Núñez.

"We're a lot closer," said Benítez, days after the season ended, when referring to how near he felt the team was to challenging for the title. "We need to make the right decisions for the future. The next step we have to take is the most difficult. This is a time when we must be careful with our decisions. When I talk with Rick Parry and the chairman they know we are closer now than we've been in a long time. They have more experience than me of what's happened at the club and they know we must be careful with new signings. We know the areas where we need to sign the right players. I know we can improve. That's the sensation I feel now. With the players we have, and by signing the right players, we will be better. Other clubs will be looking to improve, too, and we need to be aware of what they do to make sure if they improve their squad a little, we improve even more."

Even if only half of the new signings adapt quickly and live up to expectations in their first season, that will still significantly improve Benítez's options. It will help the Spaniard in his biggest challenge: to extend the consistency seen in two amazing runs of a dozen games — at the end of 2005 and at the end of the season — across a full 38 game league programme.

Consistency

In the modern squad game, unless there is an injury crisis of the level suffered by Liverpool in 2004/05 or Arsenal in 2005/06, or an unprecedented fixture list such as the Reds encountered in Benítez's second season, inconsistency at the top clubs is less of a problem. At the point when the team should be tiring, or falling flat, changes can be made to freshen things up. Until fairly recently, between three and seven defeats in a season was commonplace for the eventual champions, with just the occasional low total of defeats, as seen with Arsenal's one in 1990/91, and Liverpool's two in 1987/88. While Chelsea lost five times this season, their record is made more remarkable by the fact that they also drew only four times and by the fact that two of their losses came after they secured the title. When Arsenal went unbeaten in 2003/04, they actually dropped more points than did Chelsea this time around, because of 12 drawn matches.

Had Chelsea experienced a disastrous season — and in Mourinho's time they've yet to contend with a truly devastating injury crisis — things might have been different. But that's all ifs, buts and maybes. Chelsea could buy their way out of any injury nightmare, should it coincide with the transfer window. But simultaneous and serious injuries to John Terry, Frank Lampard and Claude Makelele at other points in the season might make it a more interesting contest.

With three English teams reaching European finals within a year, and one of those a distinctly average team in the bottom half of the table (reflected in their 4-0 pounding by Sevilla), it's fair to say the Premiership is currently a very strong league, as the country gets back to the levels of 20 years ago in continental tournaments. Rafa Benítez arrived in England when the competition was fierce. It makes the missed opportunity under Gérard Houllier at the start of the millennium all the more galling; subsequent history tells us that 2003, when the league was won by Manchester United with 83 points, was the 'easiest' time to make a challenge, and it has since become more difficult. Since the Premiership was formed in 1992 (not that I wish to pretend the other 100+ years of top-flight football did not exist), tallies as low as 75 points have been enough to win the title; it's now three seasons since the winning figure dipped below 90. The bar has been set to a height taller than Peter Crouch.

Since 1992, no team has finished 3rd in the top division with a tally as high as 82 points. That also includes 42-game seasons, before the change to the current 38. It's interesting to note that 82 points would not have secured 2nd place a year earlier, either, with Arsenal running up a total of 83 points. The last team to finish 3rd with more than 82 points was West Ham, who accumulated 84 in 1986, although again that was from 42 games, with an extra 12 points available. Not that being the 'best' 3rd-placed side in English league history is an honour the Reds will be celebrating, of course. But it puts things into perspective.

Staged climb

And so continues the task of climbing towards the summit in significant stages. Since the inception of the Premiership, the team which won the title — if it was their first in a long time — finished 2nd (or 'joint' 2nd) the season before. Manchester United finished four points behind Leeds in 1992, but won the league a year later. In 1994, Blackburn finished 2nd, eight points behind United, and won the league in 1995. In 1997 Arsenal finished 3rd — although level on points with 2nd-placed Newcastle United and seven behind Manchester United; Arsenal won the league a year later. Then in 2004 Chelsea finished 2nd, with 79 points to Arsenal's 90, a year before landing their first title in 50 years.

With each of those 2nd-placed teams the gap to the eventual champions was fairly substantial. By becoming champions 12 months later they were not making up a difference of a point or two; on average, the difference was 7.5 points with the biggest leap being made by Chelsea, who were 11 points in arrears of Arsenal in 2004. While 37 points is an impossible gap to overhaul in one single year, especially with the pursued team showing no signs of under-performing, nine points makes it far more interesting. The problem is that while it's highly unlikely that Chelsea will push beyond the mid-90 point mark, they've also shown little sign of falling far below it.

Room for improvement

The Reds had two difficult patches in a season of otherwise near-faultless results; as such, the season was split into four unequal quarters. Early on, performances were mostly good, but games could not be won. A similar thing happened in the New Year, although this time the performances were a little more inconsistent, with the team looking tired. This period also coincided with the Great Strikers' Drought. At the time one newspaper described it as Liverpool's worst strikeforce for 40 years. While that may be true — if only because the Reds have had some unbelievably good strikers in that time — in the next seven weeks, Benítez's four heavily criticised strikers scored 20 goals. And that's not including three further goals by sometime-striker, Luis Garcia. While any team would love forwards who could score as regularly or play as skilfully as Roger Hunt, Ian St John, Kevin Keegan, Kenny Dalglish, Ian Rush, John Aldridge, Peter Beardsley, Robbie Fowler (in his prime) and Michael Owen, it's also clear that Chelsea won the league in 2005 and 2006 with a strikeforce arguably inferior to any seen at Liverpool in the past 40 years.

Liverpool played all four league fixtures against Chelsea and Manchester United during the two fallow periods. The game at Manchester United actually came when the Reds were still just about eking out good results, but had been looking tired after the trip to Japan and the busy festive schedule. Rio Ferdinand's last-minute winner started what would turn into the second mini-slump of the season, as the sharpness ebbed out of the Reds' play.

These games were the six-pointers, and the timing was not beneficial. The FA Cup semi-final showed how much better the Reds could fare against Chelsea when going into the game in form and full of goals. But you have to play teams when the fixture list says. That's all part of the unpredictability of football. These will be the four most crucial games next year, and if the Reds can go into them in better form, as is distinctly possible, it should have a big effect on the league table. Victory in these games could help keep Chelsea's points tally down to the mid-80s: a total that shouldn't be beyond Benítez's team if the manager spends astutely this summer.

Final thought

Can Liverpool finally secure that elusive 19th league title?

Despite Chelsea dominance, and their intent to sign a number of world-class players, the Reds have not been in such good shape since 1987/88. Indeed, in all competitions Liverpool actually won four more games than Chelsea this season, although this came from eight extra matches. In 2002/03, when the chance last presented itself, the Reds had a less challenging field to gallop past, but a less talented jockey at the reins. It's hard to see Benítez making the same mistakes that derailed his predecessor four years earlier, and blowing his entire transfer budget on a collection of duds. He is also more tactically adaptable, with a broader range of talents in his squad.

So there you have it — 2007 will be Liverpool's year, finally ending a 17 year wait.

-------------- *Cut out, remove and burn if proven horribly wrong* --------------

* * *

Note: *the statistics used in this book for assists were compiled by Oliver Anderson and awarded to the two players who touched the ball directly before it reached the goalscorer.*

Anderson goes into far greater depth on all statistical issues in The Red Review, which takes more of an almanac approach to 2005/06.

the red review

A Liverpool FC Almanac

An in-depth statistical analysis of 2005/06

Oliver Anderson
Paul Tomkins

Available autumn 2006. ISBN 0-9549580-5-5

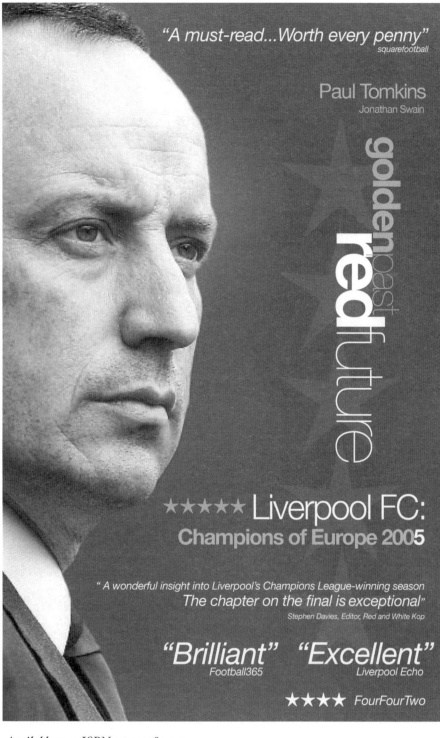

Available now. ISBN 0-9549580-2-0